Slavery, Colonialism, and Racism

Essays by

J. F. Ade. Ajayi
E. J. Alagoa
Michael Banton
Roger Bastide
Edward Kamau Brathwaite
Philip D. Curtin
David Brion Davis
Sidney W. Mintz
J. H. Kwabena Nketia
Benjamin Quarles
Thomas Sowell
Per Wästberg

Slavery, Colonialism, and Racism

Edited by SIDNEY W. MINTZ

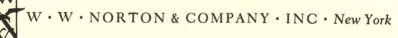 W · W · NORTON & COMPANY · INC · *New York*

CI

EI

LC# 75-305060

Copyright © 1974 by the American Academy of Arts and Sciences
ISBN 0-393-01115-1 (Cloth Edition)
ISBN 0-393-09234-8 (Paper Edition)

All Rights Reserved
Published simultaneously in Canada
by George J. McLeod Limited, Toronto

Printed in the United States of America

1 2 3 4 5 6 7 8 9 0

CONTENTS

PREFACE

THIS volume has been many years in the making; for a long time the working title for the study was "The Historical and Contemporary Experience of Black Peoples." If we desisted from using so grandiloquent a description of our work for a title, it is because we know that the contents of the volume cannot possibly sustain so vast a claim. It is doubtful that any single volume could! Our purposes are, in fact, considerably more modest.

To begin with, we have tried to say something about the state of scholarship on certain critical issues that any study of the black experience must necessarily concern itself with. We open the book with articles on slavery, colonialism and imperialism, and race relations. Each of these subjects might easily have justified a whole volume. Our purpose, however, has been to draw attention to certain new trends in scholarship on all these subjects, suggesting also some of the more important historical changes in perception and interpretation. It is not entirely accidental that many of the references are to works published recently, to studies about to be published, and to some that are available today only in manuscript or dissertation form. These fields are clearly burgeoning, though not always in ways that are recognized.

We have tried to give particular attention to the black experience in places other than the United States. Our decision to give such abundant space to the societies of the Caribbean was a very deliberate one. The region is still massively unknown in many parts of the world, regrettably so. As will become obvious from the articles we have published, this general ignorance about the area is a loss to all who are interested in social diversity and historical complexity. The same thing, incidentally, can be said of the Afro-American experience in Latin America; as Roger Bastide explains, "Black culture is not, as it appears, frozen into a system of defense mechanisms too rigid for change, but a living culture, capable of constant creation, keeping in step with the rhythms of change in the global society, of which it is not a marginal but a dialectical element."

On Africa, we publish articles that reflect the interests of the historian, the literary critic, and the musicologist. Ideally, we would like to have had, in addition, at least one contribution from someone interested in the plastic arts. Indeed, this is a dimension we would like to have introduced throughout the book; it was only considerations of space that prevented us from doing so.

A volume devoted to the historical and contemporary experience of black peoples that neglected the United States entirely would be unthinkable. Yet, it was the considered judgment of many who helped to plan this volume that the North American material should not predominate. We have tried to respect that wish. No one will say that the United States is neglected in this collection, but it certainly does not intrude at the expense of other areas.

From the beginning, our purpose was to emphasize the international character of this undertaking. Those who planned the study came from many parts of the world; those who have written articles come from Europe, Africa, the Caribbean, and the United States. There is, we believe, significance in the fact that even the European authors come from different countries: the United Kingdom, France, and Sweden. Black studies, however defined, cannot be considered a purely national enterprise; indeed, their international character may be one of their greatest potential strengths.

Thanks are due to the Ford Foundation for its generous support of this effort. We are grateful also to Mme. Adriana Salem for making her home in Paris available to us for one of our major planning meetings. The Rockefeller Foundation is to be thanked also for permitting us to use the Villa Serbelloni for another of our conferences. We greatly appreciated the hospitality of Mr. and Mrs. William Olson in those incomparable surroundings. Finally, thanks are due to Sidney Mintz, who has been of inestimable help in every aspect of the planning and execution of this volume.

STEPHEN R. GRAUBARD

Slavery, Colonialism, and Racism

DAVID BRION DAVIS

Slavery and the Post-World War II Historians

Five Turning Points in the Postwar Historiography of Negro Slavery

IN THE opening paragraph of *Slavery: A Problem in American Institutional and Intellectual Life* (1959), Stanley M. Elkins refers to "certain inhibitions" that had continued to govern discussions of American Negro slavery. He also speaks of "a painful touchiness in all aspects of the subject."[1] These words may puzzle young historians who have cut their academic teeth on Elkins' much-gnawed Sambo bone, and who have no memory of the awkwardness and embarrassment surrounding the study of slavery in the early 1950's.

The tension arose from two lines of conflicting pressure. On the one hand, however parochial their discipline, historians had by then become aware of the growing sociological literature on racial prejudice and "the Negro problem," a literature that had culminated in Gunnar Myrdal's *An American Dilemma* (1944). The postwar students who eagerly read Myrdal, Franz Boaz, Sinclair Drake, E. Franklin Frazier, John Dollard, and Melville Herskovits discovered that their parents' quiet convictions—the half-whispered "truths" about Negro character—were dangerous stereotypes that had no place in a nation that had crushed Nazi racism and committed itself to the defense of the free world. By 1950 it was an embarrassment to find a passage like the following in a popular history that had won acclaim from New Deal liberals:

The slave system . . . did incalculable harm to the white people of the South, and benefited nobody but the negro, in that it served as a vast training school for African savages. Though the regime of the slave plantations was strict it was, on the whole, a kindly one by comparison with what the imported slave had experienced in his own land. It taught him discipline, cleanliness and a conception of moral standards.[2]

It was hardly less disturbing when the most prestigious and respected textbook of the early 1950's introduced the subject of slavery with the phrase, "as for Sambo," and then proceeded to describe the carefree, happy-go-lucky Negro.

On the other hand, if I may borrow Gene Wise's recent labels for models of historical explanation, the counter-Progressive mode had only begun to appear by the early 1950's; the Progressive mode still reigned.[3] The ghosts of Turner, Parrington, and Beard had by no means been slain. And for the Progressives, including the younger disciples of the school, slavery had always been peripheral to the major forces and struggles that explained the rise of American civilization. Indeed, in the Progressive view, the nineteenth-century obsession with slavery had obscured the fundamental cleavages in American society: the cleavages between

1

labor and big business, between farmers and middlemen, between self-seeking con-
servatives and liberal men of vision. In the ante-bellum era, as in the later New
Deal years, the children of light had included Southern white supremicists. The
search for a usable past, like the search for progressive public policy, required a
"realistic" view of America's racial burden. W. E. Woodward's *A New American
History* (1936), from which I quoted the above defense of slavery, is simply a popularization, Southern style, of the dominant themes of Progressive historiography. It
was not by accident that the Progressive school relinquished the subject of slavery
to a Southerner and a disciple of Frederick Jackson Turner, Ulrich Bonnell Phillips.
Nor was it accidental that Phillips helped to rehabilitate the South's progressive image by picturing slavery as a system of racial adjustment which had arisen in
response to environmental pressures and human needs.

Although Phillips' *American Negro Slavery* appeared in 1918, it was still the
only comprehensive scholarly work on the subject when I attended graduate school
some thirty-five years later. My teachers supplemented assignments in Phillips with
Frederick Law Olmsted's eye-witness accounts of slavery in the South, apparently
assuming that Olmsted's antislavery sentiments would balance some of Phillips'
more blatant apologies. For the most part, however, the "inhibitions" described
by Elkins helped to consign slavery to a marginal place in the curriculum. For example, a course on the history of religion in America never touched on the slaves'
religion or on the religious controversies over slavery. We simply took note of the
dates when the major Protestant denominations had divided along sectional lines.
At best, slavery could be perceived as a variant on the history of immigration and
ethnic conflict. After preparing for my Ph.D. orals in 1954, I remained totally ignorant of the work of such black historians as W. E. B. Du Bois, Carter Woodson,
Charles H. Wesley, Benjamin Quarles, Eric Williams, C. L. R. James, and John
Hope Franklin. I am confident that few graduate students had at that time encountered Herbert Aptheker's *American Negro Slave Revolts* (1943) or even Frank
Tannenbaum's pioneering essay, *Slave and Citizen* (1946), which Stanley Elkins
rescued from undeserved obscurity.

There is an astonishing contrast between the inhibitions of the 1950's and the
scholarly saturnalia of the past few years. The institution of slavery has now been
probed at every spot, often with passionate intensity, and the explosive debates
have left few questions settled. Virtually no "fact" or opinion of the earlier
scholarly wisdom has gone unchallenged. Phillips has been dethroned as a racist
Progressive and then reenlisted in the armies of the Left. Kenneth M. Stampp has
been hailed for resolving the tensions between Progressive historiography and
postwar racial enlightenment—for recognizing "that one must know what slavery
meant to the Negro and how he reacted to it before one can comprehend his more
recent tribulations." Stampp has also come to symbolize the unwitting arrogance of
white integrationists who assumed "that innately Negroes *are*, after all, only white
men with black skins, nothing more, nothing less."[4] Stanley Elkins' calmly
reasoned study, which promised to escape the "moral coercions" of a century-long
debate, has provoked sufficient warfare to provide an entire volume of critical essays.[5]

Meanwhile, we have been offered new and often startling conclusions regarding
the history of racial prejudice; the demographic patterns of the Atlantic slave trade

and of various slave populations; the nature of slave occupations and the adaptability of slave labor to skilled or industrial employment; the relative efficiency of slave and free labor; the profitability of the institution and its relation to economic growth; the various forms of slave resistance, including insurrection; the place of slavery in American political and Constitutional history; the nature of slave subcultures, including religion, folklore, and various adapted forms of African culture; and above all, the similarities as well as the contrasts between the slave systems of the New World.

Looking back on the profusion of scholarship during the past eighteen years, I would identify five major turning points which have opened new lines of inquiry and have transformed the character of debate. First, Kenneth Stampp's *Peculiar Institution* (1956) ended the era of inhibition by insisting on the "peculiar urgency" of understanding the history of slavery as "a key to understanding the present." By issuing an authoritative answer to Phillips—and indirectly to the entire Progressive tradition of scholarship—Stampp sanitized the subject and thereby placed it on the profession's agenda. As Elkins later noted, Stampp's book was the "culmination and quintessence" of an anti-Phillips reaction which had been signaled as early as 1944 by a cautious and deceptively objective essay by Richard Hofstadter. Elkins shrewdly added that "the strategy of *The Peculiar Institution* was still dictated by Ulrich Phillips," suggesting that the book represented an end rather than a beginning. No doubt many historians greeted Stampp's long-awaited achievement with considerable relief, assuming that Phillips had at last been replaced. In addition, even for Elkins, Stampp opened the way for new and more dispassionate modes of inquiry. Never again, presumably, would it be necessary to debate the moral wrongs of slavery or to rehearse the evidence concerning food, shelter, working hours, police regulations, medical care, and punishments.

The Peculiar Institution is a transitional work that exhibits both Progressive and counter-Progressive characteristics. Stampp expressed little of the Progressives' faith in continuing human betterment. He did not see the slave system as the creation of reactionary or self-serving groups. Rather, Southerners "built it little by little, step by step, choice by choice . . . and all the while most of them were more or less blind to the ultimate consequences of the choices they were making." He spoke of "irony," "paradox," and "tragedy," all key terms in the counter-Progressive vocabulary. Yet unlike the counter-Progressives, Stampp opposed "myths" to "facts," in this case the myths of inherent racial characteristics to the facts of postwar social science. His unmistakable theme is the conflict between the oppressed and oppressors, between the weak and the powerful, between the innocent and the guilty. And the prevailing mood of Stampp's book is ultimately optimistic. Even a brutal slave regime, reinforced by racist ideology, could not crush the human spirit. The slaves remained "a troublesome property," capable of resistance as well as endurance. Like the earlier Progressives, Stampp sought to resurrect a usable past, a past that could serve as the first step toward a kind of social therapy. If white Americans could understand the psychic and cultural traumas occasioned by generations of bondage, they would presumably experience the necessary sympathy and guilt to undo the wrongs of the past. The sympathy, it needs to be stressed, required some evidence of the slaves' resistance as proof of their persevering humanity.

Stanley Elkins, who can be credited with the second major breakthrough in historiography, represents the more conservative wing of the counter-Progressive school. It is significant that both Elkins and Stampp paid tribute to Richard Hofstadter, the virtual godfather of counter-Progressivism.[6] Hofstadter, who did not share Elkins' pious respect for ancient institutions, directed the doctoral dissertation which ultimately emerged as *Slavery*. Aside from Hofstadter's initial critique of Phillips, he himself shied away from the subject of slavery. The same can be said of one of Hofstadter's most distinguished senior admirers, Perry Miller. Indeed, the representative figures of the counter-Progressive school—Louis Hartz, Henry Nash Smith, Leo Marx, John William Ward, William R. Taylor, Cushing Strout, and Marvin Meyers—either avoided slavery or treated the subject as a peripheral and embarrassing misfortune. Curiously, the scholars of myth and symbol seemed to take slavery no more seriously than had their Progressive forebears. They recognized Stampp as the new official authority on empirical detail. But much as the Progressives had delegated the last word to Ulrich Phillips, so the counter-Progressives tended to acknowledge Stanley Elkins as their theoretician on slavery and antislavery. Initially, Elkins drew fire from Avery Craven, Oscar Handlin, and David Donald; John William Ward, Nathan Glazer, Eugene D. Genovese, and C. Vann Woodward applauded his originality and boldness. Later on, Elkins would receive his sharpest criticism from blacks, New Leftists, and Marxists.

If Phillips dictated the strategy of Stampp's rebuttal, Elkins dictated the framework of much of the ensuing debate. There is no need here to review all the heated controversy over Sambo and the Nazi concentration camp. It is sufficient to note that a considerable amount of energy has been expended in attempts to refute Elkins on three fronts: to show that Latin American slavery was not necessarily more open, flexible, and humane than North American slavery; to show that North American slavery did not bring a fundamental personality change in its victims, reducing the typical bondsman to a childlike, submissive, carefree, and self-depreciating Sambo; and to show that American abolitionists were not irresponsible, guilt-obsessed antinomians, whose contempt for institutions precluded a rational solution to social problems. The latter debate is still in its early stages and is not central to a discussion of the recent historiography on slavery. The battles on the first two fronts appear to have been won, or rather to have shifted to new ground after the neutralization of Elkins' salient positions.

I have chosen the word "neutralization" with some care, since Elkins shielded his arguments from the possibility of refutation. His portraits of Latin American and North American slavery are essentially ideal models, illustrating the polar extremes of open and closed slave systems. The "Sambo thesis" is a corollary to Elkins' view of North American slavery as the creation of "unopposed capitalism," an exploitive impulse unmitigated by institutional safeguards or a balance of political and cultural interests. Numerous critics, among them Sidney W. Mintz, Arnold Sio, Marvin Harris, David Brion Davis, Orlando Patterson, Carl N. Degler, Roy Simon Bryce-Laporte, Herbert Gutman, and Franklin W. Knight, have marshaled empirical evidence which clashes with Elkins' paradigms. It has been demonstrated that the more humane provisions of Latin American slave law were often not enforced, and that North American slavery was more complex, varied, and open than the laws imply. We have also learned that the sugar boom in nineteenth-century Cuba and the coffee boom in nineteenth-century Brazil led to highly regimented, exploitive forms of plantation slavery which approximate Elkins' model of "unopposed capitalism" in the United States; that the Sambo stereotype was by no means confined to the United States; that slaves in the United States had considerably more psychological and cultural "space" than Elkins suggests, and that they maintained a surprising stability of family life and succeeded in creating and preserving their own religion and folklore.[7] On the other hand, empirical evidence by itself cannot disprove Elkins' arguments. If Latin American culture significantly modified men's response to human bondage, and there can be no doubt that it did, Elkins can dismiss a sugar boom or nonenforcement of laws as exceptions that merely qualify a model that he never intended to be taken literally. If slaves in the United States generally accommodated themselves to white dominion, and no one could deny that they did, then Elkins can leave open the question of "internalization" and express his willingness to settle for a "broad belt of indeterminacy between 'mere acting' and the 'true self.'"[8]

As conceptual categories, Elkins' models had the great merit of raising key questions that went beyond the earlier fruitless debate over the cruelty or humaneness of American slavery. The key questions centered on two points: the relationship between cultural heritage and the economic pressures of plantation agriculture, and the relationship between the slaves' accommodation and resistance. Both points have been most thoroughly and imaginatively examined by Eugene D. Genovese, who has proved to be Elkins' most effective critic. I shall have occasion to return to Genovese's work later in this essay, and will now simply emphasize Genovese's indebtedness to Elkins. If Genovese questioned the utility of Elkins' models, he also incorporated them into his own explanatory framework. He rightly complained that Elkins' models were too rigid, oversimplified, and deterministic. Elkins ignored large bodies of conflicting evidence and often blurred the distinction between a hypothetical construct and historical reality. The Sambo thesis was objectionable "not because it fails to account for hostile behavior, but because it proves too much and encompasses more forms of behavior than can usefully be managed under a single rubric." Yet Genovese had little patience with Elkins' critics who had been content merely to point to instances of slave rebelliousness or to Latin American cruelty. Elkins had raised the more subtle challenge of conceptualizing contradictions. How could one explain the docile, childlike slave who becomes a Nat Turner or Toussaint L'Ouverture? How could cruelty and paternalism be expressions of the same class position? How did the master-slave relationship modify cultural heritage and Old World traditions of lordship and bondage? If the dominion and dependency of the master-slave relationship tended to gravitate toward certain universal norms, what was the effect of geography, ecology, population distribution, and economic organization? It was Elkins' methodological breakthrough, and the ensuing controversy it provoked, that led Genovese to the ambitious task of encompassing all variables and contradications within a dialectical theory of class and ideology.[9]

In his first and rather unseasoned book, *The Political Economy of Slavery* (1965), Genovese cautiously took issue with Alfred H. Conrad and John R. Meyer, two economists who in 1957 had ushered in what is now termed "the Cliometric Revolution." The burden of Genovese's book was to prove that slavery had been disastrous for the South's economy, which could only be saved, within the exploitive framework of national capitalism, by territorial expansion.[10] According to Genovese, slavery led to soil exhaustion, low productivity of labor, technological retardation, a restricted market, and numerous other competitive disadvantages. Conrad and Meyer had used sophisticated mathematical and statistical models to show that the purchase of a slave in the ante-bellum South was a highly profitable investment which yielded rates of return comparable to those from investments in Northern manufacturing. Since Genovese was concerned with the larger social and ideological effects of slaveholding, the narrow question of profitability appeared to be a minor annoyance. Theoretically, slavery might be profitable for slave owners and still give rise to the values and attitudes of a "precapitalist class," values and attitudes antithetical to balanced economic growth. Genovese sought to give a Marxian reformulation to the traditional picture of the South's economic backwardness. Since the Cliometric Revolution has now challenged every point of that traditional picture, it is clear that the initial paper by Conrad and Meyer must be classed as a third major turning point.[11]

The swelling Cliometric literature culminates in Robert William Fogel and Stanley L. Engerman's *Time on the Cross: The Economics of American Negro Slavery* (1974), a book which incorporates the previous work of many economists and historians, and which rests on the quantification of prodigious empirical research.[12] In their attempt to correct "past errors," Fogel and Engerman go far beyond the question of profitable investment. They maintain that slaves were highly efficient and productive workers; that slave agriculture was 35 percent more efficient than the Northern system of family farming; that slave labor was successfully adapted to urban and industrial conditions; that slave owners encouraged the stability of slave families, and provided their workers with a material standard of life that compared favorably with that of free industrial labor; that slavery did not retard economic growth; that between 1840 and 1860 per capita income increased more rapidly in the South than in the rest of the nation; that slavery as an economic system had never been stronger than on the eve of the Civil War, when slaveholders rationally anticipated an era of unprecedented prosperity. These startling conclusions are bound to provoke continuing controversy, though most skeptical historians are ill-equipped to dispute the Cliometricians' technical apparatus and procedures. I shall later take note of some of the nontechnical implications of Fogel and Engerman's work, which is certain to influence discussions of slavery for a long time to come.

Like everyone else, the Cliometricians have been heavily indebted to a fourth seminal study which has transformed our view of New World slavery, Philip D. Curtin's *The Atlantic Slave Trade: A Census* (1969).[13] Frank Tannenbaum and Stanley Elkins had helped to break the barriers of provincialism that had long distorted perceptions of slavery in the American South. Curtin not only put the demography of the slave trade in a hemispheric setting, but came to the remarkable conclusion that North America (excluding Mexico) received no more than 4.5 percent of all the slaves imported into the New World. Curtin's breakdowns of estimated slave imports were even more dramatic than his evidence that previous studies had greatly exaggerated the total number of African slaves brought to the New World. His careful assessments underscored the importance of the natural increase of the black population in the United States, of the net natural decrease of the slave populations in the sugar colonies and in Brazil, and of the long dependence of the latter regions on a continuing labor supply from Africa. Though Curtin modestly limited the scope of his inquiry, it opened the way for much-needed studies on regional mortality and morbidity rates, on the sex and age structure of slave populations, on African origins and changing patterns of slave-trading. Above all, Curtin demonstrated the significance of demography for any comparison of slave systems. For example, the relative independence of the United States from the Atlantic slave-trading system raises a host of unanswered political, social, and ideological questions.

The fifth turning point for the study of slavery is not a single work but is rather the availability in published form of the evidence of slaves themselves. Although a few white historians had earlier made use of the autobiographies of ex-slaves, such sources had commonly been regarded with extreme caution, on the assumption that fugitive slaves could not write and that their accounts were fabricated to fit the needs of abolitionist propaganda. It is only recently that John W. Blassingame and other scholars have subjected the autobiographies to critical scrutiny, and have found that many of the ex-slaves were not fugitives and that many had no abolitionist amanuenses. We now have a rich library of reprinted autobiographies, as well as critical criteria for their evaluation. An even richer mine of information is Greenwood Publishing Company's nineteen volume series, *The American Slave: A Composite Autobiography*, containing more than 2,000 WPA interviews with ex-slaves.[14] If allowances must be made for the biases of nineteenth-century autobiographies, allowance must also be made for the biases of WPA interviewers. Nevertheless, historians have begun to shed the prejudices which long defined as inadmissible the most revealing kinds of eye-witness evidence. One point on which the United States is indisputably unique among former slaveholding nations is in its abundance of documented slave testimony. The significance of that fact has not yet received the attention it deserves. In any event, the future course of historical inquiry will be no less dependent on the personal reminiscences of ex-slaves than on the demographic and econometric calculations that flow from the pioneering work of Curtin, Conrad, and Meyer. And if Stampp and Elkins addressed themselves to issues which now seem to have been superseded, it is only because the issues themselves have been incorporated into new frames of reference.

The Rewards and Perils of Presentism

American historians often write with a message for the present, assuming that their subject has, as Kenneth Stampp put it, a "peculiar urgency." But historians have little say about the public's definition of "relevance." In the 1950's no one could have predicted the astonishing upsurge of interest in American Negro slavery. Neither Stampp nor Elkins wrote for a bullish market. For some years specialists alone took note of their books. The research for most of the scholarly landmarks of the 1960's, such as Winthrop D. Jordan's *White Over Black* (1968), originated in an era of relative public indifference toward slavery and race. No doubt Little Rock, the lunch counter sit-ins, and the Freedom Rides all quickened a limited public interest in "historical background." But the true black studies boom commenced in 1963, fed by the unforgettable images of the Birmingham boycott; of Bull Connor's police and of the unconvictable Sheriff Lawrence Rainey; of Malcolm X exhorting Black Muslims; and of Martin Luther King electrifying the massed throngs in Washington.

How had America arrived at such a crisis? Where had the traditional assumptions and expectations gone astray? The presses churned out a small library of answers, flooding the literate public with paperbacks, essays, feature stories, scholarly monographs, and reprints of long forgotten works. If the modern reading public has generally abandoned history as a source of entertainment and edification, it retains a spasmodic need for quick historical orientation to immediate crises. The questions of the early 1960's were ethnocentrically self-evident. Why had Negroes failed to "assimilate" like other immigrant groups? Had the old schoolbooks been wrong in portraying slaves as relatively happy and well-treated? Why had Negroes ever been brought to America in the first place? The more popular explanations were not the work of historians, but often drew on Elkins and other recently established authorities. By the mid-1960's black writers began raising strident voices of dissent. The crisis, they insisted, was not one "in black and white," or in "race relations." White scholars who studied "the Negro problem" were simply the intellectual heirs of slaveholders who had studied problems of slave management. Black history, when controlled by whites and when dominated by the psychological needs of whites, was simply another weapon to preserve the cultural hegemony of the dominant race. The black critics grasped a crucial point, but soon blurred it by silly disputes over whether whites could legitimately write or teach about the black experience.

This is not the place to review the violent clashes over black studies programs in colleges and universities, or to examine the complex effects of public pressure on historical scholarship.[16] I shall content myself with three observations. First, it is obvious that the racial concerns of the 1960's channeled public and private funds into various programs for the study of Afro-American life and culture. Many of these programs sought to collect and disseminate well-known information. But in England and South America, as well as in the United States, the renewed interest in slavery also led to scholarly symposia, conferences, and coordinated research. By the late 1960's, scholars working on various aspects of New World slavery were closely in touch with one anothers' work. They also enjoyed an apparently insatiable market, by academic standards, for their outpouring of books and articles. It needs to be stressed, however, that the fruits of historical research take long to ripen. The serious revaluation of slavery began long before the public demand for historical background. The faddishness of Afro-American studies has produced a shelf of fly-by-night books of questionable merit. The classroom and textbook market has long been saturated. By now many students must be weary of readings on slavery and racial conflict; the memories of CORE and SNICC are as remote and distantly heroic as were the memories of Bastogne and Iwo Jima to the early 1950's. Yet we still await the full harvest of a decade's seeding: for example, the publication of the Frederick Douglass papers, the completion of Louis Harlan's masterful biography of Booker T. Washington, Eugene Genovese's monumental study of slave-master relations, the fruition of the Cliometric Revolution, to say nothing of studies that begin to compare the Negro slavery of the New World with various other historical forms of slavery and involuntary servitude. In other words, the civil rights and

Black Power movements gave an impetus, sometimes distorting, sometimes enriching, to a scholarly enterprise which really began with the pioneering work of C. L. R. James, Eric Williams, and Frank Tannenbaum, and which has hardly begun to reach its crest.

My second observation is that the urgency of the civil rights movement focused attention on white racial prejudice, particularly on its psychology and historical origins. Postwar historians, enlightened by the earlier environmentalist school of social science, have understandably been preoccupied with the origins of their forebears' Negrophobia. In a sense, their interest in slavery has been derivative. Was New World slavery a product of the colonizers' racial prejudice, or did the prejudice arise from a functional contempt for slaves? And is slavery the ultimate source of America's continuing racial malaise? These and related questions have been fruitful guides to inquiry, and have perhaps been definitively explored in such works as Jordan's *White Over Black* (1968), Carl N. Degler's *Neither Black nor White* (1971), and George M. Fredrickson's *The Black Image in the White Mind* (1971). It is conceivable, however, that the racial focus has cropped out questions of equal importance. Degler and others have underscored the point. For example, the attention devoted to racial conflict and racial adjustment—problems easily consigned to the realm of group psychology—may well have obscured questions of class, culture, and power that lead to the structural foundations of American society. I think it is not improbable that future studies of slavery will be less concerned with race as the ultimate reality, especially as we more accurately locate slavery on a spectrum of labor systems. Similarly, I suspect that future historians will be less certain about the importance of slavery in explaining post-emancipation patterns of racial oppression. Thus far, we have no comparative studies of the "reconstruction" patterns of apprenticeship, peonage, and share-cropping in post-emancipation societies.[16] Nor has anyone ventured to explain why, in the years immediately following the Armistice of 1918, race riots erupted in Liverpool and other English cities as well as in the United States.[17]

My final and broader observation, in this connection, is that postwar historians have not only striven to dissociate themselves from any taint of racism, but have defensively suggested that their own interpretation of slavery is the only one free from racist implications. The antiracist protestations are laudable, but the game of dodge ball has led to considerable confusion. Thus Kenneth Stampp proved his faith in equality by arguing that slaves suffered unspeakable hardships and deprivations, but were never crushed in spirit. His readers could conclude (1) that the deprivations helped to account for later seeming incapacities; (2) that slave resistance, which for Stampp included lying, stealing, sabotage, and work slowdowns, gave cause for hope; (3) that since the nation had sanctioned a system that wrought private profit at such a heavy human cost, the aggrieved heirs of slavery deserved some form of restitution.

But according to Stanley Elkins, even Stampp underestimated the deprivations. The typical slave had been broken in spirit, or in Elkins' terms, psychologically "infantalized." Only the harshest and most hopeless system of slavery could account for the American Negro's degradation—that is, for his servile dependence on whites, for his self-deprecation, for his lack of family stability, for his irresponsibility, and for his alienation from any cultural heritage or institutional identity.

This environmentalist thesis, presented as a rebuttal to theories of biological inferiority, opened Elkins to the charge of racism in disguise. Black critics, especially,
sensed that Elkins had accepted the racist terms of his presumed antagonists. Yet
the black critics could not easily free themselves from another bind. They hardly
wished to minimize the sufferings of their ancestors; yet they clearly saw the
hazards of being Elkinized. Who, after all, would want to claim Sambo for his
grandfather? Yet who, in the 1960's would want to claim that slavery was not as
bad as Elkins said? In point of fact, Elkins provided two escape routes. First, he insisted that Latin American slaves had not been reduced to Sambos. Hence the infantalization process could not be attributed to the African temperament or even to
slavery per se. It may have been little comfort for North American blacks to know
that their Latin neighbors had escaped the psychological traumas of slavery. But
Elkins also contended that the infantalization process had ended with emancipation. After the closed system had been broken, progress was possible. Time and
therapy could heal. Unfortunately, the historical evidence—especially that accumulated by Herbert Gutman, Genovese, Fogel, and Engerman—suggests that
American blacks had greater family stability and access to skilled occupations prior
to the Civil War than afterwards. It is clear that Elkins intended his harsh portrait
of slavery to provide the grounds for continuing white patience and forebearance.
In the 1950's, at least, it appeared that a more sanguine image of slavery could only
reinforce unenlightened complaints that enough allowances had been made, that
enough time had elapsed for Negroes to begin to behave like white men.

Genovese, in his earlier essays, attacked Elkins for underestimating the slaves'
capacity for resistance, the integrity of their separate culture, and their sustaining
ties with an African past. Genovese also frankly acknowledged the corollary to this
thesis: Southern slaveholders were not SS guards, systematically intent on torture
and human debasement. Indeed, they desired nothing more than the genuine
loyalty and gratitude of their slaves. Unlike the paid functionaries who managed
the West Indian plantations for absentee owners, the Southern proprietors had an
interest in creating a viable society. Genovese agreed with Elkins that Southern
planters were not content with labor discipline alone. They could accept nothing
less than total cultural hegemony, which required psychological dominion and the
shaping of slave personality. But to achieve these objectives, Genovese insisted, the
planters relied far less on coercion than on paternalism—that is, on alternating acts
of kindness and cruelty, on flattery and rebuke, on bribes and deprivations. In a
sense, Genovese turned Elkins upside down. White paternalism posed a far more
serious threat to black autonomy than did any coercive attempts at dehumanization. And the slaves' only hope for resisting total dominion lay not in self-defeating
insurrections or even in petty acts of theft and sabotage, but rather in responding
to paternalism on their own terms. That the slaves succeeded in transmogrifying
their masters' paternalism is the thesis of Genovese's *Roll Jordan Roll* (1974), one of
the crowning achievements of the entire postwar scholarship on race and slavery, a
work which brings a rich empathy, warmth, and humor to the dialectic of accommodation and resistance, a dialectic both subtle in process and deadly serious in
conflicting objectives.

The immense learning and human concreteness of *Roll Jordan Roll* may satisfy
critics who have objected to the abstractness of Genovese's categories and to the

fuzziness of his concept of paternalism. Yet his professed Marxism may no longer provide protective coloration against the charge of sentimentalizing or romanticizing slavery. There are still ideological risks in softening the conventional, neoabolitionist view of Negro slavery, notwithstanding Genovese's attempts to pay homage to the integrity of black culture and to assimilate racial conflict into a larger structure of class conflict. It remains to be seen whether radical credentials will allow Genovese to get away with his bold and brilliant rehabilitation of the black Mammy who ministers to the whites in the Big House, or of the black driver whose mediating role depends on a faithful execution of the master's discipline. Genovese has suggested that the unwitting racists are those who measure black religion and family life against white middle-class norms, who conclude that slaves were defenseless and emasculated victims, and who fasten the guilt for America's continuing racial oppression on a small group of malicious planters.[18] More than any other modern scholar, Genovese has defied the pressures and compromises of presentism, and has fought to lift historical scholarship above the irresponsible rhetoric of racial conflict. Yet Genovese's work is saturated with defenses against racial bias, defenses which have sometimes implied that only radical scholars can escape the liberals' typical condescension on race. And when unfairly accused of racism himself, Genovese has delivered shrill attacks on black students of "dubious political connections," who may well have been, as he asserts, "agents-provocateurs" bent on exploiting racial antagonisms for political purposes.[19]

My point is simply that even the bravest and most honest historians have not been able to escape the coercions of the times, and that each new interpretation of slavery has professed to be more antiracist than the ones it replaces. The supreme irony, in this curious pattern of protestation, comes with Fogel and Engerman's *Time on the Cross*, a work which in most respects would bring a smile of approval from the grim lips of John C. Calhoun.

Time on the Cross is at times a self-defeating book. Its critically important contributions, presented in the guise of scientific objectivity, are often muddied by an emotional style and animus which reflect two nonscientific compulsions of the age: first, the compulsion to replace the uncertainties of traditional, impressionistic history with "hard" scientific facts, verified by computers and mathematical techniques; second, the compulsion to prove that the findings of Cliometrics will not only "expose many myths that have served to corrode and poison relations between the races, but also help to put into a new perspective some of the most urgent issues of our day." Fogel and Engerman do not consider the possibility that the findings of supposedly impartial Cliometrics might further corrode and poison the relations between the races, or that the "new perspective" on the most urgent issues of our day might clash with their own personal values.

To be fair, the authors acknowledge the limitations of scientific history and profess the laudable goal of integrating Cliometrics with humanistic values. They contend that rigorous mathematical and statistical methods, combined with "formal behavioral models," will help to clarify moral issues and reduce the number of questions on which speculation is the only option. Fogel and Engerman also admit that they have not been entirely successful in expunging all ideology from their book (they define ideology as "an unverified proposition which is held to be true," as distinct from "knowledge" which has "been verified according to a set of objective criteria such as those employed in statistics or in various fields of science"). But despite the authors' homage to the humanities, despite their indispensable contributions to knowledge, their prose is redolent with the stale battlesmoke from the war of the Two Cultures. Their tone is both defensive and belligerent. They speak of their "passion for discovering the facts," of their unremitting search for "hard" evidence, of their disdain for the "easy solutions" evoked by ideological debate. In a lengthy appendix, which provides an invaluable analysis of "the traditional interpretation of the slave economy, 1865-1956," they nail Kenneth Stampp to the cross, taunting him for his statistical errors, his nonscientific methodology, and his failure "to effect a fundamental break with racist depictions of the antebellum Negro, despite his enormous desire to do so." To the quaking and besieged humanist, Fogel and Engerman speak casually of their legions of research assistants, of their mobile SAM computers, of their electronic weaponry, of their occupation of every hidden and unknown strategic site—in short, we are told that we are encircled, cut off, and cannot fight back unless we have weapons-systems equal to those of the Cliometricians.

Yet we are not told why objective scientists baptise their book with the evangelical title, *Time on the Cross,* or why they allow themselves the indulgence, for example, of accusing the abolitionists of helping "to fasten the spikes that have kept blacks in the agony of racial discrimination during their century of freedom." The tone of *Time on the Cross* is often similar to that of a modern sex manual. The scientific researchers not only promise to give us the inside dope, but candidly confess that they offer us a "disturbing book," one which requires the "forebearance" of its readers (presumably, mature adults). After the warning of X-rating, we learn that "some of the discoveries were at one time as unbelievable to the Cliometricians as they will be to the readers of this volume. Indeed, many of the findings presented in the chapters that follow were initially discounted, even rejected out of hand as being too absurd to be true." This sort of sensationalism whets the reader's appetite. Is it possible that heterosexuality or monogamous marriage are founded on unscientific data? Is it possible that slavery was a positive good, both for blacks and whites? Like most sex manuals, *Time on the Cross* startles us and then comes down on the side of righteousness.

The startling arguments would be unobjectionable if they had not been grouped as a series of revelations, if they had carried some sense of human meaning and of the individual personalities involved, if they had referred to specific situations and environments instead of to vague statistical aggregates, and if they had not been followed by antiracist protestations,which sound much like sermons on spontaneous sexuality after statistical tables on the incidence of orgasm. To be specific, Fogel and Engerman marshal considerable statistical evidence to show that Southern masters encouraged the family stability and promoted the material welfare of their slaves. The typical field hand, we learn, received during his lifetime approximately 90 percent of the income he produced. The slave system in no way thwarted the economic development of the South; in material terms, the slaves were no worse off than contemporary unskilled free workers. The blacks' opportunities and well-being declined after emancipation. Hence the Cliometricians would seem to have resurrected the essential arguments of proslavery philosophy. Of course Fogel and Engerman quickly deny this conclusion. The capital mistake of Kenneth Stampp and other neoabolitionist historians, they claim, was to focus attention on treatment and physical welfare. Slaves did suffer cultural and psychological deprivations—such as the denial of education and of access to the higher professions (we have no comparisons on such matters with Irish immigrants or women). From one point of view, according to Fogel and Engerman, the slaves did suffer exploitation. The true beneficiaries of the remarkably profitable system were the consumers of cotton textiles, whose diffused and therefore attenuated gains could not be justified by the concentrated losses of the slave labor force.

Yet Fogel and Engerman say very little about the implications of exploitation or the long-term effects of cultural deprivation. Of all the variables they consider, it is slave productivity that emerges as the dominant theme. They tell us that they have "attacked the traditional interpretation of the economics of slavery not in order to resurrect a defunct system but in order to correct the perversion of the history of blacks." The disastrous flaw in the abolitionist and neoabolitionist argument was to denigrate blacks by depreciating their performance as slaves, even when attributing the cause to an economic system. Hence Fogel and Engerman assert their own antiracism by detecting a subtle and lingering racism in those historians who have attributed "stunted development" not to biological inferiority but to "unfortunate sociological circumstances." With *Time on the Cross* we thus come full circle. A sanguine view of slavery, including its economic viability and its relative lack of deprivation, becomes a weapon in defense of black capability—of capability, it must be stressed, as defined by the standards of capitalist economics.

Convergence?

The weakest sections of *Time on the Cross* rest on a naive moralism and on a conviction that scientific history can resolve moral issues by at last setting the record straight. Fogel and Engerman's statistical data may or may not be modified over time, but they have already shaken conventional assumptions on the economics of Negro slavery. The substantive conclusions of *Time on the Cross* will not be easily brushed aside. On the surface, at least, the work of the Cliometricians would seem to be directly at odds with the work of Genovese. Like Stampp and Elkins, Fogel and Engerman insist on the capitalistic character of Southern slavery but argue that the forces of the market and of individual self-interest protected the slave from dehumanization. For Genovese, on the other hand, it was precisely the noncapitalist character of slaveholding that gave blacks room for maneuver and for preserving a cultural identity of their own. And according to Genovese, it was the noncapitalist aspects of slavery that ultimately defined the ideology of the master class and the fatal weaknesses of Southern society.

Insofar as *Time on the Cross* and *Roll Jordan Roll* represent the historiographical trends of the 1970's, they promise continuing controversy and point to diverging lines of interpretation. Yet further commentators may also be struck by certain lines of convergence. Genovese, no less than the Cliometricians, stresses the excellence and diversity of the slaves' occupational skills. As a result of the pioneering and tragically unfinished work of Robert Starobin, no one has recently questioned the adaptability of slave labor to mining and industry.[20] Michael Craton and James Walvin have shown that the most prosperous sugar estates of Jamaica depended on a tapping of slave talent, on an encouragement of slave skills and managerial ability, and ultimately on a slave elite of "Head People" who received preferential treatment.[21] When Fogel and Engerman offer statistical evidence on the stability of American slave families, they simply add strength to the arguments of Genovese, John Blassingame, and a host of other scholars—scholars who have also stressed the persistence and adaptability of African folklore, religion, iconography, and linguistic forms. In short, we have come a long way from the 1950's, when Elkins' concentration camp analogy seemed to explain the anomie and cultural disorientation which probably had less to do with slavery than with the Negroes' later migration to the ghettos of racially volatile cities. It is now at least conceivable that the share-cropper's "voluntary" move to Chicago or New York was at least as traumatic as the original slave trade.

Yet we must always be wary of presentist influences. The Birmingham of 1963 now seems almost as remote as the Mississippi plantation of 1853. Today the once intransigent South seems almost as benign as did Brazil, in the 1950's, to North American eyes. We are less prone to sectionalize our dilemmas and responsibilities, but thereby run the risk of idealizing the preurban slavocracies. If the emerging interpretations of slavery mark an undoubted advance in complexity and sophistication, we should also be suspicious of the interests they serve—the desire to prove that American Negroes preserved a degree of cultural autonomy; that they escaped the scars of psychic impairment; that a free market economy does not produce insoluble social problems; that a precapitalist labor system allows for more honest human interaction than does a wage-and-profit system; that our fundamental ills stem from urbanization and its accompanying lack of regional and familial identity.

To their credit, Fogel and Engerman refer constantly, if somewhat hazily, to the psychological costs of Negro slavery. It is precisely this realm which Stanley Elkins overdramatized, and which Eugene Genovese has sought to redefine in terms of class and ideology. The nonmeasurable realm of human dominion and resistance, which the Cliometricians helplessly classify as moral and ideological, is for Genovese the heart of the entire problem. If Genovese is right, and I think he is, the fundamental insight does not lie in Marx, or in the history of abolitionist propaganda, but in some highly condensed and eternally relevant passages "on lordship and bondage" in Hegel's *Phenomenology of the Mind*.

REFERENCES

1. Stanley M. Elkins, *Slavery: A Problem in American Institutional and Intellectual Life* (Chicago: University of Chicago Press, 1959), p. 1.

2. W. E. Woodward, *A New American History* (New York: Farrar & Rinehart, Inc., 1936), p. 412.

3. Gene Wise, *American Historical Explanations: A Strategy for Grounded Inquiry* (Homewood, Ill.: The Dorsey Press, 1973).

4. Kenneth M. Stampp, *The Peculiar Institution: Slavery in the Ante-Bellum South* (New York: Alfred A. Knopf, 1956), pp. vii-viii. It should be emphasized that Stampp's words have often been interpreted out of context, and that even his harshest critics, including Robert W. Fogel and Stanley W. Engerman, have striven to correct the misinterpretation.

5. Ann J. Lane, ed., *The Debate Over "Slavery": Stanley Elkins and His Critics* (Urbana, Ill.: University of Illinois Press, 1971).

6. Richard Hofstadter's counter-Progressive leadership culminated in his masterful critique, *The Progressive Historians: Turner, Beard, Parrington* (New York: Alfred A. Knopf, 1968).

7. See Lane, ed., *Debate Over "Slavery,"* and also Franklin W. Knight, *Slave Society in Cuba During the Ninteenth Century* (Madison: University of Wisconsin Press, 1970); Robert Brent Toplin, *The Abolition of Slavery in Brazil* (New York: Atheneum, 1972); Robert Conrad, *The Destruction of Brazilian Slavery, 1850-1888* (Berkeley: University of California Press, 1972); John W. Blassingame, *The Slave Community: Plantation Life in the Ante-Bellum South* (New York: Oxford University Press, 1972).

8. Lane, ed., *Debate Over "Slavery,"* pp. 350-359.

9. Eugene D. Genovese's initial essays have been collected in *In Red and Black: Marxian Explorations in Southern and Afro-American History* (New York: Pantheon Books, 1971). His thesis on the varying relationships between cultural heritage and the pressures of plantation agriculture can be found in *The World the Slaveholders Made: Two Essays in Interpretation* (New York: Pantheon Books, 1969), Part One. Genovese's detailed explorations of slave accommodation and resistance will appear in *Roll Jordan Roll* (1974). I am much indebted to Professor Genovese for allowing me to read the latter manuscript.

10. *The Political Economy of Slavery: Studies in the Economy and Society of the Slave South* (New York: Pantheon Books, 1965).

11. The essay, "The Economics of Slavery in the Ante-Bellum South," has been reprinted in Alfred H. Conrad and John R. Meyer, *The Economics of Slavery and Other Econometric Studies* (Chicago: Aldine Publishing Co., 1964). For a review of the literature on profitability, see Harold D. Woodman, "The Profitability of Slavery: A Historical Perennial," *Journal of Southern History,* 29 (August 1963), pp. 303-325, which has been reprinted, along with many other valuable selections, in Allen Weinstein and Frank Otto Gatell, *American Negro Slavery: A Modern Reader,* 2nd ed. (New York: Oxford University Press, 1973).

12. I am extremely grateful to Professors Fogel and Engerman for allowing me to read various manuscript versions of their forthcoming book, which will be published early in 1974 by Little, Brown and Company. Unfortunately, the deadline for this essay has prevented me from having access to more than limited portions of the revised proof of *Time on the Cross.* Some of my references therefore refer to manuscript. Although it is hazardous to offer judgments on a work that has not yet been published in final form, it would be even more hazardous to ignore a work which is bound to make 1974 a landmark in the historiography of slavery, and which in manuscript has already evoked international respect and controversy.

13. Philip D. Curtin, *The Atlantic Slave Trade: A Census* (Madison: University of Wisconsin Press, 1969).

14. George P. Rawick has written a valuable introductory volume to the series, *From Sundown to Sunup: The Making of the Black Community* (Westport, Conn.: Greenwood Publishing Co., 1972). It should be stressed that various black historians and social scientists, including Carter Woodson and E. Franklin Frazier, had earlier made valuable use of the black autobiographies and WPA narratives.

15. I have expressed some thoughts on this subject in a collection of essays which also provides a sampling of the black critique of white scholarship, *Black Studies in the University: A Symposium,* ed. Armstead L. Robinson, Craig C. Foster, and Donald H. Ogilvie (New Haven, Conn.: Yale University Press, 1969).

16. C. Vann Woodward has long been working on such questions, and provides intriguing suggestions of what his forthcoming studies may accomplish in *American Counterpoint: Slavery and Racism in the North-South Dialogue* (Boston: Little Brown, 1971).

17. For England, see James Walvin, *Black and White: The Negro and English Society, 1555-1945* (London: Allen Lane, the Penguin Press, 1973).

18. I should stress, however, that Genovese has scrupulously avoided accusing other scholars of racism.

19. Genovese, *In Red and Black*, p. vi. His reference was to the explosive conflicts at Sir George Williams University. It is a mark of the extreme pressures of presentism that Genovese felt it necessary to refer to such conflicts in dedicating a collection of historical essays. Although his phrasing gives the opposite impression, Genovese's mention of "agents-provocateurs" referred to whites, not blacks.

20. Robert Starobin, *Industrial Slavery in the Old South* (New York: Oxford University Press, 1970).

21. Michael Craton and James Walvin, *A Jamaican Plantation: The History of Worthy Park, 1670-1970* (Toronto: University of Toronto Press, 1970).

PHILIP D. CURTIN

The Black Experience of Colonialism and Imperialism

THE SERIOUS STUDY of African history in American and European universities began only in the 1950's, and detailed studies of African experience under colonialism are only now beginning to appear. Two traditions formerly dominant in Western historiography discouraged an earlier concern about Africa. One was a deep ethnocentric bias: history was the study of "our" past, which emphasized English history in England, French history in France, and American history in the United States. Africa was simply beside the point. And history was also elitist—concerned with those who governed countries, won battles, invented, discovered, and innovated. It was not much interested in the ordinary people of Europe and America, much less of Africa.

These beliefs were more serious for colonial Africa than they were for precolonial Africa, when Africans were in charge and their affairs could be emphasized in the same way those of European kings and prime ministers were in European history. But in the colonial period the obvious leaders, those who gave the orders and made policy, were European. Historians following the normal elitist tendencies of the discipline found themselves writing African history of the colonial period without leaving a place for African initiative. Nine-tenths of recent scholarship dealing with the colonial period has to do with the European conquests, European colonial policies, colonial government, economic development plans, and occasionally with the growth of the Western-educated elite that was to take over when the colonial period ended. Next to nothing is said about the way African societies responded to colonial rule, or about the impact of colonial policies on individual Africans.

This tendency is heightened by the fact that historians are used to working from written sources, and the main written sources for the colonial period are those of colonial governments, missions, European business firms, and European travelers. Much the same is true of American history, for that matter; nonliterates leave no record here either. There is a difference, however, in the fact that the elite who left the records here were members of the same society, and shared the common way of life or culture in the broad sense. Having grown up in contact with those who left no record, they had some opportunity to understand the submerged mass of their own society. Their record is therefore some reflection of the whole society, even though it has to be read and interpreted to allow for class prejudice.

In colonial Africa, on the other hand, the Europeans who left the records had rarely grown up in the society they observed; they rarely understood its language

17

or culture, and were unsympathetic with the parts they did understand. Thus their record is inadequate in the extreme. The research done by anthropologists was, of course, a notable exception, and studies of particular societies provide some of our best insights into the history of the colonial period. But the dominant anthropological tradition of that period was a kind of functionalism that stressed the description of a static society, purposely setting aside the consequences of the colonial impact in order to describe an "undisturbed" African culture.

Fortunately, many Africans are still alive who remember the colonial period very well, and new field work by historians using interviews rather than written documents has begun to yield a number of microcosmic studies, not unlike those of the anthropologists except that they are concerned principally with change through time and the impact of European rule.

These have begun to emerge only in the 1970's, however, and many of them are still available only as unpublished Ph.D. theses.[1] The standard works on African history in one or two volumes have not yet been affected. Their authors now treat the colonial period with a self-conscious sense of the problem, but still without benefit of the new work on the subject. Most, in fact, pass over the colonial period as a kind of postscript to the "real" African history.[2]

The history of the colonial period thus lagged, even behind the general rediscovery of African history in the West. Meanwhile, however, historians dealt with some outstanding questions of importance for understanding the colonial era. One of the central issues was the attitude of Europeans toward race difference, which lay behind all the policies they tried to follow in colonial Africa. In the wake of the Second World War, scholars began to look intensively at the racist ideology of the National Socialists in Germany, and this concern spread in the 1950's and 1960's and led to studies of European racial thought about Africans and Euro-American thought about Afro-Americans.[3] In the process, the roots of racial prejudice began to come into better focus, and it could be recognized as an influence on the course of history, not merely a present problem. Ordinary xenophobic prejudice has, in fact, been a common feature of past societies where differences in physical appearance ran parallel to differences in culture or social class. An observer sees a bundle of traits that appear to go together among another group of human beings. It is only natural to assume that they went together in other times and places and to associate them with the most obvious trait in the group, usually physical appearance. Words that begin with an ethnic meaning frequently gain a cultural or social meaning through time, and, in some instances, the original ethnic meaning drops away altogether. The word "slave" is an example. The classical Latin for "slave" was *servitus,* but slaves were so frequently slavs from the east that *servitus* dropped out of Medieval Latin beginning in the ninth century and *sclavus* took its place, becoming the root of "slave" in English and of cognates in Arabic and most European languages.[4] The same thing happened to "Negro" in some varieties of West African English and French. From its first meaning of "black" in Spanish, the root led to words like *nègre* and "nigger" in eighteenth-century French and English respectively, which designated a person's status as a slave rather than his race as such. In some varieties of West African English, the racial sense disappeared and "nigger" came to mean simply an employee or social subordinate, so that a European ship's captain arriving at a port in the Niger delta might be met with a polite request to know whose "nigger" he was—who, in other words, were the owners of the ship?

Early Western racism was based on prejudice in the original sense of prejudging an issue before all the facts were known. Africans were assumed to be of slave status, but only until they were found to be otherwise. Then treatment of them changed. European slave dealers on the West African coast treated African kings with the greatest deference. They dealt with African merchants as equals, and sometimes took their sons to Europe for education, treating them as members of their own families. In much the same way, Pushkin's African grandfather cut an impressive figure at the Russian and French courts of the early eighteenth century because the Czar's patronage had established his position in society. Prejudice rooted in simple ignorance could be removed when the ignorance was removed.

But that changed in the nineteenth century, when ordinary xenophobic prejudice gained the support of what then passed for science. The origins of this shift go back to certain ideas that were common in eighteenth-century Europe, especially to the idea of the "great chain of being" which held that the universe of living things was arranged in hierarchic order from the highest to the lowest. As biologists began to classify species, they tended to rank them, and it seemed natural enough to rank the varieties of mankind as well. Since European biologists did the ranking, it was only natural that they should put themselves at the top. And, since skin color is the most obvious physical trait, it seemed natural to give the lowest rank to people whose skin color was most different from their own. The fact that Africans in the Western world were mainly slaves helped to confirm this prejudice. The great material progress of industrial Europe made nineteenth-century Europeans even more arrogant about their own achievements, in contrast to the "barbarism" they thought they saw in the civilizations of India, China, and Africa—and it is worth remembering that Africans were classified by Europeans as "barbaric" through the first half of the nineteenth century, not as "savage" the way American Indians usually were. After the 1860's Darwinian biology made biology in general appear in a new guise as the science that could explain how the world came to be as it was. Darwin himself had little to say about racial differences, but his views were at least consonant with "scientific" racism, and others wrote about race struggle in much the same terms he had used in discussing the struggle for survival among species.

This "scientific" support of the new racism was serious because it was virtually uncontested, and it meant that a person's prejudice could no longer be removed by new information. The eighteenth-century slave traders visiting the Gold Coast had adjusted rapidly enough to the fact that their African counterparts were intelligent men. At least one midnineteenth-century visitor was struck with the same fact, but, since he *knew* the teachings of "science" about the inferiority of Negroes, he decided that the Akan must not be Negroes, in spite of their physical appearance.[5]

The timing of "scientific" racism was of the greatest importance because this development in European intellectual history happened to intersect with quite independent trains of events in Africa and in the United States. The peak of unchallenged "scientific" racism fell between about 1880 and 1920. In North America, federal efforts to reconstruct the defeated Confederacy had recently been abandoned, and the Euro-Americans of the southern states were again in charge and free to establish a new relationship between the races. The result was Jim Crow segregation and effective removal of political rights throughout the South. These decades also saw the first mass migration by Afro-Americans from the former slave states into the northern cities, and was hence a formative period in northern race relations as well. A recent revisionist interpretation of United States, based on quantitative indices, shows that Afro-Americans were materially better off under slavery than they were in the late nineteenth-century phase of racial oppression.[6]

In Africa, the high tide of "scientific" racism coincided with the European conquest of Africa and the first imposition of colonial rule. Imperialist thought of that period was thoroughly impregnated with the view that the ruled were permanently inferior to their new masters. They were to be ruled in their own best interest, and the period of "trusteeship" was assumed to stretch far indeed into the future. The high-minded Covenant of the League of Nations promised ultimate independence to the "white" Arab provinces of the Ottoman Empire, but it promised no such thing to the former German colonies in Africa.

Thus, on both sides of the Atlantic, the era of "scientific" racism ushered in a period when Europeans and Euro-Americans accepted racial subordination because they thought it was part of the nature of things. The abolitionists, who had secured the end of slavery, allowed Jim Crow laws without protest. The British, who had ended West Indian slavery and done more than any other nation to suppress the Atlantic slave trade, allowed South Africa to become independent with full power in the hands of a minority of overseas Europeans; and racial oppression continues in southern Africa to the present.

One problem in discussing imperialism and colonialism is the words themselves. Like "nationalism" and "tribalism," any narrow meaning they may once have had has long since expanded into a cloud of loose implications and emotional overtones. Both "imperialism" and "colonialism" will have to be redefined or abandoned before the history of colonial Africa can be set straight, and the process will not be easy. Men from William of Occam to Humpty Dumpty (speaking for Lewis Carroll) have argued that a word can mean whatever a writer wants it to mean, "neither more nor less."[7] But a long gap lies between the truth of formal logic and the art of communication, and these words bear such emotional weight from past usage that no amount of propping up with redefinition can give them strength enough to carry an unambiguous message.

The strange death of the long historical controversy over the "Marxist interpretation" of European "imperialism" is a case in point. The quotation marks are necessary partly because Marx himself had next to nothing to say on the subject, initially raised to prominence by J. A. Hobson's *Imperialism: A Study,* published in 1902. Hobson was writing in the political context of the Anglo-Boer War in South Africa, in which Britain's desire to protect her investment was an obvious and important motive. On the basis of economic arguments more pre-Keynesian than Marxian, he concluded that one underlying cause of the European overseas conquest and seizure of new territory in the decades just past had been a need to invest in places where interest rates were higher than they could be in the saturated capital market of Europe. Lenin's pamphlet, *Imperialism: The Highest Form of Capitalism,*[8] came out during the First World War and appeared to adopt Hobson's arguments as its own. With that, the controversy was fully launched, but it never went very far. In the African context at least, the value of the Witwatersrand was clear enough, but no capitalists showed a clear desire to invest large amounts in tropical Africa—either before the conquest or after.

In fact, historians of Africa over the years have taken to giving brief notice to the Hobson thesis, and then passing on to other subjects. No recent historian has tried to take up Hobson's case and argue it with new evidence. It was dying from old age and lack of revision when it was killed off by a theoretical analysis by Winslow in 1948 and a frontal attack on its implications for Africa by Gallagher and Robinson in 1961.[9] In recent years, several of the more prominent Marxist historians and economists have dropped the idea that economic motives prompted the Europeans to conquer Africa; at least one attributes the exploitation of Africa to the proverty of European capitalism, rather than to its drive for expansion.[10] This is not to say that the European conquest of Africa was innocent of material motives, only that the line of argument which tied these motives to particular aspects of the European economy never had a prominent body of advocates.

In retrospect, even Lenin's association of "imperialism" with an economic interpretation of the conquest of Africa turns out to be a case of mistaken identity in the semantic jungle of loaded words. "Imperialism" has its linguistic roots in a Latin word meaning "to command." Once it entered the name of the Roman Empire, "empire" came to mean any maximal political unit and was passed down through a sequence that included the Holy Roman Empire, the French Empires of Napoleon I and Napoleon III, the Russian Empire of the Czars, and Bismarck's *Deutches Reich*. None of these states had anything to do with the most common English sense of "imperialism"—the policy of imposing political control over distant and alien societies. That sense of the term came rather late in English for that matter: the British rarely called their colonies an "empire" before the middle of the nineteenth century, and the word carried Napoleonic overtones in England until the 1870's, when Disraeli gave Queen Victoria the title "Empress of India." Even then, the word "imperialist" referred to a person who believed that Britain should have close ties with self-governing colonies like Canada and Australia. Its meaning changed only gradually from 1880 to 1895, by which date "imperialist" clearly meant "expansionist." It was another curious accident of timing that the word spread to America at that stage with only the final expansionist meaning.

That set the trap to confuse a half century of students with an American background who set out to read Lenin's *Imperialism*. In fact, Lenin referred not to the jingo imperialism of the English-speaking world but to the continental imperialism of Imperial France, the Kaiser's Germany, or the Czar's Russia. Lenin wrote about the historical stage of monopoly capitalism, defined as ". . . capitalism in that stage of development . . . in which the partition of all the territories of the globe among the great capitalist powers has been *completed*."[11] Lenin's imperialism, in short, began only after Hobson's imperialism was finished. This point, however, managed to slip past the general notice of historians until Eric Stokes recalled it to their attention in 1969.[12]

By that time it made little difference, since historians already tended to divide the study of any specific act of overseas conquest into two parts. One group went on dealing with its diplomatic aspect—the European impetus, and the relations among the European powers. With the rise of African history into professional respectability, quite another group began to be concerned with the results of that act of conquest in Africa itself. It was as though one group took "imperialism" as its field, while the other took "colonialism"—the distinction following one set of the many meanings of these two terms.

"Colonialism," like "imperialism," carries a comet's tail of burnt-out meaning. Its Latin root, *colonia*, meant farm or estate, and came from a verb meaning to till the soil. This was stretched to mean first a new agricultural settlement, then a settlement in a new country. "Plantation" had the same origins and significance in seventeenth-century English, but it kept its agricultural connotation. "Colony," on the other hand, came to mean first the body of people who moved to set up a new offshoot of their old society, then the political unit that governed such settlers, and then, in still another extension, any distant dependency, especially overseas. (The United States and Canada, for example, are always careful to call their dependencies "territories" when they are contiguous with the self-governing states or provinces.) Finally, "colonialism" came to mean simply alien rule, though the earlier meanings were not quite extinguished.

Meanwhile, in the first half of this century, "colonialism" began to acquire an opposing -ism—"nationalism." The beginnings of this term go back to nineteenth-century Europe, where "nationalism" was the dream of having one's nationality incorporated in an independent state, such as a unified Germany or a reborn Poland. Indians under the British Raj called their independence movement "nationalist," and consciously compared their aspirations with those of the Greeks and the Irish. In the wake of the First World War, movements in opposition to colonial rule appeared in Africa and called themselves "nationalist," although they lacked the idea of resurrecting pre-existing "nations." They might have chosen that goal and sought to regain independence for the Asante or Oyo, but instead organizations of the 1920's, like the National Congress of British West Africa, worked first for specific reforms in colonial rule, then for the distant goal of independence for the territorial units that Britain used to govern Africa. Once the concept of "nation" was dropped from the African variant of "nationalism," the term meant nothing more than opposition to alien rule. It is, of course, these new and stripped-down meanings that militant Afro-Americans use when they claim to be "colonized" within the United States, and describe their own movements as "nationalist."

It may be worthwhile to start fresh and look at the actual content of situations labeled "colonialism" in usual, common-sense, recent usage. The point of reference is a government by people of one culture over people of a different culture—usually of Europeans over non-Europeans because that situation has been common in recent history. Today "colonialism" also carries overtones of disapproval. The Colonial Dames are not likely to choose "colonialism" as the most apt word to describe the eighteenth-century British migration to the thirteen colonies. Nor would present-day Africans choose "colonialism" to describe a government by fellow-Africans, however despotic. Within Europe, it is not used to refer to rule over national minorities, thus recognizing a real difference between Italian rule over the German-speaking minority in Alto Adige and Italian rule over Libya. Even Portugal, which theoretically rules its colonies as "overseas provinces," has to recognize that the Azores, which are inhabited entirely by people of Portuguese origin, are very different from provinces like Angola where the vast majority of the people are African.

This common usage of "colonialism," however, needs to be narrowed and honed still more to become a useful concept.[13] It sometimes fails, for example, to distinguish sharply between race and culture—between the inherited physical traits and the way of life, which is learned. "Scientific" racism made the same mistake, and racism pervaded European thought in the colonial era. The Europeans always imagined that colonial rule involved rule over people of another "race," even when the physical differences were as insignificant as those between French and Algerians. In retrospect, it is obvious that the physical difference, however striking or obvious, was only a kind of badge of the cultural difference that best identifies colonial rule and separates it from other forms of oppression. However disagreeable, both German anti-Semitism and American segregation, for example, need to be distinguished from "colonialism." Jews were persecuted in Nazi Germany ostensibly on grounds of race; Afro-Americans have met a hundred kinds of adverse discrimination on similar grounds, yet neither German Jews nor Afro-Americans were very different in culture from other Germans or Americans of the same region and social class.

Still another aspect of the older definitions needs to be set aside. This is the factor of distance from a ruling metropolis. The narrower meaning I am suggesting—domination by people of another culture—is equally possible within an independent state. When South Africa became legally independent of Britain in 1931, the change made no significant difference in the status or experience of the majority of South Africans. The Quechua of the Peruvian Andes in the first half of this century were just as fully in a colonial situation as their ancestors were two centuries earlier when the overseas Europeans in Lima were themselves ruled from Spain.

The narrower definition of colonialism as cross-cultural political domination thus helps to point up the very different experience of "black" Americans and "black" Africans in recent decades. It helps to explain why historians who attack and historians who defend the colonial record in Africa reach such different conclusions on nearly the same evidence. And it provides a key to important variables distinguishing the different *kinds* of colonial experience in different parts of Africa.

One obviously important factor is the relative numbers of people in the subordinate and dominant cultures of a particular colony. At one end of the African scale is Nigeria, where the census of 1952-1953 showed only 0.03 percent Europeans in the total population—and that census is notorious for undercounting Africans. For convenience, colonial rule in which a minimal number of Europeans are present can be identified as the Nigerian type. At the opposite pole, on a world-wide scale, is Australia, where settlers came in such numbers and with such disastrous epidemiological consequences for the local people that the native population all but disappeared. In Africa, the closest approach to the Australian type came in South Africa, where 30.1 percent of the population was Western in culture in about 1956. Census data accumulated by the United Nations for that period shows the range of possibilities between South Africa and Nigeria (see Table 1). The top group of South Africa, Algeria, and Southern Rhodesia are the three places in

Table 1

European Settlement and Per Capita Productivity at the End of the Colonial Period[14]

Country	Percentage of Population Classified European (1956)	Per Capita National Income in Dollars (1958)
Union of South Africa	30.1°	346
Algeria	10.9	221
Southern Rhodesia	7.2	no separate data
Tunisia	6.7	176
Morocco (former French zone)	5.4	191
Federation of the Rhodesias and Nyasaland	3.5	132
Northern Rhodesia	3.0	no separate data
Nyasaland	2.7	no separate data
Angola	2.5	no data
Mozambique	1.0	no data
Kenya	0.9	78
Belgian Congo	0.8	76
French West Africa	0.5	133
French Equatorial Africa	0.5	126
Tanganyika	0.3	48
Ghana	0.1	194
Uganda	0.1	57
Nigeria	0.03	69

° Counts the "colored" population as culturally Western. On racial basis alone, percentage "European" is 20.8.

Africa where European settlers have fought or declared their intention to fight for their local dominance, even if it meant opposition to the home country as it did with the OAS in Algeria and the declaration of unilateral independence by Rhodesia. Another significant break in the scale comes between the Belgian Congo and French West Africa; from that point down the scale toward Nigeria, the colonial regime followed comparatively lax policies of racial segregation.

Though it reflects broad patterns in race relations, Table 1 does not reflect the situation with precise accuracy or detail. Parts of south Kivu in the Belgian Congo, the region around Nairobi in central Kenya, the cities of Dakar in Senegal and Abidjan in the Ivory Coast, for example, all had regional concentrations of Europeans that fail to show up in gross statistics. The importance of the settler presence also differed according to whether the settlers intended to make a home in Africa, or simply to make a fortune and go back to Europe. The French, for example, tended to take frequent vacations in France and meant to retire there. The English who acquired estates in the countryside of highland Kenya more often hoped to stay into retirement and raise their families in Africa, and this intent helped to form their attitude toward African aspirations.

The scale of cultural demography in Table 1 is also faulty in another respect. Just as it necessarily leaves out the Australian type, it also leaves out certain New World types of colonialism that hardly existed in Africa. In Africa, most people met the European invasions with their societies intact, even though they were eventually defeated and subjected to alien rule. The form of cultural interaction was very different where Africans were uprooted as individuals and set down in another country where the whole social structure was created by Euro-Americans and run for Euro-American ends. Here too, a range of different cultural-demographic mixtures came into existence. At one extreme are countries like Haiti and Jamaica, where the input of slaves from Africa was so intense over the centuries that today virtually everyone is at least partly of African descent. This Jamaican type of minimal European presence can be seen as a New World parallel to the Nigerian type in Africa, but the differences are more striking than the similarities. The social fabric that might have helped the African immigrants to protect and transmit their way of life to new generations was pulled away in the passage through the slave trade. Each individual found himself assigned a social niche, surrounded by strangers. He was forced to learn the ways of the new society, and he found it hard indeed to pass on much of the old culture to his children. The new culture was not necessarily a distinctly Western culture. It was more often an amalgam of cultures from several "old countries" set in a matrix of Western language, religion, and social structure.

North America, however, was different. The northern colonies began as an approximation of the Australian type, but the southern colonies were a mixed case where the slave plantations were close to the Jamaican type while small farmers in the same areas were a separate community closer to the Australian pattern. The local cultural amalgam was not as African as that of the West Indies, but it was assimilated by "white" as well as by "black" southerners. This took a long time, but Afro-Americans and Euro-Americans lived side by side in the South for a long time. The Afro-American time of arrival in North America is indicative. The median date, at which half of all African immigrants had arrived, falls in the 1760's, while the equivalent for Euro-Americans falls at about 1900. The prolonged separation from their African roots caused Afro-Americans to become thoroughly Western in all important aspects of culture. The strains in New World societies were therefore primarily between racial groups with only minor cultural differences. In North Africa, they were between cultural groups with only minor racial differences. In sub-Saharan Africa, they were both cross-cultural and racial.

That long digression is important as background for the paradoxes and controversies that surround the colonial period in Africa. One group of historians—broadly speaking the defenders of the colonial record—point to the colonial experience as a form of enforced modernization, painful at times, but necessary for the ultimate benefit of Africa.[15] They draw attention to the impact of education in Western languages, to the contribution of missionary schools and hospitals, to economic growth with the opening of export markets and the exploitation of untouched mineral wealth. Especially in South Africa, the defenders of *apartheid* make much of the material well-being of the African population which is, though far worse off than the overseas Europeans, sometimes a little better off than some African populations in tropical Africa. Lewis Gann and Peter Duignan make a special point in favor of the settlers' Africa—that colonies with relatively numerous settlers experienced the most rapid economic development and arrived at the end of the colonial period with the highest per capita incomes. Table 1, compiled independently from data assembled by the U. N., seems, at first glance, to support their contention. Only Ghana and the two French-ruled federations of colonies do not show close correlation between percentage of Europeans and per capita income. Ghana's large per capita incomes are explained by its special position as the world's biggest cocoa producer, while those of the two French federations also rest mainly on the agricultural and timber wealth of the tropical forest. These resources required comparatively little European capital or technology. The table may also fail to reflect certain African earnings outside the modern economy. The main problem, however, is not the probable high level of inaccuracy of the numbers themselves, but the interpretation they can be made to yield. The argument that material well-being resulted from European settlement mistakes correlation for causation; it's like blaming the police for traffic tie-ups because, at the center of any traffic jam, you find a policeman directing traffic. Having conquered all of Africa by the end of the last century, Europeans were free to choose where to place their investment, where their skill and technology would pay the highest dividends. By making the right decisions for their own self-interest, they went where the resource endowment was ripe for development. The greater wealth of settlers' Africa is therefore the result of men and capital following resources. Given their superior technology, it could be argued that they should have done far better than they did in comparison with countries like Ghana, where economic development remained largely in African hands.

The defenders of the colonial record, however, are not concerned with material things alone. Gann and Duignan cast up a balance sheet in *Burden of Empire* and come to this summary conclusion: "In our view, the imperial system stands out as one of the most powerful engines of cultural diffusion in the history of Africa; its credit balance by far outweighs its debit account."[16] Indeed, the degree to which Western culture has replaced the original African culture follows the cultural-demographic types. The greatest Westernization occurred where the Africans were uprooted and remained a minority, as in North America, and the next most where they were uprooted but formed the bulk of the population, as in Jamaica. In Africa, the degree of cultural change also tends to be greatest where most Europeans have settled, though with variations depending on the index used to measure it. Conversion to Christianity follows one pattern, for example, while literacy in a Western language follows another. As a proposition with admitted exceptions, the generalization stands: cultural change was greatest among the uprooted who were moved to the Americas, next greatest in those parts of Africa where Europeans were most numerous, while African cultures survived most successfully where Africans were left alone.

On this point, anticolonialists and procolonialists agree, but many anticolonialist historians see the "powerful engine of cultural diffusion" as a monster to be feared, not praised. They see the European impact as a massive homogenizing steamroller that tended to destroy the variety and value of human experience in Africa.[17] A similar point of view appeared in the radical anticolonialism of the New Left in the 1960's. Frantz Fanon was far more concerned with psychic injury than with mere material exploitation. He put aside claims on the solidarity of the working class everywhere in favor of another kind of solidarity for the non-Western world as a whole. *Les damnées de la terre* ends with an appeal to the third world not to follow the European course toward modernization but to strike out in new directions.[18]

The survival of African cultures was not merely of sentimental value. Racism hurt least where African culture was most intact. An accusation of permanent and inherent inferiority obviously caused no mental anguish among Africans who knew nothing about it. Those who saw Europeans only at long intervals could lead their lives within a framework of ideas and social relations that protected their sense of identity and self-respect. Even those Africans in frequent contact with Europeans were protected if they had a community of their own where nearly everyone shared values and attitudes different from those of the alien rulers. At the other end of the scale, the most difficult situation was one in which Africans were in constant contact with those who claimed superiority. Where overseas Europeans were in the majority, as they were in North America, they could dominate the channels of information so thoroughly that many Afro-Americans in the early decades of this century were led to a half-belief that they were indeed inferior and that their place in society was "proper." The racial accusation was probably more damaging in North America than it was even in South Africa because Afro-Americans were at the mercy of the Euro-American media. The differences in language and communication patterns had long since been erased. By the same token, the racial accusation was more damaging in settlers' Africa than it was in tropical Africa, where protecting cultures were better preserved.

Thus, while a rough hierarchy of material well-being for African and Afro-Americans can be traced from the Afro-North-Americans at the top, through a range of settler societies, down to the most out-of-the-way parts of tropical Africa; there is a reverse hierarchy of cultural change toward Western norms and consequent psychic damage from racist accusations. The parallels between the two are not perfect, especially when it comes to the great variety of different social and economic conditions found in the tropical Americas but they are close enough to suggest that the current controversy between pro- and anti-colonialists is still another case of mistaken identity. What one group sees as Europe's theft of culture and identity, the other sees as an "engine of cultural diffusion."

Perhaps the controversy will simply die out of its own accord. The main voices in contention are, after all, those of outsiders—mainly British or South African on the pro-colonial side, while Fanon was Afro-French from the Antilles and only African by adoption. African historians from the new universities in tropical Africa have not, in fact, been very much concerned to argue about the colonial period, which they see as a comparatively brief period in the whole history of Africa, though one of unusual importance. They are not much concerned about the loss of African culture, because they recognize that African culture is not lost in their countries. Their historical revision is not so much a series of low marks for the colonial rulers as an insistence—in which they are absolutely right—that much of the initiative and direction of historical change in Africa, even in the colonial period, came from Africans.

REFERENCES

1. Of those recently published, see, for example, Steven Feireman, *The Shambaa Kingdom: A History* (Madison: University of Wisconsin Press, 1973).

2. American Heritage, *The Horizon History of Africa* (New York: American Heritage, 1971); Basil Davidson, *Africa: History of a Continent* (New York: Macmillan, 1966); E. Jefferson Murphy, *History of African Civilization* (New York: Crowell, 1972). The emphasis on the precolonial period is even there in works by African historians dealing with relatively recent history. See J. B. Webster and A. A. Boahen with H. O. Idowu, *History of West Africa. The Revolutionary Years—1815 to Independence* (New York: Praeger, 1967).

3. Philip D. Curtin, *The Image of Africa* (Madison: University of Wisconsin Press, 1964); David B. Davis, *The Problem of Slavery in Western Culture* (Ithaca: Cornell University Press, 1966); Winthrop D. Jordan, *White Over Black* (Chapel Hill: University of North Carolina Press, 1968); P. D. Curtin, *Imperialism* (New York: Harper and Row, 1971).

4. Charles Verlinden, *The Beginnings of Modern Colonization* (Ithaca: Cornell University Press, 1970), pp. 35-37.

5. Curtin, *op. cit.*, p. 320.

6. Robert Fogel and Stanley Engerman, *Time on the Cross* (Boston: Little Brown, 1974).

7. Lewis Carroll, *Through the Looking Glass*, Ch. IV (New York: Modern Library, 1924).

8. V. I. Lenin, "Imperialism: The Highest Stage of Capitalism," *Selected Works* (New York: International Publishers, 1943), 5:5-119.

9. E. M. Winslow, *The Pattern of Imperialism: A Study in the Theories of Power* (New York: Columbia University Press, 1948); Ronald Robinson and John Gallagher with Alice Denney, *Africa and the Victorians* (London: Macmillan, 1961).

10. Samir Amin, *L'Afrique de l'ouest bloquée: l'économie politique de la colonisation 1880-1970* (Paris: Editions de Minuit, 1971), Introduction.

11. Lenin, *op. cit.*, Ch. 6.

12. "Late Nineteenth-Century Colonial Expansion and the Attack on the Theory of Economic Imperialism: A Case of Mistaken Identity?" *The Historical Journal*, 12 (1969), pp. 285-301.

13. Simply to keep the record straight, I should add that I have used somewhat different terminology in the past, referring to the situation here called "colonialism" in the narrow sense "true empire," and reserving the term "true colony" for the actual dispatch of settlers to form a new community.

14. United Nations, Department of Economic and Social Affairs, *Economic Survey of Africa Since 1950* (New York: 1959), pp. 13, 15.

15. The principal spokesmen for this point of view have been L. H. Gann and Peter Duignan especially in their *Burden of Empire. An Appraisal of Western Colonialism in Africa South of the Sahara* (Stanford: Hoover, 1967). The larger *Colonialism in Africa, 1870-1960* (London: Cambridge University Press, 1969–), which they are editing in five volumes, represents many different points of view in addition to those of the editors. For an English representative of the procolonial school see Margery Perham, *The Colonial Reckoning* (New York: Knopf, 1962).

16. Gann and Duignan, *Burden of Empire*, p. 362.

17. Like the generally procolonialist view, this point of view is not found so much in particular historical works where it is argued at length. It turns up, rather, as an accompanying attitude in a number of different works by principal historians of Africa. One of the leading figures is Terrence Ranger whose first important work was *Revolt in Southern Rhodesia, 1896-97* (Evanston: Northwestern University Press, 1968). He has recently been concerned with the role of religion in African history. A second anti-assimilationist is Yves Person whose major work, *Samori. Une revolution Dyoula*, 3 vols. (Dakar: Institut fondamental d'Afrique noir, 1969-), is again a study of African resistance to European conquest. It may be worth noting that these two men are from Ireland and Brittany respectively, which may account for some of their sympathy for cultural diversity.

18. Frantz Fanon, *Les damnées de la terre* (Paris: 1961), translated into English as *The Wretched of the*

Earth (London: Penguin, 1965). Meanwhile, a still newer criticism is beginning to appear from the Left, concerned not with colonial rule as such but rather with the possibilities of manipulation inherent in the enormous industrial power of the developed world. It is associated, first of all, with the plight of the primary producers faced with fluctuating world prices for their products. It first became a guiding idea for historical re-interpretation with regard to Latin America—in English notably A. Gunder Frank, *Capitalism and Underdevelopment in Latin America* (New York: Monthly Review, 1967). The key issues are not colonialism and anticolonialism, or even capitalism and anticapitalism, but rather the relations between the more and less developed worlds. Walter Rodney made a broad and popular sweep over African history with some of these ideas in *How Europe Underdeveloped Africa* (London: Bogle-L'Ouverture Publications, 1972). The principal spokesman for a similar position in French is Samir Amin in several works of which *L'Afrique de l'ouest bloquée: l'economie politique de la colonisation 1880-1970* (Paris: Editions de Minuit, 1971) is representative, while the most serious scholarly study to take these issues into account so far is A. G. Hopkins, *An Economic History of West Africa* (London: Longman, 1973).

MICHAEL BANTON

1960: A Turning Point in the Study of Race Relations

RECENT YEARS HAVE seen a revival of interest in the question whether race relations are ultimately reducible to class relations.[1] Some writers have maintained that race relations situations can be distinguished from other kinds of social situations and that the field of race relations study can therefore be defined by its subject matter.[2] In my view it is more illuminating to see this field—like others—as defined by a tradition of inquiry, for this enables us to take account not only of what is studied but of who does the studying and the context within which they work. As in any academic field, the problems which have interested race relations scholars have changed from generation to generation; so have their theories, and the boundaries of their field.

A Tradition of Inquiry

If one attempts to define a field by its subject matter, boundaries are important, for the definition must plot a fence around it. If, on the other hand, one defines a field in terms of a tradition, this puts the focus on the core problems at the center, and it is not important to put up a fence at the edges. This is particularly relevant when discussing any international field of study, for there are often different traditions or subtraditions in different countries. A scholar engaged in the field can identify foreign scholars as working on topics of common interest though the areas of overlap do not fall into any simple pattern. The historian of science can describe the way in which traditions of inquiry have developed and locate the points in time when one paradigm of problem-finding and problem-solving has been overthrown in favor of something new. At any particular moment in time the general picture is apt to be one of confusion, but the course of change becomes comprehensible afterwards. We can learn a great deal from studying the history of our tradition, especially from the mistakes and experiences of our predecessors. They too are our colleagues.

The tradition of race relations study began in the middle of the nineteenth century. If one seeks an event and a date to mark the beginning, the best is the publication in 1850 of Robert Knox's *The Races of Men*. A new phase opened with the attempt to apply in sociology the principles uncovered by Charles Darwin; a convenient marker for this is the publication in 1875 of Ludwig Gumplowicz's *Rasse und Staat*. For a considerable period the study of race relations put the stress on race rather than on relations, and took its guidelines from biology. With the rise of sociology in the United States a new approach extricated itself from the coils of social Darwinism. There was no sharp transition but as good an indication as any of the change was the publication in 1921 of the textbook edited by Robert E. Park and Ernest W. Burgess, *An Introduction to the Science of Sociology*. Later in this essay I shall argue that in about 1960 there was a change in the study of race relations every bit as profound as the previous ones. Before coming to that, however, it will be well to describe the previous phases. In the advance of a science any new theory must explain everything accounted for by the previous theory, plus something new. It should be possible to find such a sequence in the study of race relations.

Racial Typology

In the first half of the nineteenth century the framework within which scholars contemplated the interrelations of peoples was drawn from the Old Testament. The dominant view was that all peoples descended from Adam and Eve. The word "race" was used in what now seems a loose fashion to identify many different categories of humans. That some peoples were less advanced technologically than others was seen as the will of God, the consequence of environment, or the outcome of differences in their moral life—culture, as we would now say. As the study of man's physical nature advanced, all this changed. The conviction grew that mankind had consisted originally of a limited number of independently created races of varying capacity and with distinctive abilities. Some mixing had occurred, but it still made sense to see each man or woman as the representative of a particular race. Knox was the first to express this new outlook in book form. He argued that race was the key to history, explaining the outcome of the major events in man's story. Race or physical nature determined culture. Moreover, it explained the relations between races, for according to Knox each race displayed an innate antagonism toward its enemies. In the 1840's and 1850's Englishmen, stimulated by novelists like Scott, Lytton, and Kingsley, were coming increasingly to think of themselves as a distinctive race and nation, and to look at other peoples in terms of race rather than of Biblical anthropology. The brutal treatment of conquered or captured peoples was not strange to the ancient world and the slave trade provided many ferocious examples of man's inhumanity to man, yet a new dimension seems to have been added to relations between blacks and whites in the middle of the nineteenth century and there is a sense in which one can say that race relations, as well as the study of race relations, started at that time. The sharper formulation of race as a physical category, and its rapid spread in popular consciousness, made a difference in the attitudes white Europeans and Americans expressed toward others, both white and black. The racist theories of the 1850's provided a justification for Negro slavery and for the harsh treatment of peoples in the colonial world.

Knox's book was followed within four years by Arthur de Gobineau's *Essai sur l'inégalité des races* and J. C. Nott and G. R. Gliddon's *Types of Mankind*. These French and American versions of contemporary racist theory resembled Knox's in the supposition that there had once been pure races. Change, therefore, could only be for the worse. Indeed, Gobineau remarked, "We do not come from the ape but we are rapidly getting there." Knox considered it useless for Europeans to emigrate because they were not adapted to live in other habitats, and human races could not acclimatize themselves to new environments. It had long been believed in Europe that white men would degenerate in America, but not all of the mid-nineteenth-century racists were so pessimistic. A more popular supposition was that races were populations which could migrate to a new country without changing their essential character. These theories resembled those of eighteenth-century typologists in botany, in seeking to find behind the diversity of forms natural categories which would explain that diversity. The idea of originally pure races passed into popular thought and has remained influential long after its shaky scientific basis was destroyed.

Social Darwinism

The work of destruction was started by Charles Darwin with his demonstration that plant, animal—and therefore human—species were not fixed but subject to a process of natural selection by which they became adapted to their environment. In Britain and America this new line of thought was applied most readily to social relations because of the popularity of Herbert Spencer's writings. In the German-speaking world Ernst Haeckel's popularization of Darwinian doctrine enjoyed great acclaim and inspired its application to race relations by the Polish sociologist Ludwig Gumplowicz, who presented human history as a process of amalgamation by which small groups became big ones: "The means by which all this was accomplished, by which tribes became peoples, peoples nations, nations grew into races and developed themselves, is something we know already; it is the perpetual struggle between races for dominance, the soul and spirit of history."[3] Social Darwinism dominated the study of race relations for two generations. It lay behind the physical anthropology of Otto Ammon, Georges Vacher de Lapouge and John Beddoe. It lay behind the sociologies of Walter Bagehot, William Graham Sumner and F. H. Giddings. It saw the main determinants of social life as those of heredity and selection. The factor of heredity restricted the possibilities of social reform by stressing the limitations of human capacity. The idea that nature was continually selecting for fitness also suggested that humanitarian attempts to promote equality were of little avail.

Two strains in social Darwinist thought were of particular significance for race relations studies. Although they were present in the early writing, they were more sharply formulated after the establishment of scientific genetics, and can be most clearly observed in the writing of a latter-day social Darwinist like Sir Arthur Keith. First, social Darwinists contended that whether or not pure races had ever existed in the past, they would exist in the future because natural selection would lead to the emergence of specialized interbreeding populations. Second, racial prejudice had an evolutionary function: by causing members of one group to hate those of another and identify with their own, it accelerated the process of race-building. This theory explained everything that Knox's had. In addition, it provided a more sophisticated answer to questions about why Europeans had an advanced technology and Australian aborigines did not; it also claimed that racial antagonism was innate, but gave a more plausible reason for thinking it so. It was a better theory than that of the 1850's racists in that it commanded more and better supporting evidence; it claimed to account not only for differences between races, but also for differences within them. Where the earlier theory was one of structure and pessimistic, this was a theory of process and optimistic, offering a vista of continuing improvement, with the supremacy of the whites becoming ever more secure. The earlier conception used race as a concept in comparative morphology, but the social Darwinists had shown that race modification and race-building were to be seen as a process. They represented this process as conforming to immanent principles (like laws of historical development) rather than as an adaptation to environment. Only in the 1920's and 1930's, with the establishment of population genetics, did a more satisfactory approach become possible. Social Darwinism was an influential train of thought which contributed an important element to the ideology of late-nineteenth and early-twentieth-century white imperialism and may have been partly responsible for the vicious streak often apparent in it. In the United States the social Darwinist theory also fashioned the arguments advanced in favor of the immigration quotas of 1922 onwards.

The Era of Robert E. Park

The social Darwinist theory was attractive to those who wished to bring the methods of natural science to the study of social processes, yet it had manifest weaknesses: its propositions were difficult to test, and it was formulated at too generalized a level to provide any fruitful interrelation with the study of human history. After an enthusiastic reception, doubts about it multiplied. A new phase began with Park's presentation of race relations as the product of European expansion—a view faithfully represented by his pupil E. Franklin Frazier in *Race and Culture Contacts in the Modern World* (1957). Park was profoundly influenced by social Darwinism and the theoretical structure he put in its place still showed a Darwinist pattern, in, for example, the prominence it gave to the four major processes: competition, conflict, accommodation and assimilation. But Park insisted that society was grounded in a moral order and considered the shared values of human communities a more or less autonomous element. Though he came late in life to academic sociology, his own thought developed progressively, not least because he sent his students out to study contemporary social relations and reformulated his conceptual schemes to take account of empirical findings. Park reoriented the study of race relations by shifting the emphasis from the first word to the second. He defined the field in terms of people's consciousness of racial groupings. "Race relations . . . are the relations existing between peoples distinguished by marks of racial descent, particularly when these racial differences enter into the consciousness of the individuals and groups so distinguished. . . ."[4] Park presented racial hostility as the product of norms of social distance and prejudice which individuals learn when they are socialized into their communities. In this he was part of a wider movement. The view of prejudice as innate was attacked as inconsistent with the evidence, and new studies soon persuaded most scholars that prejudice was not a drive but an attitude, and that it was learned. Indeed the chief characteristic of the third phase of race relations study was this focus upon the prejudice of majorities.

The 1930's saw the fruits of this reorientation in a brilliant series of contributions by some very talented American scholars. W. Lloyd Warner formulated the two-category model of race relations in the Old South, picturing it as a closed social system split into two mutually exclusive racial categories called color-castes. Each caste was divided internally by social class, but some class links across caste lines could be discerned. One set of norms governed caste relations, another class relations, and the system was managed in such a way that there was rarely any doubt about which norms were appropriate to any particular situation. The South has changed since then, but recent studies of the Chinese and Indian minorities there have shown that the model still has utility for sociological analysis. That no social system works by force alone was demonstrated once more in John Dollard's *Caste and Class in a Southern Town*. One of the few classics of race relations study, this book laid bare basic psychological features of racially divided societies. The striking contributions of Charles S. Johnson, Hortense Powdermaker, Alison Davis, Burleigh Gardner, Kingsley Davis, Robert Merton, St. Clair Drake and others culminated in that magisterial judgment of their generation, Gunnar Myrdal's *An American Dilemma*. Shortly afterwards, the study of Chicago by Drake and Horace R. Cayton, *Black Metropolis*, appeared, inadvertently demonstrating that the two-category model was of no real help in elucidating the complexities of race relations in a big city with a less closed social system. It was followed by Oliver C. Cox's impressive book, *Caste, Class and Race*. Cox sharply criticized the prevailing orthodoxy. He asserted that any conception of prejudice was inadequate which failed to build upon its function of justifying exploitation in capitalist society. Yet in some respects Cox's book shared the assumptions of his generation and did not prefigure the break in tradition which was to come later. The publication in 1950 of the massive study by T. W. Adorno and others, *The Authoritarian Personality*, attracted research away from the questions raised by Cox and toward studies of the sources of prejudice in personality dynamics. This volume profoundly influenced the social science of the 1950's, a decade when research into the socio-structural origins of prejudice ran the risk of being accounted an un-American activity.

Though social Darwinist ideas have been a long time dying, the new paradigm banished them from race relations studies. It furnished an explanation of interracial contacts in terms of the socially transmitted values of the groups, but shifted interest away toward the study of smaller-scale problems using sociological concepts such as ideas of the marginal man, racial etiquette, social distance, and the race relations cycle. Sociologists were now more free to concentrate on the questions suggested by their own theoretical frameworks because biologists were correcting the extravagances of those who had thought to explain so much in racial terms. Research in the 1950's on the inheritance of the sickle-cell trait and other abnormal hemoglobins provided telling illustrations of the need to see physical characteristics not as morphological traits, but in statistical terms as part of a process of biological or organic adaptation. In many respects, this operates independently of cultural or superorganic evolution and the latter could therefore be the subject matter of an independent field of study. During this period, however, progress in sociological theorizing was dependent upon American universities where teaching in race relations was often regarded as part of a process of training undergraduates to be good citizens. Textbooks were of a low standard and heavily oriented toward American social problems. As a specialization within sociology, race relations was perceived as a low-status and theoretically undeveloped field.

The Tradition Challenged

1960 was the year which saw the admission of so many new African countries to the United Nations and, by no means coincidentally, the forward surge of the civil rights movement among black Americans. It was followed by vehement attacks upon white American institutions and white American sociology. Activists, white as well as black, rejected out of hand the existing tradition of race relations study and demanded something new. Black studies were to be part of it. For a while, I understand, it was impossible to hold conferences on race relations in the United States because of the likelihood of their being disrupted by dissidents. This change in political mood was of decisive importance. The three phases of race relations study I have so far described were inaugurated by changes in the thoughts of scholars. This one was inaugurated by changes in the behavior of the people who constituted a major portion of the subject matter, and it quickly communicated itself to black peoples elsewhere through the rapidly expanding audience for the mass media. Furthermore, it coincided with a growing internationalization of sociology and with a new phase in the development of that subject. In the 1960's sociology teaching in countries outside the United States expanded rapidly and scholars elsewhere began to play a part in fashioning its character. Around 1960 the system-building of Talcott Parsons lost its dominant place and, with the rediscovery of the young Marx, an important tradition of critical analysis took a new lease on life. New enthusiasms for symbolic interactionism, phenomenology, ethnomethodology, and so on, while leading to advances, have also brought about a revival of interest in some more traditional European approaches and have so widened the scope and character of sociology that it is sometimes difficult to think of it as a single subject.

Prior to 1960, the terminology of race had been used chiefly by white peoples as a way of defining others. Marcus Garvey had been an exception when he exhorted his potential followers, "Up you mighty race!" A striking feature of the new phase was that black activists, like Garvey, used popular conceptions of racial difference as a way of recruiting support and mobilizing their potential followers. "Black" had been an adjective of disparagement, a possible insult lying behind gentler adjectives like "colored." The activists transformed it, persuading their followers to display "black pride" and to elevate "black culture." All nonwhites were invited to join the struggle, so that in 1973 even the British Broadcasting Corporation could advertise a T. V. program with an "all-black multi-racial audience." The cry for "black power" marks the beginning of a process whereby a variety of subordinated groups are coming to a consciousness of their position, defining it in opposition to what they represent as an exploiting white power structure and using "race" to recruit the support of their fellows instead of letting it be used as an excluding principle by those occupying more powerful positions. Those who have raised the cry are not worried by the charge that they are cultivating "black racism" because they are sure their doctrine can never do as much harm as white racism has done. Their movement has upset the deterministic streak in the sociology of race relations, showing that the behavior of the subordinated is not completely determined by the social structure, for they have some power to choose the sort of group they will be.

If my analysis of the break in the paradigm for problem-finding and explanation in race relations studies is correct, it helps to account for the relatively disorganized state of research in the field at present. When an intellectual tradition is fractured, a period follows when every man must act on his own appreciation of the course of advance. (Dædalus must construct wings to escape from the labyrinth he has built!) About 1960 there was a great expansion of African studies in the United States. I have been told that at this time money was poured into race relations studies, though I cannot testify from personal knowledge that this was so or explain just what kinds of studies were favored. Many of them may have been of a local, fact-finding character. It is probable that the reports of the 1961 Commission on Civil Rights and the 1967 National Advisory Commission on Civil Disorders made a significant impact on public opinion, but these were compilations of relatively accessible evidence rather than scholarly research. It might well be interesting now to have an evaluation of the race relations strategies inaugurated in the Kennedy years. Having watched from the other side of the Atlantic, my impression is that the concern for race relations expressed in high quarters contributed virtually nothing to the development of a systematic body of knowledge and scholarly understanding of the social processes at work. It has to be remembered that, with the rising mood of black assertiveness, this was not an attractive research area for the white social scientist. But it is more important, I think, to acknowledge the wastefulness of trying to develop a field of study by pouring money into research on current "problems" without re-evaluating that field's intellectual heritage. More recently, many American universities have instituted black studies and ethnic studies programs and there are several institutes for race relations research. Yet no institute or university department has made an international mark with race relations research or is generally recognized as preëminent. There seems to be no sociological work with the excitement and penetration that characterizes the books of leading American historians interested in racial patterns, especially those who have been examining black slavery. It is also noteworthy that with the possible exception of *Phylon*, the Atlanta journal of race and culture, there is no learned journal in the United States which specializes in race relations.

The major specialist journal is *Race: A Journal of Race and Group Relations,* published by the Institute of Race Relations in London. The Institute was founded in 1958 as an offshoot of the prestigious Royal Institute of International Affairs, and it started with an overseas orientation. In the mid-1960's the Institute moved to a closer concern with domestic relations. The tensions generated by political struggles over race and immigration policy in Britain played some part in the 1972 crisis in the Institute's affairs when most of the Council resigned and were replaced by members anxious to pursue policies sympathetic toward Britain's own racial minorities. The Community Relations Commission in London also publishes a quarterly journal, *New Community*, which contains research reports that are essential reading for anyone interested in British race relations. In British universities, race relations studies have been pursued chiefly at Edinburgh, Sussex, Bradford, and Bristol where there is a special graduate course. Ethnic studies are now attracting a lively interest in Canada, as a consequence of that country's varied sources of immigration. In France, an Institut d'Etudes et de Recherches Interethniques et Interculturelles has been established at the University of Nice and publishes an annual entitled *Ethnies*. In Southern Africa, an institute of race relations has been created at the University of Cape Town and there is a special research program at the University of Rhodesia. The South African government has been harrassing the Institute of Race Relations in Johannesburg and the political climate makes it very difficult for race relations studies to develop there. All the signs suggest that international interest will grow and that the new paradigm will need to be useful in the study of a much greater diversity of circumstances than the previous one. In particular, it will need to assist in the study of situations that are less closed and more open to change by political action than those previously studied.

Individual teachers and research workers in race relations have felt themselves under pressure to fashion their work in a way that reflects the new criticisms. The best sociological work of the previous era retains its validity, however, and, like any work with socioscientific pretensions, should be extended. But, in the 1960's, the issues were seen in such emotional terms that there was a tendency to renounce earlier approaches. Especially in the United States, many of the younger scholars sought modes of analysis which would assist the oppressed by exposing the sources within the white power structure of the attitudes and practices which maintained inequality. The expression "racism" was used to cover all manner of ills so that it lost its analytical value as a concept identifying a particular kind of doctrine. "Colonialism" has been used almost as loosely. Most Americans and many of the younger generation in Europe assume that colonialism is something of which nothing good can be said, and for which no excuses can be accepted. "Exploitation" is another in this family of concepts that can also be used as epithets, but it is difficult to employ it with any precision unless one presupposes a labor theory of value. In the new atmosphere of riot and confrontation there was an audience for superficial analyses based on emotive but ill-defined terms. Sociologists have been slow to undertake the detailed work of theory-building and empirical inquiry which is called for, and even in the United States very few scholars of recognized distinction specialize in this field. Perhaps some are deterred by the immensity of the task. How, after all, does one set about constructing a new framework of analysis that has to fulfill so many demanding requirements?

Insofar as any trend can be observed, the leading writers argue that it is necessary to formulate a highly general framework and then work downwards to empirical inquiries. Pierre L. van den Berghe has contended that if race relations study is to make a significant contribution to sociology it must be studied (1) historically—that is, as part of the development process of a given society; (2) holistically—that is, in the context of the total society in which these relations take place; (3) from a cross-cultural perspective so that generalizations can be formulated; and (4) with a commitment to explicit value premises so that those involved in the debates have the opportunity "to reach a state of conscious, disciplined, explicit subjectivity."[5] A similar starting point is adopted in a remarkable work by R. A. Schermerhorn, *Comparative Ethnic Relations*, in which the author maintains that "a comparative study requires a view of race relations in macrosociological perspective, i.e., in their relation to total societies."[6] This book defies summary. It proposes a highly complex classification of societies in terms of power relations, economic structures, and forms of domination. A similar commitment to macrosociology is evident in the work of John Rex, and a number of writers who approach race relations from dissimilar philosophical standpoints also believe that the first priority for the present is to concentrate on understanding the major determinants of social trends. Philip Mason (whom the nonspecialist will find the most readable of the authors in this field) contends that "the study of race relations is concerned with the total behaviour of men when they find themselves in a certain situation."[7] Julian Pitt-Rivers insists "if the subject is to attain coherence it will have to take more account of social structures in their totality and the cultural premises on which they are founded."[8] This concern with total social structures and situations gave impetus during the 1960's to a lively interest in the concept of the plural society, and to the possibility of considering race relations within a framework made up of groups differentiated in ways other than race but locked together by the structure of power. Exploration, however, showed that the problems were even more intractable than they had appeared. Most proposals for a comprehensive approach to the conceptual problems run into two difficulties. First, they tend to define race relations in terms of its subject matter and this is problematic since the biological concept of race cannot be a basis for differentiating social relations. Pitt-Rivers, indeed, believes that although the word "race" in biology and the word "race" in social science have a common etymological root, they are to all intents and purposes homonyms. For him and others, race relations situations are characterized by the participants' racial consciousness, something that is continually changing. Second, the "given society" all too easily becomes the nation state, a tendency which underemphasizes the significance both of differences within societies and of relations between nations. Nation states have so many peculiar characteristics that research of the kind envisaged quickly becomes more historical than sociological.

Despite the demand for a general theoretical structure to encompass the race relations field, most research tends to start with the analysis of smaller-scale problems in the hope that it may be possible to work upwards to more powerful theories (this is not to say that such research presupposes an inductive methodology; everyone acknowledges the need for two-way traffic between theory and observation, and indeed Schermerhorn has usefully classified the forms of induction and deduction used by theorists in this field). Prominent among contributions on smaller problems have been those stemming from the new interest in urban ethnography revitalized in the United States by Elliott Liebow's *Tally's Corner* and developed by Ulf Hannerz' *Soulside* and Lee Rainwater's *Behind Ghetto Walls*. These studies have their parallels elsewhere in works such as Graham Watson's *Passing for White*, which explains why a school near Capetown is kept in being although it has a more mixed population than is allowed for by South Africa's laws concerning racial classification. They must also be compared with the great public interest in recent years in books by authors like Frantz Fanon, Claude Brown, Eldridge Cleaver and George Jackson, who have compiled gripping descriptions of social institutions as they appear to members of the minorities. Yet local studies and imaginative insights could accumulate for decades without leading to any general theory. In my own work I have used different models for different regions without trying out different models on the same region or fully justifying my eclectic choice of models, and this, as my critics have told me, can be excused only temporarily. Somehow or other, the pre-1960 way of looking at race relations must be extended, but not so much that it becomes as inclusive as the study of society itself, or so amorphous that research workers can no longer get a grip upon it.

The immediate response to the upsets of the 1960's was for political analysts to see race relations as a polarity between blacks and whites. But the successes of blacks encouraged the political movements of all the other minorities in the United States and of many outside it. Other ethnic minorities asserted themselves, sometimes in opposition to the blacks, and interest grew in cultural pluralism as a design for living in a heterogenous state. Such minorities include the Spanish-speaking population of California, who sometimes—and perhaps significantly—call themselves *La Raza* as well as Chicanos; North American Indians; and Puerto Ricans. They possess some, but not all, of the attributes of black Americans as a minority. It may be that a new paradigm for race relations studies can best be developed by paying considerable attention to such groups—to white ethnics and intermediary populations like the Chinese in Southeast Asia or the Asians in Africa—for this might enable the student to enumerate and separate the many variables involved instead of being blinded by the starkness of polar oppositions. In this connection it is worth taking note of Michael Lyon's suggestive distinction between *racial* minorities whose group boundary is maintained by the majority, and *ethnic* minorities which maintain their own boundary. At some periods of time, certain groups are both ethnic and racial minorities.[9] The utility of this distinction can be illustrated by the case of Ashkenazi Jews who in Eastern Europe had their collective identity reinforced by the persecution of the majority; with a lower level of prejudice in the United States their descendants have the new problem of preventing assimilation. The institutions which served them when they were a racial as well as an ethnic minority are not so well adapted to their new status as a purely ethnic minority.

Class, Race, and Nation

In seeking a better conceptual framework for race relations studies it can be helpful to reconsider the decision unreflectively taken in the sociology of the late nineteenth century. In the work of writers like Gumplowicz there are three large-scale social units: class, race and nation. European sociology fastened on the first of these; indeed, in the Marxist schema class is a privileged concept. Race was neglected partly because the concept was being misused: for sociologists at that time to have given serious consideration to race as a kind of grouping would have been to suggest that they had been taken in. But nation was equally neglected and most modern textbooks pay even less attention to the significance of national groupings than they do to racial ones. Elie Kedourie's argument that nationalism is a doctrine invented by European philosophers at the beginning of the nineteenth century[10] deserves the closest attention. Before that, the people of Europe were divided and united along many different lines of language, religion and region; nation was not predominant. Germany, after all, was united only in 1870 and Italy in 1871. What the nineteenth-century movement achieved was to persuade people that it was natural to a man to possess a nationality; that it was to be expected that he should wish to be ruled as a member of a national unit; and that nationalist sentiments were politically legitimate. As Ernest Gellner explains, these claims involved philosophical-anthropological, psychological, and normative propositions which do not look very persuasive when they are subjected to critical examination. Nationalist movements, he says, have invented nations where they did not exist. And why have they done so? Because individuals and groups have agitated for their own ends.

Nineteenth-century economic liberals did not expect nationalism to become important because the expanding network of world trade would create so many counter-balancing interests. Nor did the Marxists: according to their philosophy of history, the ultimate determinants of social patterns lay in the means and relations of production, and all else must eventually be subordinated to these. But if the Marxist prediction is being fulfilled, the process is a slow one. The consciousness of peoples has been having a profound effect on their productive activities. Nationalism has become one of the most potent and legitimate factors in twentieth-century politics. The name of our highest organ is the United *Nations*. It has taken the place of the League of *Nations*. The development of nationalism follows no simple laws because it forms in opposition: so much depends on the neighbors or rulers of a territory and the issues which bring the masses into conflict with them. There is an important difference between a nationalist movement trying to mobilize its forces and the situation in which it has succeeded in persuading others that it is now a new nation, and faces the problem of cultivating unity in new circumstances. Bangladesh succeeded and is now accepted. Biafra did not. The difference between the before and after situations is such that one authority reserves the term nationalism for the former alone, preferring to speak of "national sentiment" in the established nation.[12] Nineteenth-century sociologists had good, though perhaps not sufficient, reasons for denying to national groupings an important place in their conceptual schemes. But they have been proven wrong. The new doctrine of nationalism, whether for good or ill—and Kedourie at least thinks it was for ill—captured men's imaginations and nations have become important units.

Similarly, nineteenth-century sociologists had good but insufficient reasons for considering race unimportant to the formation of major social units. It seems as if they may be proven wrong in this connection also. Yet an important distinction must be noted. By definition, no nation could be inherently better than any other, whereas all the early discussion of racial classification assumed that races were unequal. Race could start being a major kind of grouping, comparable to nation if less significant, only when the bogey of inequality was dispelled. Only then could previously subordinated groups accept racial designations. Such a process, I suspect, may have started around 1960. It was as if black leaders in the United States declared, "You define us as a racial group. Right. We will accept that label. We will prove that our subordinate position is not the outcome of our physical nature but of our social and political position. We will put an end to our subordination while retaining our racial characteristics."

The parallels between racial minority movements and nation-building are close, as E. U. Essien-Udom suggested when he presented his research on American black Muslims as a study of *Black Nationalism*. Just as feelings of national solidarity have arisen in opposition, so blacks became a more self-conscious group in response to white conduct. New nations need myths about themselves and their past, and they have an acute problem when their past seems to be one mainly of slavery and the acceptance of subordination. Their history has to be rewritten to give a heroic stature to the leaders of protest. The Republic of Eire took valiant steps to preserve and revive the use of the Erse language. Black Americans and Caribbeans have looked to Africa for language, costume, music and art forms which they can use in creating a black culture. The process results in an amalgamation not unlike that sketched by Gumplowicz in 1883 except that it comes about by social means and not by interbreeding. Social anthropologists have described the way it works in Central Africa. Men leave their ethnically homogeneous homelands and come to the cities where they meet other Africans who speak different languages and follow different customs. In these circumstances the migrants welcome as brothers Africans who might previously have been enemies but with whom they have more in common than with strangers from farther away. New groupings are precipitated: migrants from one region as opposed to those from another, and all Africans as opposed to Europeans. Similarly, in the United States, blacks scattered across the Southern states, whose ancestors originally came from different cultures, have, in opposition to whites, cultivated what they had in common and come to feel that they are one people. They have been making themselves an ethnic as well as a racial minority. Lester Singer perceptively named the process *ethnogenesis*[18] and it is not limited to black Americans.

The American situation is of special sociological interest in that black nationalism probably cannot follow the course of other nationalisms and capture a separate territory for itself. Nor can white America expel the blacks as Uganda ejected the Asians. The parties are being forced to agree on a new social contract and, since developments in the United States probably have a greater demonstration effect than those in other countries, the implications will be far-reaching. New minorities are emerging which do not at present have any racial or ethnic label. With the changing structure of the employment market young people have become more independent of their parents and elders, and instead of identifying with them, they often choose to react against them. Old hierarchies and social groupings are weakening and have to compete actively for the allegiance of the new generation. This process will in time affect black Americans as it has affected Jewish Americans and it will not be confined to the United States. The governments of industrial countries cannot afford to allow racial or ethnic minorities to control important sections of their economies. If the so-called "guest workers" of the European Economic Community establish themselves and their families in European societies in the way West Indians, Indians, and Pakistanis have in Britain, they will have to be assisted to spread themselves over a range of occupations and residential areas if these countries are not to experience disorders of a kind previously characteristic of nonindustrial multiracial societies. American experience will serve as a guide both to governments and to minority leaders. Though for a while minorities like black and Spanish-speaking Americans may appear to be subnations within the United States, feeling solidarity with citizens of other states who share their physical or cultural background, the loosening up of majority social structures may well change them so that they lose their racial minority and nationalist features and become purely ethnic minorities in Lyon's sense.

A Multidisciplinary Field

Colette Guillaumin has observed that race relations research in Europe has tended to take for granted the institutional structure of the majority societies. It has concentrated on the attitudes of the majority and the structures of the minorities, ignoring the "structural" factors within majority society which generate those attitudes and playing down the attitudes of minority members on the assumption that they have no alternative but to adjust. There is truth in this description, though it should be acknowledged that the individual research worker, especially in so new a field, does well to select for study those questions that he has some chance of being able to answer. To study majority institutions as a totality is a daunting task. The same criticism may be directed to much of the American research of Park's era, though again there are qualifications to note. Furthermore, this research has since been balanced by more studies of black attitudes and the effects of prejudice upon blacks, and by studies of black movements within political structures.

Yet such criticism of earlier race relations research draws attention to one of the problems for a future paradigm. If race cannot be easily separated from the wider web of social and economic relations, research will need to call upon all the social science disciplines. One of the main weaknesses of contemporary race relations study is that so much of it is left to sociologists. One reason accepted by the Social Science Research Council in Britain for the establishment of the Research Unit on Ethnic Relations at Bristol was the need to persuade all the social science disciplines to find problems in the race relations field amenable to study within their various frameworks and to get them to contribute toward the development of this field. Research workers have been appointed from economics, geography, political science, social administration, social anthropology and social psychology as well as from sociology. The intention is to develop race relations research not as a separate specialism but as an area for multidisciplinary inquiry.

Sociologists and social psychologists have studied the ways people express various degrees of racial prejudice. They have not asked, as the economist does, what price people put on their prejudices. If, for example, a white man is selling a house, how much of the price will he forgo in order to sell to a white rather than to a black purchaser? To answer such a question, very complex research is required. Yet even to reflect on what is entailed suggests that race relations research in the future must employ multivariate modes of analysis in which the effect of race as one variable is weighed against others. While social scientists will be needed, who can relate information about the significance of race, extracted from different sorts of research, it will be increasingly difficult to define the field of race relations study by drawing a line around its boundaries.

REFERENCES

1. Sami Zubaida, ed. *Race and Racialism* (London: Tavistock Publications, 1970), pp. 3-9. Cf. Marvin Harris' claim that "a theory of race relations must be a sub-case of a theory of social stratification," *Current Anthropology*, 10 (April 1969), p. 204.

2. Notably John Rex, *Race Colonialism and the City* (London: Routledge, 1973), p. 203.

3. Ludwig Gumplowicz, *Der Rassenkampf: sociologische untersuchungen* (Innsbruck: 1883), p. 342. This book develops arguments first advanced in 1875.

4. Robert Ezra Park, *Race and Culture* (New York: Free Press of Glencoe, 1950), p. 81.

5. Pierre L. van den Berghe, *Race and Ethnicity: Essays in Comparative Sociology* (New York: Basic Books, 1970), pp. 11-12.

6. R. A. Schermerhorn, *Comparative Ethnic Relations: A Framework for Theory and Research* (New York: Random House, 1970), p. 50.

7. Philip Mason, *Race Relations* (London: Oxford University Press, 1970), p. 5. Cf. Mason, *Patterns of Dominance* (London: Oxford University Press, 1970).

8. Julian Pitt-Rivers, "Race Relations as a Science: A Review of Michael Banton's 'Race Relations,'" *Race*, 9 (January 1970), p. 338.

9. Michael H. Lyon, "Race and Ethnicity in Pluralistic Societies: A Comparison of Minorities in the U. K. and U.S.A.," *New Community* (Summer 1972), pp. 256-262.

10. Elie Kedourie, *Nationalism* (London: Hutchinson, 1960), p. 9.

11. Ernest Gellner, *Thought and Change* (London: Weidenfeld and Nicholson, 1964), pp. 147-150.

12. Anthony D. Smith, *Theories of Nationalism* (London: Duckworth, 1971), p. 168.

13. Lester Singer, "Ethnogenesis and Negro-Americans Today," *Social Research*, 29 (1962), pp. 419-432.

SIDNEY W. MINTZ

The Caribbean Region

THE DESPAIR OF classifiers, area studies programs, kremlinologists in ill-fitting sombreros, North American race relations experts, ambulent East European commissars and the CIA, the Caribbean region goes its own way, richly researched but poorly understood. Too black to be purely European, too North European to be simply Latin, too modern to be primitive, too "overdeveloped" to be accurately labeled "underdeveloped," its diversities seem contradictory, its unities artificial or obvious. "These Caribbean territories," V. S. Naipaul tells us sourly,

are not like those in Africa and Asia, with their own internal reverences, that have been returned to themselves after a period of colonial rule. They are manufactured societies, labor camps, creations of empire; and for long they were dependent on empire for law, language, institutions, culture, even officials. Nothing was generated locally; dependence became a habit. How, without empire, do such societies govern themselves? What is now the source of power? The ballot box, the mob, the regiment? When, as in Haiti, the slave-owners leave, and there are only slaves, what are the sanctions?[1]

Behold a patchwork quilt of societies, each one a patchwork itself, the whole a foreign invention, informed with reality and a scant integrity only by the lengthy presence of the oppressors. "It is the brevity of the [British] West Indian's history," asserts George Lamming,

and the fragmentary nature of the different cultures which have fused to make something new; it is the absolute dependence on the values implicit in that language of his coloniser which has given him a special relation to the word, colonialism. It is not merely a political definition; it is not merely the result of certain economic arrangements. It started as these and grew somewhat deeper. Colonialism is the very basis of the West Indian's cultural awareness. . . . A foreign or absent Mother culture has always cradled his judgement.[2]

That Naipaul and Lamming should appear to agree epitomizes the Caribbean condition, for they must surely agree on nothing else. Naipaul, the child of Indian contract laborers from Uttar Pradesh who migrated to Trinidad in the nineteenth century, is regarded as one of the most gifted—surely the most sardonic—of Anglo-Caribbean writers. The sympathy he manifests for Caribbean folk is always diluted by his—and, he contends, their—alienation. Lamming, a black Barbadian, hopes for more; his anger is less with the tawdriness of Antillean life than with the forces he feels have made it so. But that these two sensitive writers, so different in their perspectives, should find common ground in their conviction that an utter emptiness typifies the Caribbean scene makes the question they raise all the more urgent.

Naipaul wonders what sanctions to govern by, once the masters have gone away. On balance, however, Caribbean self-rule has surely turned out to be no more disastrous than national experiments in self-government elsewhere. At the same time, the Caribbean region has produced a quite staggering number of political critics and activist leaders, given its size and its relatively brief trajectory within Western history. No need to go back to the first warriors of Haitian independence, or to the leaders of the antislavery struggle elsewhere in the islands. It should be enough to mention the names of the twentieth-century figures—Marcus Garvey, Frantz Fanon, Aimé Césaire, Eric Williams, George Padmore, C. L. R. James, Eugene Chen and Fidel Castro. The truth is probably that this coruscating if ideologically heterogeneous array has been as much the *product* of colonialism and a disjunct past, as a measure of achievement in the face of such obstacles.

For Eric Hobsbawm, the Caribbean region is

a curious terrestrial space-station from which the fragments of various races, torn from the worlds of their ancestors and aware both of their origins and of the impossibility of returning to them, can watch the remainder of the globe with unaccustomed detachment.[3]

Indeed, if enslavement disjoined once-free men from a past they would have preferred to cling to, then renewed freedom—freedom from slavery—must prove a very different state from preslavery. The special enigma of Caribbean peoples may well lie in their never having settled for a vision of history as something that must or should repeat itself.

The "Caribbean" is a region of perhaps fifty insular societies scattered over more than two thousand miles of sea, as well as certain mainland subregions—the Guianas in particular—which all passed through broadly similar historical experiences. These societies range in scale from a few square miles and populations of a few hundred or a few thousand inhabitants, up to the 44,000 square miles and nearly ten million inhabitants of contemporary Cuba.[4] Whether one examines the region from a racial, a demographic, or a sociocultural perspective, it is as differentiated as it is complex. Any attempt to evaluate the experience of Afro-Caribbean peoples must lead the generalizer to despair.

The moment Columbus decided to build a settlement on the north coast of Española (today's Santo Domingo and Haiti), and to leave there a reputed thirty-nine crewmen from the sunken *Santa María,* the conquest, settlement, and "development"—the word is used advisedly—of the Caribbean region began. No part of the so-called Third World was hammered so thoroughly or at such length into a colonial amalgam of European design. Almost from the very first, the Caribbean was a key region in the growth of European overseas capitalism. The German historian Richard Konetzke has pointed out that, before Columbus, there were no *planetary* empires; the Antillean islands were Europe's first economic bridgehead outside itself.[5] Nor were these islands mere ports of entry, ports of trade, or ports of call; in fact they were Europe's first overseas *colonies.* As keystones in ultramarine economic "development," they required labor in large quantities. For a long time, that labor was African and enslaved; free men do not willingly work for agricultural entrepreneurs when land is almost a free good. Philip Curtin estimates that 28 percent of the total number of enslaved Africans who reached the New World ended up in the islands alone—something more than two and one-half million—between the first decades of the sixteenth century and the latter decades of the nineteenth.[6] Before and after slavery, however, other groups supplied labor—before slavery: indentured servants, convicts, whores, petty thieves, labor organizers, the pariahs of Britain and France,[7] as well as countless native Americans from the islands themselves and from the New World mainland; after slavery: contract laborers from India, China, Java, Africa, the Iberian Peninsula and elsewhere. Nor have such movements of people ever really ceased. They help to explain the unusual ethnic and physical heterogeneity of the Caribbean region; but they also reveal the economically motivated intents of distant rulers. It would be fair to say that almost no one who was not European ever migrated to the Caribbean region freely; and surely no non-European born in the region was ever consulted about the advisability of additional migration.[8]

This demography by fiat was remarkable, first of all, because it represented the *replacement* of indigenous populations by outsiders—unlike events in most of Africa, Asia, and even mainland Latin America;[9] and secondly, because it was, in the context of the time, always massive. More than half a million Indians, both Moslem and Hindu, were shipped to the Caribbean region, most going to Trinidad and Guyana (erstwhile British Guiana), with smaller numbers to Dutch Guiana, Jamaica and Martinique; about 150,000 Chinese were imported, principally to Cuba; more than 30,000 Javanese, entirely to Surinam (Dutch Guiana); even a few Indo-Chinese ended up in the canefields. Whatever their biases in other regards, the European planters of the Antilles were apparently quite free of prejudice when it came to brute labor—even fellow-Europeans would do. Spaniards and Portuguese, in particular, reached the Caribbean colonies in large numbers in the nineteenth century, proving—as if it had to be proved—that Europeans, too, could cut cane beneath a broiling tropical sun.

Such movements forged societies of a special sort, in which people became accustomed to jostling with strangers matter-of-factly, accustomed to the presence of different habits, different values, different ways of dressing and of looking, accustomed to anonymity itself, as an expected part of life. That such goings and comings have been occurring for nearly 500 years—as long, that is, as the colonial domination they express—says much about the particularity of the region. The principal motive for such movements was the provision of unskilled labor in quantities sufficient to make European investment in plantation agriculture profitable. Hence the most advanced, the most "developed" enterprises in the islands for a long time—in many places, to this day—were rural, so that the rainbow-hued spectrum of Caribbean peoples and cultures is spelled out in the shacks and canefields of the countryside, as much as in the alleyways of the cities. That these societies are ethnically, culturally and racially various is just as important in understanding their true nature as that they are agrarian, rural, and poor. By putting these two axes of description together, we begin to see that, whatever the so-called Third World really is, the Caribbean region can only be part of it figuratively. Naipaul's assertion that the islands are merely the "Third World's third world"[10] is false; these lands were being force-fit into the First World, the European World, before the Third World even existed. It is being rural, agrarian and poor that makes Caribbean folk look like Third World peoples elsewhere; it is being so anciently heterogenized, enslaved, colonized, proletarianized—yes, and Westernized—that makes the Third World label inappropriate for them today.

From one perspective, of course, the Caribbean region is merely American—for

all American societies are migrant societies, and all are composed in some measure
of the descendants of strangers. But with several significant exceptions—the
hispanophone societies in particular—the peoples of the Caribbean region are
marked by the absence of a central tradition through which migrant populations
could mediate their relationships to each other. The lack of just such a tradition has
affected qualitatively the emergence of an ethnically based national consciousness,
and has required of Caribbean peoples a social innovativeness more in tune with
the modern world than with the world of the eighteenth and nineteenth centuries.
Neither perceived differences in physical type nor in ethnicity has been irrelevant
in the development of that innovativeness, but such differences may well have intensified one variety of consciousness. In one of his most evocative tales, told in the
first person by a Grenadian black who becomes Trinidad's most successful baker,
Naipaul manages to put both race and ethnicity into their special Caribbean context.[11] Youngman, the hero, is apprenticed to a Chinese baker, and finally strikes
out on his own. But no one will buy his bread, in spite of its superior quality.
Bewildered and discouraged, Youngman engages in some amateur sociology, and
discovers the secret of his failure—and, thereby, of his eventual success:

> When black people in Trinidad go to a restaurant they don't like to see black people
> meddling with their food. And then I see that though Trinidad have every race and every
> colour, every race have to do special things. But look, man. If you want to buy a snowball
> [flavored ice], who you buying it from? You wouldn't buy it from a Indian or a Chinee or a
> Potogee. You would buy it from a black man. And I myself, when I was getting my place in
> Arouca fix up, I didn't employ Indian carpenters or masons. If a Indian in Trinidad decide to
> go into the carpentering business the man would starve. Who ever see a Indian carpenter? . . .
> And, look at the laundries. If a black man open a laundry, you would take your clothes to it?
> I wouldn't take my clothes there. . . . And then all sorts of things fit into place. You
> remember that the Chinee people didn't let me serve bread across the counter? I used to
> think it was because they didn't trust me with the rush. But it wasn't that. It was that, if
> they did let me serve, they would have no rush at all. You ever see anybody buying their
> bread off a black man?

Armed with his insight, Youngman hires a young Chinese to stand in the front
of his shop, hangs Chinese calendars inside, and changes his sign to read Yung
Man, instead of Youngman. He triumphantly concludes:

> I never show my face in front of the shop again . . . my wife handling that side of the
> business, and the wife is Chinee. . . . As I say, I only going in the shops from the back. But
> every Monday morning I walking brave brave to Marine Square and going in the bank, from
> the front.

The baker's story tells us that Caribbean societies, when multi-ethnic, are
differentiated, among other things, in terms of ethnic and/or "racial" expectations;
but it also tells us about the West Indian's remarkable capacity to observe and act
with "unaccustomed detachment." Ethnic succession—which has meant a succession of peoples, languages, religions, costumes, customs, cuisines and all else—has
eventuated in being a valuable instrument of empire, even now when the empires
are gone or going. It is not yet enough that class interests may be the same;
perceived ethnic and "racial" differences may continue to divide groups, and it
would be erroneous to claim that this forced heterogeneity has now led to the
emergence of any pan-Caribbean commonality, or even to a strong national identity in many Antillean lands. Yet a consciousness of the way these societies were

formed, by those who are their citizens, and the general lack of any elite tradition through which culturally different peoples could relate to each other, have been critical factors in the creation of that detachment of which Hobsbawm speaks.

We might be inclined, were it not for so much contrary evidence, to suppose that these differences among Caribbean peoples sort themselves out along some simple continuum from white to black, or even from non-European to North European. But most societies are more complicated than that, at least in the Caribbean region. The waves of migration, to which we have referred, of peoples from nearly everywhere, have made this region today the seat of as much ethnic and physical heterogeneity as can be found in any region of comparable size in the entire world.

II

Fernando, Isabel's spouse, when mentioning a shipment of seventeen African slaves to Santo Domingo in 1505, declared a need for a hundred more in order that "all of these be getting gold for me."[12] It was not until 1886—more than 380 years and more than two and one-half million enslaved and transported Africans later—that slavery was abolished in Cuba, thus ending it for all time in the Antilles.[13] Denmark illegalized the trade in 1802, England in 1808, Sweden in 1813, France in 1814, and Spain in 1820; but the illegal trade continued at least until the 1860's, and free (or freed) but contracted African laborers were also imported during much of the nineteenth century. Emancipation was accepted as reluctantly as the end of the trade had been: 1838 in the British colonies, 1848 in the French colonies, 1863 in the Dutch colonies, 1873 in Puerto Rico, and 1886 in Cuba. Though the abolitionists frequently argued on principle, the complaints of the planters always originated in the want of labor; the vaunted congenital inferiority of the slaves was an embellishment upon far more basic arguments. At every stage, then, slavery was defended because it was first of all profitable, and only thereafter because it was rationalized as benign. It followed that every concession to freedom would be accompanied by demands for more labor of whatever sort, so that the tides of new migrants might keep pace with the ebbing of a system of perpetual servitude.

It is a commentary on slavery that Caribbean slave populations did not maintain themselves by reproduction. In the most lunatic periods of plantation expansion—Saint-Domingue in the late seventeenth century, Jamaica in the eighteenth century, and Cuba in the nineteenth century, for instance—high mortality rates typified the plantation regimen, and the trade could barely keep pace with the proclaimed need for new slaves. But the slave trade eventuated in the "Africanization" of the Caribbean region, culturally as well as genetically. While the question of "racial" identity—who is "black" and who is not—is surely one of the most vexing in the interpretation of Caribbean social structure, it is reasonable to suppose that at least three-quarters of the population of the Antilles and the Guianas today carries some African genetic inheritance. This may amount to some twenty million persons, nearly one-third of the "black" population of the hemisphere, and equal to more than two-thirds of the black population of the United States. Such estimates attest to the immense importance of the slavery of Africans and their descendants in the economic, social and political history of the

New World and, in view of its relatively limited size, of the disproportionate importance of the Caribbean region in that history.[14]

Any reflective view of the experience of black peoples in the Antillean islands and their surrounding mainland shores must take account of the intricate and tormented past embodied in slavery and the struggles against it. "It is a good region," Hobsbawm writes, "in which to be born black." The meaning is clear, at least for countries such as Jamaica or Haiti, where being black has always meant being one of the overwhelming majority; better to be born black in Kingston or Port-au-Prince than in Harlem. But for most blacks, in most of the Caribbean, for many generations it might have been better not to have been born at all. For much too long, life was unbearably hard for most human beings in these islands; for most, it still is. The lands which Columbus described so rapturously in his accounts were soon to become the first overseas agricultural factories of Europe; to a large extent, that is what they remain. But their relative importance to the European heartland is now vastly diminished, and little of new economic significance has grown in the intervening centuries. Now tourist havens, playgrounds for scuba-divers and social scientists, their last century has been a century of eclipse; a scattering of luxury hotels, aluminum mines and oil refineries amounts to too little now, and is certain to amount to less in the future. Here, too, is part of the Afro-Caribbean patrimony. After a historical experience surely the most bitter in modern times, a future as dim as the past can sour the taste of freedom, whether already achieved or simply anticipated.

This is a provisional framework into which to fit some consideration of the past and present of Caribbean black peoples: lengthy and intense colonialism of particular kinds; slavery and the various struggles against it; economic deprivation and a scarcity, partly genuine and partly spurious, of economic opportunities; socioracial and ethnic heterogeneity, and the political and identity problems created by such heterogeneity. The study of these peoples has not consistently taken account of such background conditions, and European models and preconceptions have often been transferred uncritically to the analysis of contemporary Caribbean life, and to formulations of policy. Though such research has been massive, and sometimes even marked by good intentions, it often fails to speak to the needs of the societies with which it has been concerned, and our ignorance of Caribbean realities remains substantial. Part of the difficulty appears to originate in a common unwillingness to take the Caribbean region seriously; for the most part, seriousness of intentions is exhibited only when the danger to European and North American interests appears to be genuine, as in the case of contemporary Cuba, the invasion of Santo Domingo, etc. But there are other reasons why the region has not attracted enough problem-oriented research workers, which deserve at least passing notice.

One might begin by remarking that, except for occasional hurricanes and their political equivalents, the Caribbean is not thought of as a "dangerous" research area. Reasonably close to both Europe and the United States, endowed with a generally agreeable climate, free of most serious contagious diseases, it may look humdrum, homogeneous and "easy" to the Western eye. To the extent that it is not "dangerous," of course, it can hardly be glamorous for some social scientists. Yet a more contemplative and modest perspective suggests that the region is possibly not quite as easy as all that. Moreover, its apparent homogeneity turns out to be rather deceptive, once one decides to take it seriously. Some of the insights one acquires in society A are not, in fact, readily transferrable to society B; and some of the insights that seem so complete and penetrating on first examination turn out to be more enigmatic than they appeared, when reapplied to other societies. Most of all, superficial overviews of the region, which see it as being as accessible intellectually as it is geographically, often misgauge the ways in which complex phenomena may appear simple, if one begins by imputing simplicity to them.[15]

To work effectively as a Caribbean specialist (rather than as a specialist in one island or mainland society, or one "language group") ideally requires reading and speaking knowledge of at least four principal European languages: English, Spanish, French and Dutch. Historical research would require in addition some reading knowledge of earlier variants of these languages, and of others—for instance, to work on the history of the U.S. Virgin Islands, formerly Danish possessions, one would need to read Danish. Any research based on fieldwork in the region without an interpreter would call for more specialized knowledge of local languages, such as Sranan Tongo, Saramaccan, or Djuka in Surinam; Haitian Creole in Haiti; Papiamento in the Dutch islands of Aruba, Bonaire and Curacao; other creole languages employing English or French lexicons in many of the Lesser Antilles, and so on.[16] Moreover, while these societies share many features based on broad and common historical experiences, each is in its own way particular and distinctive. Though knowledge of some similarities might ease the undertaking of research in Haiti, for instance, after prior work in Martinique, the differences between these societies—culturally, politically, and otherwise—would prove as important as any likenesses. Local cultures are profoundly affected by political relationships; not only is this true as between, say, Haiti (long independent) and Martinique (an overseas Department of metropolitan France), but also as between Jamaica and Trinidad, both now independent, but with strikingly different demographic, cultural and political pasts in relation to their former imperial ruler, Great Britain.

Yet, though the learning necessary to become a competent scholar of the region is considerable, this is not matched by any general feeling that such learning is "worthwhile." In fact, Caribbeanist research is not held in very high regard by European and North American social scientists, in part for the very reasons that should make its study significant. The absence of "indigenous" populations, of attractive crafts, of monumental architecture, of lengthy literate traditions goes together with the presence of people from everywhere, handicrafts based on toothbrush handles and flour sacks, belief systems that are "hybrid" or "mixed," grass shacks shored up with rusty Coca Cola signs, illiteracy, and the medley of reworked traditions that give the region its startlingly Western, modern and imputedly "corrupt" cultural character. In anthropology, for instance, the rarely articulated underlying assumption of traditional ethnography, with its emphasis on the isolated, remote, "primitive," and "pure" has meant that the islands would serve best as a training ground, a laboratory, a place "to get your first fieldwork under your belt," before turning to the "real" anthropology of Africa, Asia, or the tropical forests and frozen wastes of the New World. Though the terms of reference are of course different, similar perspectives appear to dominate the thinking of scholars in the other social sciences.

Such views also seem to be matched to some extent by their opposite in the region itself. There, the social sciences have often been seen as the ancilla of Western imperialism, making out of civilized humankind a theater for the pursuit of colonialist preconceptions. Though it is debatable in some regards, this view is by no means entirely wide of the mark. Too often, visiting scholars have left no copies of their work in local institutions, published none of their papers in local journals, and cooperated with no local scholars in the pursuit of their research. Only in recent years have these practices begun to change, particularly as top-flight local professionals have begun to staff local institutions, to edit local journals, and to conduct research of their own. Here, too, of course, the limitations implicit in colonial or erstwhile colonial educational centers have held back both local efforts and international intellectual cooperation. Heavy teaching loads in Caribbean universities, the lack of research funds, and other problems have resulted in the draining away of social-science talent to European and North American institutions; and the absence of substantial local readerships has meant that no local scientific journal was likely to survive without heavy dependence upon the world outside.

Thus, in spite of the accumulation of a great deal of social-science research, some of it of very good quality, internal limitations and external reserve have hampered the integration of findings into any analytically effective picture of either the past or present of the region as a totality. Most Caribbean societies, now politically independent in name at least—Puerto Rico and some of the Lesser Antilles, together with the French Antillean overseas departments and the Dutch Antilles, are the glaring exceptions—remain culturally tributary to their former colonial metropolises, and geopolitically tributary to the presence of the United States. To point to this deficiency, however, is no more than to ask a core question in a different way: how will these societies achieve a national identity on the one hand, while building a pan-Caribbean solidarity on the other?

III

Caribbean "racial" composition is highly diverse. First, the phenotypic variety of Caribbean peoples is unusual, due both to the circumstances of immigration, and to the lengthy colonial careers of their component societies. Second, the codes of social relationships typifying these societies take account of phenotypic variety, but each society employs its code in its own distinctive fashion. Hence, while "race" is important throughout, its significance and its particular uses in social assortment vary from one Caribbean society to another. If one conjures up a "racial map" of the region, employing the criteria common to white middle-class North Americans, one finds societies such as Haiti or Jamaica, in which nearly everyone appears to be of African or largely African origin, and others such as Puerto Rico, Cuba, Saba or the Cayman Islands, where this is much less the case. But since perceptions of physical type are culturally conventionalized, such a map does violence to the realities of Caribbean social life. A more effective map would depict *perceived* "race," for those persons who fall within all of the *locally defined* categories between black and white. While a number of writers[17] have contributed significantly to our understanding of what this map might be like, it remains largely imaginary, and its complexity is difficult to grasp.[18] Yet a third such imaginary map could deal with ethnic divisions—with those population segments falling outside any black-white scale—for which perceived cultural differences (including stereotypes), rather than perceived physical differences, appear to constitute the primary basis of social assortment or allocation.

But "maps" of these societies in terms of "race," perceived race, and ethnicity evade what many theorists would regard as a much more obvious and fundamental basis of assortment: the class structure. Caribbean societies are, of course, stratified and class-differentiated entities. Color and ethnicity are not neatly correlated with class membership, even if it was once generally true—and, to a very large extent, still is—that lightness or whiteness and upper status tend to accompany each other, much as do darkness and lower status. What is more, the introduction of large populations that are not perceived to be aligned along any single gradient from blackness to whiteness, such as the Indians in Trinidad or the Chinese in Cuba, has made much more complicated any analysis of the relationship among economic status, physical type, and ethnic identity.

While many features of the traditional stratification systems of the region are still operative, changes in class structure have proceeded along different lines, such as the decline of local planter classes, the emergence of corporate, foreign plantation systems, the growth of tertiary, service-rendering sectors, the development of externally oriented consumer economies, the emigration of large populations, etc.[19] These changes have affected the distribution of persons of particular physical or ethnic identities within local social systems, and the linkage between these identities and class membership has accordingly become more nuanced. Changes in political arrangements have also altered the traditional picture. To note but two very different cases, in recent decades in both Cuba and Haiti a clear upward movement in position or in life-chances for substantial numbers of darker persons has marked political change; many would argue for parallel phenomena in other parts of the region as well. In these ways, the sociological complexity of these societies may be seen to have increased significantly, in accord with political, economic, and demographic processes that extend themselves over time.

For the scientist interested in abstractions, it is clear that physical characteristics are genetically inherited, while culture (as described, among other things, by the term "ethnicity," and expressed in such forms as dress, speech, food preferences, etc.) is not. For the Caribbean person, however, perceived differences, "racial" and/or ethnic, are guides to behavior and a source, however unreliable in individual cases, of prediction. Naipaul's baker knows whereof he speaks. The social scientist's task, then, is not that of contenting himself with exploring the difference between inherited and socially acquired denotata of group membership, but of learning how particular taxonomies of distinction are employed. Adequate approximations of Caribbean social systems—how these societies are organized, and how they work—must take account of both differences, and different *kinds* of differences, in terms of how people perceive themselves, how they perceive others, and how they are themselves perceived. In this connection, one research direction has been enough pursued, in attempting to make sense of Caribbean societies in these terms, to be worthy of a digression here.

That these societies were not only racially but also ethnically complex did not become a serious research concern until long after politicians, businessmen and novelists were aware of it. In 1949, the sociologist R. A. J. van Lier employed in modified form the concept of the "plural society," first developed by J. S. Furnivall to describe Burmese and Javanese societies under European domination.[20] Furnivall's thesis, as Raymond T. Smith has pointed out,[21] had two parts: first, that colonial rule and laissez-faire capitalism had destroyed group norms and values, resulting in an extreme variant of economic individualism; and second, that they led to the crystallization of differential ethnic norms within a single, externally dominated polity. It was the second of these assertions, however, that has most attracted Caribbeanists. For van Lier, Surinam (Dutch Guiana) was a plural society because it was

marked by the absence of unity of race and religion, while there is a typological difference between the religions; and furthermore, the different groups live in different economic spheres. The differences that arise in this type of society are not gradations within one and the same culture, but are the result of the descent of different groups from different ethnic groups with differing cultures. Social strata usually coincide for the greater part with groups which differ on the basis of racial, cultural and economic factors as well.[22]

Van Lier's pioneering application gave rise to what might almost be called a "plural society school" of Caribbean sociology, the most creative exponents of which have been Michael G. Smith and Leo Despres.[23]

But the fundamental questions raised by the concept of the plural society do not appear to be significantly different from those addressed in the study of any complex stratified society, Caribbean or other. The United States, for instance, which M. G. Smith does not consider to be a plural society, certainly manifests many of the sociological characteristics attributed to a society such as Jamaica or Grenada, including the presence of ethnically and racially differentiated segments whose cultures are by no means homogeneous.[24] Perhaps the important fact in the case of Caribbean societies is not whether the "plural society" concept fits them, but whether the specific economic and historical experiences that endowed them with their ethnic and racial heterogeneity, and the particular systems of power which order the relationships among their component groups over time, and at present, can explain their particular sociological character.

In many or even most Caribbean societies, we are confronted with single political orders within which two or more groups, differentiated by physical type and/or other sociostructural and cultural features, may coexist without necessarily mingling.[25] We have already noted that, in this region, successive migrations of different peoples, conditioned by the political and economic objectives of the colonial powers, were part of the "solutions" to a largely spurious labor scarcity. Such groups as the Javanese in Surinam, the Indians in Trinidad and Guyana, the Chinese in Cuba (and, at later points, the Haitians and Jamaicans who were imported to Cuba as well) were introduced into what were already stratified and heterogeneous societies. The masses of the "host" populations—themselves newcomers all, at earlier points—had absolutely nothing to do with the original decisions to encourage or facilitate immigration. Moreover, the major economic benefit deriving from the presence of any such newcomer group was, in all Caribbean cases, enjoyed by only a tiny minority of the host population, at best. Finally, the opportunities for any host group materially to improve its economic condition, rare even before the new migrant wave, could be expected to become even rarer after the advent of new competitors. These historical and structural aspects of ethnoracial heterogeneity, formed within rigidly stratified societies controlled by Europeans, can probably reveal more of the nature of the Caribbean case than any particular theory of pluralism. And it is against a background of these quite special conditions that the particular experiences of Afro-Caribbean peoples can most profitably be viewed.

IV

No general article can treat more than a limited number of the research problems now under investigation, which deal with the historical and contemporary experiences of Afro-Caribbean peoples. The historical span, the number of societies encompassed, and the diversities, both past and present, that characterize the Caribbean region are daunting; while the interests of Afro-Caribbeanists range from the origins of creole languages and the nature of Afro-Caribbean religions, to peasant economics and the differential character of race relations. Rather than attempt to summarize shallowly this spectrum of research topics, it is more useful to concentrate on two complex themes, both of particular interest for the student of the development of Afro-Caribbean cultures. The first such theme inheres in the special history of Afro-Caribbean peoples, as defined by enslavement, transplantation and acculturation: that of continuities and discontinuities with the African past. The second theme, though related, has to do with the plantation system—within which the experience of Afro-Caribbean peoples was so largely encapsulated—and with the unusual nature of "escape" from that system, as represented by such diverse developments as the growth of maroon (runaway) communities, forms of resistance to slavery and to the plantation regimen, and the evolution of Caribbean peasantries. Though neither theme can receive here the full treatment it deserves, each may provide useful perspectives upon the field of Afro-Caribbean studies.

In recent years, the concern with Afro-American culture which swept North American intellectual life has been joined to the somewhat belated recognition of the presence of Afro-American societies elsewhere, and particularly in the Caribbean region.[26] This "discovery" has been made not only by historians of slavery, linguists, folklorists and ethnologists, but also by black North Americans in general, for many of whom the Caribbean had once been only a rather obscure cluster of distant and unimportant lands. Underlying the recent upsurge of interest, there has been an expectation on the part of some that, beneath differences in history, language, local culture and all else, there would prove to be some kind of African unity or commonality that is ultimately identifiable—and the expectation is by no means naive. But the significant fact about "the search for Africa" is the growing recognition that each Caribbean society has its own particular history; that each creation of an Afro-American culture occurred under particular conditions; and that the innovativeness and originality of the first Afro-Americans and of their descendants played a central role in building new cultural forms, and new institutions through which to perpetuate them. Thus the search for Africa is a genuine one, but it has come to be predicated upon a more sophisticated view of the processes of social and cultural change. Richard and Sally Price, whose investigations among the Bush Negroes of Surinam are setting a new standard in Afro-Caribbeanist research, provide a striking example of this new trend. By carefully tracing Saramaka woodcarving during more than a century of change, Richard Price has demonstrated that some features previously regarded as direct continuities from Africa are relatively recent developments, within fluid and highly innovative aesthetic frameworks:

> This dynamic aspect of Bush Negro cultures, the importance of fads and fashions, should serve as a caution to the researcher seeking African survivals. And it might encourage skepticism toward any African attributions based on formal rather than specifically historical evidence, such as the idea that Saramaka decorative tackwork is "the survival of the African ornamentation of woodwork with iron." Noting a greater use of brass tacks in the Upper than in the Lower River region, Herskovits suggested that in "the deep interior . . . where the African elements have been most faithfully retained," the use of metal has somehow survived. I would argue that it is more useful to view the use of tacks in the general context of changing artistic fashion, noting, for example, that they were apparently first used in the mid-nineteenth century (when trading contact with the coast was regularized), became popular on the Upper River only after the turn of the century, and were used far more by some carvers than others within any village. Moreover, the differing use of tacks on the Upper and Lower River during the 1920's, which puzzled Herskovits, was almost certainly related to the very different patterns of wage labour and attitudes toward coastal goods in these two regions at that time. . . .[27]

Price certainly does not mean by this to deny the significance of the African past in the aesthetic world of the Bush Negroes or any other Afro-Caribbean people. Rather, he locates its significance on a different level, concluding that:

> My own preliminary research into Saramaka art history certainly suggests that particular formal similarities between "Bush Negro art" on the one hand and "the art of West Africa" on the other are more likely to be products of independent innovation and development within historically related and overlapping sets of aesthetic ideas than direct retentions or survivals.[28]

This more sophisticated approach, concerned less with formal similarities and more with what might be called a "grammar" of African cultures, has begun to turn up in the study of other expressive media, including music, dance, and language itself. Such a view requires the scholar to remember that Afro-Americans were vibrant, resilient individuals who, while they often resisted slavery and fought it to the death, also lived, observed and acted, even while enslaved. Ralph Ellison, referring to the Afro-American experience in North America, has said it most eloquently, perhaps for music:

> For as I see it, from the days of their introduction into the colonies, Negroes have taken, with the ruthlessness of those without articulate investments in cultural styles, whatever they could of European music, making of it that which would, when blended with the cultural tendencies inherited from Africa, express their own sense of life—while rejecting the rest.[29]

As it happened in North America, so it doubtless happened in Caribbean societies as well: Afro-American culture is African—and American.[30] Its distinctiveness lies partly in the unusually repressive conditions under which enslaved, transplanted and heterogenized groups had to create new cultural forms, interpreting their own heritages and creating new ones.[31]

And as with crafts and music, so, too, with language. The enslavement and transportation of individuals from many different language groups meant that the New World situation would impose a need to acquire or develop new media of communication, under extremely difficult conditions.[32] A relatively sudden revival of interest in pidgin and creole languages on the part of both linguists and historians has tended to unify the study of Afro-American speech, with special emphasis on the processes of formation of such languages. This, in turn, has revealed a sphere of inquiry in which the pasts and present of Afro-Caribbean peoples are of particular importance. Though there is emphatically no consensus on the origins of these languages, nor even on the locus (or loci) of their origins,[33] it is clear that enslaved Africans and their descendants must have played a particularly creative linguistic role. Syntactic and other similarities among languages as diverse as the lexically differentiated creoles of the Caribbean, and their presence in certain creoles in other world areas, may argue for a common origin, followed by later processes of "remodeling" and relexification, in which certain West African languages may have figured importantly. In these new studies, discourse and syntax have been stressed—fruitfully, it seems—more than lexical features. For the layman, what may be the most interesting finding of all is the fact that, hidden behind entirely different lexicons, common or near-universal grammatical features seem to typify most creole languages. The studies of pidgin and creole languages have now converged with interests in bilingualism and "code-switching," in class differences in speech, and in "black English." In these problems, as in the study of creole languages generally, the languages of Afro-Caribbean peoples are helping to reveal much that was unsuspected about general processes of language change.

In similar fashion, studies of folklore, oral expressiveness and performance among Afro-Caribbean folk[34] have generated renewed attention to the dynamics of change, rather than concentrating only upon the documentation of formal similarities or retentions, possibly explicable as "survivals." Such work has as its objective a more effective demonstration of the relationships between cultural "materials" and the social contexts in which these materials—such as proverbs, tales, jokes, and language forms generally—are employed. Studies of these kinds aim not at reducing the emphasis upon the role of the African past, but at identifying more fundamental stylistic and cognitive features of that past, and at systematizing methodologies for further work. Thus in these inquiries, as in the others cited earlier, the research objective has become both more sweeping and more subtle.

France's leading Afro-Americanist, Roger Bastide, has drawn an interesting contrast between "preserved" and "living" Afro-American religions,[35] implying that, in this sphere as in most others, scrupulous conservatism in form may be less faithful to the past than a readiness to change, while selective change may keep more fundamental principles alive than does total commitment to the preservation of details of form. In a similar vein, but cleaving more closely to ethnographic detail, Richard and Sally Price have demonstrated for one aspect of culture—Afro-American naming systems—that surface and subsurface phenomena may yield two quite different perspectives for the study of processes of retention and change. Some Afro-American naming systems conserve lexically African names, while giving up certain more fundamental (but also more subtle) principles associated with naming. Others may have little if any lexically African materials in their naming systems, yet remain more faithful to naming principles of deeper African origin.

If students of the African heritage in the Americas, were to turn their attention more fully to the delineation of higher-level cultural rules or deeper structure, it might be found that the more dynamic, "African" systems generate forms in some domains which are less readily traceable to specific West African sources than do the more defensive, retentive ones.[36]

If these emphases are justified, it seems fair to draw a distinction between formal similarities on the one hand—"survivals" and "retentions"—and possible underlying unities on the other. But the intellectual or theoretical importance of the scholarly aspect of Afro-Americana should not conceal a quite different distinction: that between cultural forms as part of the fabric of matter-of-fact daily life for Afro-Caribbean peoples, and the political role of such materials in the ongoing dialogues of their societies' leaders. For most Haitians or Jamaicans, for instance, the issue as to whether their cultures are "African" or not, or in what degree, has no particular significance. But it is nonetheless a very real issue in the Afro-Caribbean political arena for those who seek to build political movements phrased in cultural terms, and who see external pressures of all kinds as ultimately destructive of national cultural unity. In the hispanophone Caribbean societies, for example—Cuba, Puerto Rico and Santo Domingo—any emphasis upon the African component in local culture usually must be reconciled politically with the objective of a generalized "hispanic" cultural unity, around which all citizens can rally. Thus a stress upon the distinctiveness of Afro-Caribbean cultural components within these societies is sometimes seen as divisive, rather than as politically unifying. In those Caribbean societies in which non-European, non-Afro population segments are substantial, too heavy stress upon Afro-Caribbean solidarity, tied to a notion of cultural commonality, has indeed proved divisive at times. Thus, for instance, K. V. Parmasad, a Trinidadian of Indian descent, accepts as necessary the struggle of the Trinidadian people for a social order that transcends the colonial past, but he is not willing to be assimilated to Afro-Caribbean culture as the price of that struggle:

To boast of a national identity here [Trinidad], is to live in a world of make-believe. To claim that we are all one is to ignore the stark realities of the present. To ignore the presence of any one group is to sow the seeds of future conflict, discord and chaos. . . .

Our outmoded politicians, hunting for votes through deceit and deception, trying hard but in vain to impress the hungry masses, are in the habit of speaking of the "new national identity of Trinidad and Tobago." But what national identity can we, Indians, be proud of when the culture of 40% of our people is denied its rightful place and recognition it deserves; when the vast majority of our people exist on the fringes of society and are considered as possessing nothing more than nuisance value?[37]

Parmasad rightly asserts that the entire social system of Trinidad was geared to strip each Indian of "his name, his religion, his culture, his language, his history and become what the system demanded—that is, Christianized, Westernized, colonized, dehumanized." But as he knows well, the system had been engaged in the same exercises, practiced upon others, centuries before the first contracted Indians were brought to the islands. Thus, the assertion of ethnic identity as a political objective, rooted in such distinctions as language, cuisine, and dress, must take account of existing ethnic group differences which mark the internal composition of many Caribbean societies, as well as of the extent to which such differences may divide groups whose wider political stakes are partly shared, but also partly

different. Class consciousness and ethnic consciousness do not necessarily corre-
spond in political terms; coalitions which transcend ethnicity (and "race") in the
pursuit of common action hence commonly typify attempts to build a new Caribbean political order.

On one level, of course, these problems might appear not to concern the student of culture, who may feel free to examine the questions of Africanisms and of
continuities and discontinuities in cultural forms without reference to their political
relevance. On another level, however, the political significance of cultural—and
"racial"—differences is immense.[38] This issue ultimately turns, of course, on the
notion of "relevance" in the social sciences. Some may feel that studies of such
seemingly recondite subjects as ethnobotany, proverbs, aesthetics and children's
games have no place in a world where poverty, political corruption and despair are
rampant. But in that same world, it often appears that what is politically relevant
and what is not hinges upon forces extraneous to scientific inquiry. In the Caribbean region, cultural questions are often raised in a context of ethnic
heterogeneity, where class differences and ethnic differences intersect, but are
rarely identical. The study of the African past, in all its richness and variety, hence
inevitably carries its political coefficient in these lands. Even the most obscure
details of cuisine or gesture may have—or may acquire—ethnopolitical
significance. And ethnic differences may serve to conceal underlying economic
problems, for which such differences can become political expressions.

We have noted that most Caribbean societies are not only ethnically (and
"racially") heterogeneous, but also that they sometimes seem to lack a living core
tradition through which different groups may relate to each other. The political
crystallization of ethnicity is doubtless affected by these circumstances, particularly
if the outdated but still-powerful values of an older colonial social structure persist.
The political significance, then, of any denotatum of ethnicity—like the political
significance of its study—is more likely to become clear after the event, than
before. What is more, any politically motivated search for ethnic identity must be
evaluated in terms of the particular circumstances under which it arises. R. T.
Smith, in interpreting the case of Guyana, an ethnically heterogeneous society,
calls attention to the difficulties such a society faces as it becomes politically independent:

Grave problems must arise in trying to satisfy the aspirations of a rapidly increasing population and there is bound to be a growing reservoir of resentment and frustration just as there
is in most new nations. At the same time that those problems are being faced, there is the
problem of trying to overcome the limitations of colonial creole society at the cultural and
symbolic level. This issue may be evaded of course and some variant of the popular slogan of
"out of many, one people" used as a means of trying to erase ethnic differences.[39]

But ethnic differences, however they may have become actualized politically, do
not simply disappear in the face of slogans: ". . . before ethnic identity can be
transcended it must be *asserted*," Smith adds, "in order to ensure the stature, participation and self-respect of everyone in the local community; not because race [or
ethnicity] is a necessary basis of social identity but because it has been made so in
creole society."[40] It is in these terms that the study of the emergent and contemporary cultures of Afro-Caribbean peoples has direct and significant political
relevance; and it is in this light that the whole canvas of the Afro-American past

must be viewed. That past—or better, those pasts—live in the present; their careful documentation is in the service of millions of people, now dead, who had to build their new world under the harshest conditions in recorded history, and even more in the service of their descendants.

V

From the earliest decades of the Conquest until 1886, the ownership of human beings—and more, of their children—set the dominant tone of social relationships in the Caribbean region, and for Afro-Caribbean peoples. This patterning of life took shape in the presence of—indeed, was enacted through—the plantation system. We have stressed that the Caribbean islands and their surrounding mainland shores were the seat of the first European experiments in overseas capitalism; and while mining, fishing, and certain other pursuits played some part in these developments, they were organized principally through the plantation itself. Put simply, large estates engaged in the monocrop production of basic commodities for European urban populations—above all, sugar, but also rum, coffee, cotton, tobacco, indigo, etc.—were established by private entrepreneurs enjoying royal support. Manned by coerced and enslaved labor, such enterprises were an economic boon to their owners and to the metropolises, but agroindustrial graveyards for those who worked on them.

Some writers have attributed to the plantation such importance in Caribbean history that they see the social systems of its component societies as little more than projections of the plantation mold. While this view is perhaps extreme, particularly since the plantation system always had to deal with the specific prior character of the society within which it took shape, the development of local plantation economies typically involved the engrossment of land, labor and much of the sociopolitical structure at large. Just as the high points of plantation development in Saint-Domingue, Jamaica and Cuba were marked by a terrible mortality for the slaves themselves, so too these grotesque pinnacles of "development" meant the perversion of colonial rule to meet the needs of the plantation system.[41] Plantation systems not only determined in large measure the social ambiance of plantation societies at large; they also underlay the establishment of local codes of behavior, and influenced the emergence of new patterns of interaction, infused with many of the older values, after slavery itself had ended. This was no simple or uniform process; the abolition of the slave trade was enacted successively by one after another European power, while the end of slavery itself, usually affected by a series of stages designed to protect the interests of the planter classes and their metropolitan backers, followed more or less tardily.

But these slow and often reluctant loosenings of control were counterbalanced by two phenomena in particular, one a political convulsion of sufficient importance to rock the European world, the other a chronic accompaniment of New World slavery. The Haitian Revolution, 1791-1804, which ended in the establishment of the New World's second sovereign state, was a "nightmare" not only for Napoleonic France, but for every other land where slavery endured, including the United States. Not surprisingly, the United States did not choose to recognize Haiti until 1862. But the Haitian Revolution was only the capstone of a general resistance to slavery characteristic of the Afro-American response everywhere, both before and after the Revolution occurred. Such resistance took many forms: self-mutilation, malingering, poisoning, suicide, armed revolt—and escape.[42] Runaway slaves, whom the Spaniards called *cimarrones*, the French *marrons*, and the English "maroons," were commonly hunted down, punished, tortured, returned to their owners, or put to death. Here and there, however, maroon groups were able to establish long-term settlements, on occasion maintaining successful resistance and even maurauding, or signing treaties with the military representatives of their former owners. In recent years, the social history and significance of these groups has been rediscovered.[43] Older assertions that such groups, by virtue of their escapes and isolation, would be more "African" than other Afro-Americans, have begun to be put to the test; while general hypotheses about Afro-American culture change are now being refined in the light of new knowledge about living communities of maroon descendants.[44]

Successful escape and continued armed resistance, on the one hand, and what might be called "subversive accommodation" on the plantations on the other, suggest two of the major ways in which the slaves dealt actively with their condition. But the history of the plantation system in the Caribbean region has always been played out against a third and more elaborate form of resistance: the establishment of peasant communities. Caribbean peasantries are "reconstituted," in that they consist in large measure of Afro-Caribbean people who took advantage of every decline, lengthy or brief, in plantation domination to settle themselves on the land, as producers of a substantial part of their own needs, and of cash commodities they might sell as individuals to local or foreign markets. The best example of this form of resistance is expressed in the aftermath of the Haitian Revolution, when an entire nation turned its back upon the system of large estates, worked by forced labor, to create a peasant lifestyle; to this day, the vast majority of the Haitian people forms a thoroughgoing peasantry.[45] The process also occurred in other Caribbean lands, however, and was typified by as many failures—whenever the planter class could, by discriminatory legislation,[46] special taxes,[47] the importation of additional labor from elsewhere,[48] or by other means, defeat the peasant adaptation—as by successes. But wherever the peasantry was able to maintain itself, it represented "a reaction to the plantation economy, a negative reflex to enslavement, mass production, monocrop dependence, and metropolitan control."[49] Thus it seems fair to view the growth of Afro-Caribbean peasantries as an important form of "resistance," even though it may appear otherwise. The whole issue of resistance has been beclouded in some sense by the insistence of some that instant violence to the death is its only permissible measure. That the case is not all so simple should be obvious upon reflection:

There should be neither surprise nor disappointment in the discovery that considerable resistance involved as its precondition some processes of culture change, of adaptation, on the part of the slaves themselves. This is not an idle issue. The house slave who poisoned her master's family by putting ground glass in the food had first to become the family cook. The runaway slaves who created viable communities in the hinterlands of so many slave societies needed to learn techniques of cultivation in an alien environment. And the slaves who plotted armed revolts in the marketplaces had first to produce for market, and to gain permission to carry their produce there.[50]

The emergence of peasant communities upon the Caribbean landscape represented from the first—and to some extent, still represents—resistance to the will of the plantation system to turn every citizen into a faceless, interchangeable atom in "the labor pool," and to harness every local resource for its own needs. Accordingly, land has always had special meanings for Afro-Caribbean folk, since its ownership has so often been perceived as the key to independence and dignity.[51] This is a quite separate issue from that of the relative economic viability of plantation and peasant adaptations, since the competition for resources has never been symmetrical. Characteristically, government support, agricultural extension, water resources, transportation and all else are siphoned off by the plantations, leaving the peasantry to confirm the preconceptions of outsiders about peasant "fatalism," "stoicism," "conservatism," and "backwardness." But this is a subject that cannot be explored here.

Just as Afro-Caribbean peasantries have long been an important key to unlocking the resistant spirit of local peoples to external domination of certain kinds, so the perpetuation of the plantation system, on an ever grander and more industrial scale, reveals the unbroken thread of metropolitan interest and control. But the plantation system today is more than simply a form of agricultural organization. As in the past, it is also the framework for a particular social adaptation: that of the rural proletariat. Modified significantly now by aluminum mines in Haiti, Jamaica, Guyana and elsewhere, by the oil refineries of Curaçao, and by tourism nearly everywhere, the ancient pattern of factories in the field, modern machinery islands in seas of sugar-cane, still remains the Caribbean rural archetype. Rural proletarians, but proletarians nonetheless—landless, propertyless, wage-earning, store-buying, with naught but their labor to sell[52]—are the contemporary evidence of those demographic successions by which the region became an ethnic and "racial" potpourri.

The creation of rural proletariats, geared into the growth of large, impersonal, corporate plantations, owned and managed by foreigners, which held both land and factories, was, after the Haitian Revolution and subsequent emancipation elsewhere, the single most important sociological fact in Caribbean life in the nineteenth century. The expansion of North American economic, political and military power was a "natural" concomitant of this process, as Europe's grip upon the region began to loosen, and as the North Americans completed the post-bellum engrossment of their own mainland territories. The massive importation of new laboring populations to the Caribbean region similarly proceeded from the perpetuation and expansion of the plantation system, now on a wholly new technological level.

In these terms, the divergent but interrelated development of peasantries and rural proletariats epitomizes the social history of the Caribbean region—and of its black populations—during the last two centuries. Peasant and rural proletarian adaptations are neither mutually exclusive nor wholly isolated from each other, and it would be erroneous wholly to counterpose these socioeconomic forms or categories, or to view them as summarizing the complexity of Caribbean rural life. Yet it is nonetheless striking how differences between peasants and rural proletarians, ultimately referrable to their economic relations, are also expressed in lifestyle, attitude, and political disposition. Research on Afro-Caribbean—but *rural*—politics is still immature; yet some of the apparent enigmas of political sociology in such societies as Jamaica or Haiti may one day be unlocked by this means. Such research is likely to make clear that even in such seemingly esoteric aspects of life as those with which we dealt earlier—expressive media, performance, and the presence or absence of Africanisms—proletarian and peasant adaptations within the same society may manifest significant differences.

More significantly, perhaps, theories concerned with class consciousness and the role of different classes in revolutionary movements will probably undergo serious revision when the nature of Caribbean societies is fully understood. The historical significance of the proletariat and the supposed inertness of the peasantry, as set forth in European Marxist sociology, has already been called into serious question.[53] Deeper understanding of the evolution of classes in Caribbean societies, far from European metropolises but deeply influenced by European capitalism in their historical development, may eventuate in a more effective cross-cultural treatment of the concept of class consciousness, and a new view of the political potentialities of the anciently disinherited.[54]

The argument thus far has concentrated on several principal features of the past and present of Afro-Caribbean peoples: enslavement, forced emigration and forced labor, lengthy colonial domination, the plantation system, the rise of the peasantry, increasing ethnic heterogeneity over time, and the widening of social, political and economic horizons. In recent decades, the emigrations of Afro-Caribbean citizens to the heartland of Western society—to Britain, to France, to the Netherlands, to the United States and elsewhere—has meant the introduction of nonwhite populations into societies which (except for the United States) were previously able to deal with racism as a "colonial problem" and with ethnicity as separable from perceived physical difference. For the migrants themselves, such movement has meant a confrontation with the home-grown racism of the West, and a renewed experience with the colonial mentality, this time detached from the assurance provided by colonial familiarity. It has also meant confrontations between different sets of values and attitudes; and the high psychic costs involved express themselves in myriad ways, including the recognition that physical differences in the Western heartland are assimilated to a white-nonwhite dichotomy typical of North Europe and North America.

This latter problem is felt particularly acutely, perhaps, by hispanophone (Cuban, Dominican, and Puerto Rican) migrants to the United States, among whose intermediately complexioned members blackness becomes a badge of despair, never experienced in quite the same way at home.[55] But migrants from other Caribbean countries likewise undergo structurally similar, if psychologically different, transformations of perceptions. Haitians and British West Indians, for instance, discover not only that variant degrees of whiteness or blackness are irrelevant to the majority society, but that differences in class, education, sophistication and all else also tend to be submerged in the host population's obsession with "race."

Afro-Caribbean migrant populations are not homogeneous in these ways; Martiniquans and Guadeloupans in Paris do not see themselves as indistinguishable from francophone Africans or from each other; Cubans and Puerto Ricans in New York do not think of themselves as one people; Barbadians and Jamaicans in London are unprepared to accept the local citizen's homogeneate view of all nonwhite outsiders. This radical difference in perception and in self-identity will one day have significant consequences, some of them political, for the host countries.

On a wider canvas, these movements of colonial peoples to the doorsteps of their rulers have produced some reversals in attitudes, in the United States perhaps less than elsewhere. The United States is a special case, perhaps, because it is the geopolitical colossus of the Caribbean region, in spite of all else, and because its racism was embedded in an antislavery struggle waged on its own territory; unlike the European powers, the United States never enjoyed the luxury of "solving the color problem" in distant colonies.[56] The European powers, once able to view racism as deplorable in the absence of citizen nonwhite peoples, have some serious self-reflection in which to engage, even if they choose as Britain did to substitute fiat for courage. That the United States must one day accept its racism and begin over thereafter, *whether or not* Afro-Caribbean peoples continue to seek its shores, simply points up the difference between the Americas and the Old World.

Perhaps it is from the vantage point of this assertion that a few conclusions may be drawn, having to do with the future of social science research among Afro-Caribbean peoples. While in the past social scientists were able, however languorously, to appreciate the significance of the Caribbean region for their work, they could do so without any honest recognition of the geopolitical realities of the North American presence. Such a luxury is now (blessedly, perhaps) forever gone. Not only does a revolutionary socialist society continue to function less than a hundred miles away, having survived a wide variety of retaliations, some subtle and some less so, but that island, together with its neighbors, has been contributing significantly to the radical alteration of the North American demographic, racial, and—eventually—political scene. In New York City, one may read a Haitian newspaper, dine in a Cuban restaurant, dance to Dominican merengues, and vote for ever-larger slates of Puerto Rican candidates for office. New Haven—of all places—has the largest population of Nevisian emigrants to the United States. Puerto Rican laborers in northern Connecticut struggle against working conditions they deem exploitative and unfair, while (British) West Indians there man important posts in business and civil administration. Cuban culture in all its many forms has transformed Tampa into a Cuban city, while in New York, one may choose to attend a Puerto Rican Pentecostal service, an Afro-Cuban cult ceremony, or a Haitian *vodoun* ritual. So thoroughgoing and continuous is this two-way interpenetration of North America and the islands to its south that the writer was recently told by some market women friends in the great downtown marketplace of Port-au-Prince that their *houngan* (*vodoun* priest or leader) now commutes regularly to New York City!

It is uncertain to what extent this qualitatively different situation, in which migrants from the entire Caribbean region are now becoming living parts of the North American scene, is fully grasped by us North Americans. So far, an ingroup murder among Jamaican migrant Rastafarians or the development of a social-action movement such as the Young Lords is more likely to hold the attention of the men of decision than the plight of migrant laborers in Connecticut or Florida or the changing cultural character of the Eastern metropolises; after all, policy men are sometimes of greater interest to policy-makers than is the making of policy. But in New York City alone, reasoned guesses are that 200,000 Haitians, at least 170,000

Dominicans, perhaps 225,000 Jamaicans, over 100,000 Cubans and more than 1,200,000 Puerto Ricans are now in residence. Most of these people are perceived as nonwhites by the majority society; they share little otherwise, though few North Americans, even black North Americans, are much concerned to distinguish them from each other

Much the same lack of distinguishing perception typifies the outsider's view of Afro-Caribbean peoples at home. The first step in a new social science of the Caribbean region will be the establishment of criteria of distinctiveness, and the documentation of particularity within the Caribbean sphere, both in single societies and between societies. Such a task will not hinge, ultimately, on the exaggeration of the relativistically unique features of each Caribbean society, but upon the plotting of differences against a broader understanding of those fundamental similarities in history, economy, and society which give the region its peculiar integrity, even though the colonial experience and the growth of local multicultural communities has constantly militated against the recognition of underlying likenesses, either scientifically or politically.

The adequacy of formulations that would allow us to weigh the importance of local distinctiveness in the context of parallel histories will depend, to some degree at least, on their ultimate success in explaining precisely what perceptive and concerned observers like Naipaul, Lamming, and Hobsbawm have called to our attention: the character of Caribbean societies as artifacts of the Western thrust outside itself, and the "unaccustomed detachment" of the Caribbean perspective. That a dependence of the spirit, on the one hand, is matched by a remarkable capacity to discern realities without the burden of unconscious but profound commitment to the past, on the other, should perhaps not really surprise us. But the processes by which peoples are led—and driven—from a received historical sense of group identity to a new view of self and others are still only dimly understood. Furnivall is probably right in asserting that Western capitalistic overseas enterprise intensified in some ways the separateness of ethnic groups and "races"; but he is even closer to the mark when he notes that, in societies thus remade ". . . the individual stands even more alone." It is not paradoxical to assert that the transplanted peoples of the Caribbean had to be *homogenized* to meet the economic demands the West imposed upon them, at the same time that they were *individualized* by the destruction of the institutional underpinnings of their pasts. It is in this individualization that both the weakness and the strength of Afro-Caribbean peoples—and, for that matter, of all Caribbean peoples—can be located. That we have failed as yet to test such a hypothesis, or even to refine it so that it can be tested, may be a minor measure of the limitations of social science research in the region.

But whereas a programmatic statement of this sort might once have said something only about the Caribbean region itself, the movement of Caribbean peoples away from the periphery and to the Western core should make it clear that comparable studies are already badly needed in Montreal, Paris, London, Amsterdam, and New York, together with *their* peripheries. The Caribbean region, a medley of peoples and cultures, has now firmly extended its roots outward to the capitals of that world which brought it into being. It is not entirely grotesque to claim that, in at least some subtle ways, the West may be re-Westernized by these missionaries, who are the only peoples outside the heartland to have shared so fully—though at the other end of the stick—in the making of empires. Thus the significance of the past and present of Afro-Caribbean peoples has somehow grown greater, even as the societies from which they come, once jewels in every imperial diadem, may appear to some to matter less in the modern world. The peculiar poignancy of these lands and peoples is still only imperfectly grasped, it seems. But someday their achievements will receive appropriate recognition—for nowhere else in the universe can one look with such certainty into the past and discern the outlines of an undisclosed future.

REFERENCES

The writer is grateful to Jacqueline W. Mintz and Richard Price for their help with an earlier draft of this paper.

1. V. S. Naipaul, *The Overcrowded Barracoon* (New York: Knopf, 1973), p. 254.

2. George Lamming, *The Pleasures of Exile* (London: M. Joseph, 1960), p. 35.

3. Eric Hobsbawm, review of *Frantz Fanon: A Critical Study*, by Irene L. Gendzier, *New York Review of Books*, Feb. 22, 1973, p. 8.

4. David Lowenthal, "The Range and Variation of Caribbean Societies," *Annals of the N.Y. Academy of Sciences*, 83 (1960), pp. 786-795.

5. Sidney W. Mintz, "The Caribbean as a Sociocultural Area," *Cahiers d'Histoire Mondiale*, 9 (1966), pp. 916-941.

6. Philip A. Curtin, *The Atlantic Slave Trade: A Census* (Madison: University of Wisconsin Press, 1969), p. 268.

7. Eric Williams, *Capitalism and Slavery* (Chapel Hill: University of North Carolina Press, 1944), pp. 9-19.

8. Sidney W. Mintz, "Groups, Group Boundaries and the Perception of 'Race,' " *Comparative Studies in Society and History*, 13 (1971), pp. 437-443.

9. Sidney W. Mintz, "The Caribbean as a Sociocultural Area," pp. 916-941.

10. V. S. Naipaul, *The Overcrowded Barracoon*, p. 250.

11. V. S. Naipaul, *A Flag on the Island* (New York: Knopf, 1967), pp. 135-146.

12. Carl O. Sauer, *The Early Spanish Main* (Berkeley: University of California Press, 1967), p. 207.

13. Arthur Corwin, *Spain and the Abolition of Slavery in Cuba, 1817-1886* (Austin: University of Texas Press, 1967).

14. Eric Williams, *Capitalism and Slavery*; and, more recently, Richard Sheridan, "The Plantation Revolution and the Industrial Revolution, 1625-1775," *Caribbean Studies*, 9 (1969), pp. 5-25. Both works have stressed the importance of the slave trade and of Caribbean slavery in European economic development. Stanley Engerman, "The Slave Trade and British Capital Formation in the Eighteenth Century: A Comment on the Williams Thesis," *The Business History Review*, 46 (1972), pp. 430-443, and Roger Anstey, "The Volume and Profitability of the British Slave Trade, 1761-1807," (ms.) have argued the opposite view. Regardless of the economic importance of the Caribbean region to Europe, however, its role in New World "development," and its meaning for those who became its transplanted inhabitants, remains.

15. Naipaul, one of the most acute observers of Antillean culture alive, sometimes catches himself in the same trap. In recounting his first attempt to talk the creole language of Paramaribo, Dutch Guiana, he tells us,

Improvising an accent, the words coming from I know not where, I asked, "you no sabi waar she iss?" "*Ik weet niet waar ze is,*" the woman replied in careful Dutch, and tossed her head. "*Ik spreek geen talkie-talkie, mijnheer.* (I do not speak talkie-talkie, sir.)" So I hadn't spoken gibberish; I had spoken negerengels.
V. S. Naipaul, *The Middle Passage* (London: André Deutsch, 1962), p. 173. Wrong again; he had spoken gibberish, not negerengels. The taki-taki interrogative phrase for Naipaul's question would be *I no sabi pé a dé?* (for which I thank Mr. Adiante Franszoon). Whether or not Naipaul's informant understood him (or speaks taki-taki, for that matter) is hardly the point. But if one begins by assuming a language is "gibberish," one is hardly likely to learn that language, let alone ever to concede eventually that it *is* a language.

16. William A. Stewart, "Creole Languages in the Caribbean," *Study of the Role of Second Languages in Asia, Africa and Latin America,* ed. Frank A. Rice (Washington, D.C.: Center for Applied Linguistics of the Modern Language Association of America, 1962), pp. 34-53.

17. Harry Hoetink, *The Two Variants in Caribbean Race Relations* (London: Oxford University Press, 1967); David Lowenthal, "Race and Color in the West Indies," *Dædalus,* 96 (Spring 1967), pp. 580-626.

18. Hoetink (*ibid.*) points out with some justice that the same individual may be considered "white" in some parts of the Caribbean, "colored" in other localities, and a "Negro" in the southern United States. This important fact, however, simply calls our attention to differences in culturally conventionalized norms of perception. The problem is much more complex. Even within a single society, drawing the sort of "map" suggested will continue to prove impossible until the criteria of distinction are far better understood:
    Perception of color is not simply a matter of observed phenotype but of observed phenotype taken together with many other factors. . . . Individual judges within a society, when speaking of the color of any other individual, may be hardly conscious of the criteria they are using or of any priorities they may be giving to some criteria over others in making their judgments. Moreover, there is some reason to suppose that perception of an individual's color may vary from time to time and from situation to situation, even when the same person is making the judgment. Such variation may be unconscious for the most part, and may hinge not only upon the judged individual's social status or behavior, but also upon the judge's conception at any given time of *his own physical appearance, social status, and behavior relative to that of the man he is judging.*
    Sidney W. Mintz, review of M. G. Smith's "A Framework for Caribbean Studies," *Boletín Bibliográfico de Antropología,* 8 (1957), pp. 189-194.

19. Raymond T. Smith, "Social Stratification in the Caribbean," *Essays in Comparative Social Stratification,* ed. Leonard Plotnicov and Arthur Tuden (Pittsburgh: University of Pittsburgh Press, 1970), pp. 43-76.

20. J. S. Furnivall, *Colonial Policy and Practice* (Cambridge: Cambridge University Press, 1948).

21. R. T. Smith, "Social Stratification in the Caribbean," pp. 43-76.

22. R. A. J. van Lier, *Samenleving in een Grensgebied* ('s-Gravenhage: 1949). The citation is from the English edition, *Frontier Society* (The Hague: Martinus Nijhoff, 1971), p. 10. Richard Price, in "Studies of Caribbean Family Organization," *Dédalo,* 3 (1970), has pointed out that van Lier discarded the term "plural society" soon after; see his "Development and Nature of Society in the West Indies," Koninklijke Vereeniging Indisch Instituut, *Mededeling No. XCII, Afdeling Culturele en Physische Anthropologie, No.* 37 (Amsterdam: 1950).

23. See, for instance, M. G. Smith, *The Plural Society in the British West Indies* (Berkeley: University of California Press, 1965); and Leo Despres, *Cultural Pluralism and Nationalist Politics in British Guiana* (Chicago: 1967).

24. Leo Kuper, who espoused the plural society concept particularly in dealing with Africa, has recently given some ground on the general applicability of this framework, by noting that all complex societies may exhibit "pluralism," and by replacing the original conception of the plural society with four "dimensions" of pluralism: particularism-individualism, segregation-assimilation, cultural

diversity-homogeneity, and inequality-equality. He speaks out for the retention of the original concept for "extreme" cases; but this view seems slightly sentimental, since he does not argue that such "extreme" cases are *qualitatively* different:

> What is common to these conceptions of the plural society and of pluralism is that they have come to be applied to any society that is politically unitary through being under a single, supreme political authority, or that has a unitary organization in relation to the outside world by any other structural criteria, but is internally made up of racially or ethnically or culturally diverse groups who maintain distinguishably separate ways of life.

Leo Kuper, "Political Change in Plural Societies," *International Science Journal*, 23 (1971), pp. 598-599. Such a shift in perspective may ultimately prove salutary, for the inclination to view so-called plural societies as members of a more general order of social system could facilitate a greater unification of social theory.

25. It is impossible in a paper of this kind to examine the many different ways in which Caribbeanists have sought to classify Caribbean societies for purposes of deeper analysis. But one important axis of classification has separated the hispanophone polities (Cuba, Santo Domingo and Puerto Rico) from the others, because of two major distinctions: the relative lack of massive migrant streams other than from Europe and Africa; and the relatively late development of large-scale plantations. Cuba would be the major exception; though its African component is very ancient, most enslaved Africans were transported to Cuba after 1760. Moreover, the nineteenth-century migration of Chinese laborers was heavy, and large numbers of Haitians and Jamaicans emigrated to Cuba in this century. Taking account of these exceptions, it can be said that the hispanophone societies generally manifest a black-white continuum, without significant ethnic additions. Moreover, the nature of that continuum differs in important—though not yet fully understood—ways from the nonhispanophone cases, since it is broken up typologically and perceptually very differently from other Caribbean cases. The significance of this fact was remarked upon by North American historians of slavery, and by students of race relations, and it remains an important research area for all Caribbeanists. See in this connection Frank Tannenbaum, *Slave and Citizen* (New York: Knopf, 1947); Stanley Elkins, *Slavery* (Chicago: University Chicago Press, 1959); Sidney W. Mintz, review of Stanley Elkins, *Slavery*, *American Anthropologist*, 63 (1961), pp. 579-587; Harry Hoetink, *The Two Variants in Caribbean Race Relations* (London: Oxford University Press, 1967); and Sidney W. Mintz, "Groups, Group Boundaries and the Perception of 'Race,' " *Comparative Studies in Society and History*, 13 (1971), pp. 437-450. A number of important general articles dealing analytically with the Caribbean region as a totality have appeared in recent decades. Though some have been cited in one or another connection in this paper, it may be useful to enumerate a few of the most important for future reference: Michael G. Smith, "A Framework for Caribbean Studies," in his *Plural Society in the British West Indies* (Berkeley: The University of California Press, 1965), pp. 18-74; Raymond T. Smith, "Social Stratification in the Caribbean," pp. 43-76. Particularly insightful and provocative is a recent book by Peter Wilson, *Crab Antics* (New Haven: Yale University Press, 1973), which offers an original perspective from which to view the sociology of the anglophone Antilles. Also of possible interest are several general papers by the present writer: "The Caribbean as a Socio-cultural Area," *Cahiers d'Histoire Mondiale*, 9 (1966) pp. 916-941; "Caribbean Nationhood in Anthropological Perspective," *Caribbean Integration*, ed. T. Mathews and S. Lewis (Río Piedras: Institute of Caribbean Studies, 1967), pp. 140-153; and "Caribbean Society," *International Encyclopedia of the Social Sciences*, 2, pp. 306-319. Mention must be made of the excellent bibliography of the Caribbean region by Lambros Comitas which, though it omits Haiti and the hispanophone Antilles, is an essential *vade mecum* of any serious Caribbeanist scholar: *Caribbeana 1900-1965* (Seattle: University of Washington Press, 1968).

26. In all of North American anthropology, one individual in particular, Professor Melville J. Herskovits, anticipated by decades the "discovery" of Afro-America. A Boas-trained cultural anthropologist, Herskovits had early evinced a serious interest in Africa and, even more unusual at the time, in Afro-American cultures and societies. He began publishing on this theme in 1929, and his book, *The Myth of the Negro Past* (New York: Harper, 1941), was to become an indispensable handbook for all students of Afro-America. For Herskovits, the "myth" was that the black peoples of the New World had no past beyond slavery, and he devoted his life to disproving it, laying heavy emphasis on continuities with Africa in the life of Afro-Americans. In his debate with the black North American

sociologist-historian, E. Franklin Frazier, concerning the origins of Afro-American familial and domestic organization, Herskovits' work anticipated an embarrassingly substantial portion of so-called contemporary scholarship. While Frazier saw Afro-Americans as being, in W. E. B. DuBois' words, "nothing so indigenous, so completely 'made in America' as we," Herskovits rejected so sweeping and seemingly ahistorical a formulation. Not surprisingly, he turned to the Caribbean region most of all to document the living character of the African past. That his ethnography was exclusively concerned with Africanisms, real or putative, rather than with the whole cultures of the peoples he studied (in Surinam, Trinidad, and Haiti), and that his work is sometimes unconvincing ethnographically, hardly diminishes his importance as a pioneer in Afro-Caribbean research. For some estimates of Herskovits' contributions, see the introduction to *Afro-American Anthropology* (New York: Free Press, 1970), by its editors, Norman Whitten and John Szwed; J. L. Dillard, "The Writings of Herskovits and the Study of the Language of the Negro in the New World," *Caribbean Studies*, 4, pp. 35-41; and the present writer's "Melville J. Herskovits and Caribbean Studies: A Retrospective Tribute," *Caribbean Studies*, 4, pp. 42-51. It should be stressed that the disinterest of North American anthropologists in Afro-America was happily not matched by their colleagues to the south, among whom one must mention at the very least Jean Price-Mars and Jacques Roumain in Haiti; Fernando Ortiz, Romulo Lachatañere, and Lydia Cabrera in Cuba; and Nina Rodrigues, Artur Ramos, Edison Carneiro and Gilberto Freyre in Brazil.

27. Richard Price, "Saramaka Woodcarving: The Development of an Afroamerican Art," *Man*, 5 (1970), p. 375.

28. *Ibid.*, p. 375.

29. Ralph Ellison, *Shadow and Act* (New York: Signet, 1964), p. 248.

30. Sidney W. Mintz, "Creating Culture in the Americas," *Forum*, 13 (1970), pp. 4-11; "Foreword" to N. Whitten and J. Szwed, eds., *Afro-American Anthropology* (New York: Free Press, 1970), pp. 1-16.

31. Sidney W. Mintz and Richard Price, "An Anthropological Approach to Afro-American Culture History," (ms.)

32. Sidney W. Mintz, "Toward an Afro-American History," *Cahiers d'Histoire Mondiale*, 8 (1971), pp. 317-332; "The Socio-Historical Background of Pidginization and Creolization," *Pidginization and Creolization of Languages*, ed. Dell Hymes (Cambridge: Cambridge University Press, 1971), pp. 481-496.

33. It is impossible to treat this subject adequately here. The plethora of publications dealing with pidgin and creole languages and their possible origins has become overwhelming, and the controversies now raging in this regard seem to change almost from week to week. For a useful starting-place, the interested reader may wish to consult Dell Hymes, (*ibid.*). One of the most erudite and brilliant students of such languages is Douglas Macrae Taylor; consult his "New Languages for Old in the West Indies," *Comparative Studies in Society and History*, 3 (1961), pp. 277-288; also "The Origin of West Indian Creole Languages: Evidence from Grammatical Categories," *American Anthropologist*, 65 (1963), pp. 800-814.

34. See, for instance, Roger Abrahams, "The Shaping of Folklore Traditions in the British West Indies," *Journal of Inter-American Studies*, 9 (1967), pp. 456-480; and "Traditions of Eloquence in Afro-American Communities," *Journal of Inter-American Studies*, 7 (1970), pp. 505-527.

35. Roger Bastide, *Les amériques noires* (Paris: Payot, 1967).

36. Richard and Sally Price, "Saramaka Onomastics: An Afro-American Naming System," *Ethnology*, 11 (1972), pp. 362-363.

37. K. V. Parmasad, "By the Light of a Deya," *Tapia*, 22 (1971), p. 5.

38. That the issue is not a new one, and that these questions are by no means academic, even in the United States, is revealed in an early statement by Melville Herskovits, which prefigures so much of the North American dialogue of recent years:

   Disconcertingly enough, it is those holding extreme opinions concerning the Negro who sense the opportunity to bolster their particular theses by reference to the fact that Africanisms have been retained in the New World. On the left, the point of view taken conceives the Negroes of the United States as a subject "nation," whose true freedom and full citizenship may come only after the establishment of an autonomous Black Republic in the South shall have permitted the fulfillment of the inherent genius of this people. What better theoretical base for such a program could be found than in material which seems to show that American Negroes, under their skins, are but Africans whose suppressed racial tendencies will, when released, furnish the drive needed for working out their own destiny? At the same time, those on the extreme right, who urge social and economic segregation for the American Negro, also vindicate their position by contemplating the Africanisms retained in American Negro life. Is this not evidence, they say, of the inability of the Negro to assimilate white culture to any workable degree, and should not Negroes therefore be encouraged to develop their own peculiar "racial" gifts—always, that is, within the bounds of the Negro's "place"?

Neither conclusion is in the least justified. To say that American and New World Negroes have retained certain African patterns of behavior and certain African aspects of belief within a varying range is not to suggest that in this country, for example, they have not assimilated American culture. They have, in fact, assimilated it to the degree that their opportunities have permitted. . . .

Melville J. Herskovits, *Life in a Haitian Valley* (New York: Knopf, 1937), pp. 303-304.
Herskovits' argument is pitched directly toward the issue in North America; but it plainly possesses a wider relevance. In political terms, it calls attention to the question as to whether the assertion of Afro-American cultural continuities is a "progressive" or a "conservative" act; and Herskovits wisely responds that it is both—or neither.

39. Raymond T. Smith, "People and Change," *New World*, 2 (1966), p. 54.

40. *Ibid.*, p. 54.

41. See, for instance, Sidney W. Mintz, "Labor and Sugar in Puerto Rico and Jamaica," *Comparative Studies in Society and History*, 1, pp. 273-283; Manuel Moreno Fraginals, *El Ingenio* (La Habana: Comisión Nacional de la UNESCO, 1964); Orlando Patterson, *The Sociology of Slavery* (London: MacGibbon and Kee, 1967); and Edward Brathwaite, *The Development of Creole Society in Jamaica, 1770-1820* (London: Oxford University Press, 1971).

42. Pioneering works on this theme include Herbert Aptheker, "Maroons Within the Present Limits of the United States," *Journal of Negro History*, 24 (1939), pp. 167-184; and Raymond and Alice Bauer, "Day-to-day Resistance to Slavery," *Journal of Negro History*, 27 (1942), pp. 388-419. See also Sidney W. Mintz, "Toward an Afro-American History," pp. 317-332.

43. For a sweeping hemispheric view of the maroon saga, see Richard Price, ed., *Maroon Societies* (New York: Anchor Books, 1973). Particularly moving is the autobiography of the Cuban maroon, Esteban Montejo, available now in English: Miguel Barnet, ed., *The Autobiography of a Runaway Slave* (New York: Random House, 1973).

44. Barbara Klamon Kopytoff, "The Incomplete Polities: An Ethnohistorical Account of the Jamaica Maroons" (Unpublished Ph.D. dissertation, University of Pennsylvania, 1973).

45. James G. Leyburn, *The Haitian People* (New Haven: Yale University Press, 1966).

46. See, for example, Alan H. Adamson, *Sugar Without Slaves* (New Haven: Yale University Press, 1972).

47. See, for instance, Philip D. Curtin, *Two Jamaicas* (Cambridge: Harvard University Press, 1955), p. 130.

48. See, for example, K. O. Laurence, *Immigration into the West Indies in the 19th Century* (St. Lawrence, Barbados: Caribbean Universities Press, 1971).

49. Sidney W. Mintz, foreword to Ramiro Guerra y Sánchez, *Sugar and Society in the Caribbean* (New Haven: Yale University Press, 1964), p. xx.

50. Sidney W. Mintz, "Toward an Afro-American History," p. 321.

51. David Lowenthal, "Caribbean Views of Caribbean Land," *Canadian Geographer*, 5 (1961), pp. 1-9.

52. Sidney W. Mintz, "The Folk-Urban Continuum and the Rural Proletarian Community," *American Journal of Sociology*, 59 (1953), pp. 136-143.

53. Eric R. Wolf, *Peasant Wars of the Twentieth Century* (New York: Harper and Row, 1969).

54. Sidney W. Mintz, "The Rural Proletariat and the Problem of Rural Proletarian Consciousness," *Journal of Peasant Studies*, 1 (1974), in press.

55. Virginia R. Dominguez, "Spanish-Speaking Caribbeans in New York: 'The Middle Race,' " *Revista Interamericana*, 3 (1973), pp. 135-142; Roy Sunon Bryce-Laporte, "Black Immigrants: The Experience of Invisibility and Inequality," *Journal of Black Studies*, 3 (1972), pp. 29-56.

56. Sidney W. Mintz, "Le rouge et le noir," *Les Temps Modernes* 299-300 (1971), pp. 2354-2361.

EDWARD KAMAU BRATHWAITE

The African Presence in Caribbean Literature[1]

> in december to about april every year, a drought visits the islands. the green
> canefields take on the golden deciduous crispness of scorched parchment. the
> blue sky burns muted. the dry air rivets the star nights with metallic cold. it is
> our tropical winter. this dryness, unexplained, is put down to 'lack of rain'.
>
> but living in st lucia at this time, i watched this drought drift in towards the
> island, moving in across the ocean from the east, obscuring martinique, obscur-
> ing sails beating towards castries and i suddenly realized that what i was
> witnessing—that milky haze, that sense of dryness—was something i had seen
> and felt before in ghana. it was the seasonal dust-cloud, drifting out of the great
> ocean of sahara—the harmattan. by an obscure miracle of connection, this
> arab's nomad wind, cracker of fante wood a thousand miles away, did not die on
> the sea-shore of west africa, its continental limit; it drifted on, reaching the new
> world archipelago to create our drought, imposing an african season on the
> caribbean sea. and it was on these winds too, and in this season, that the slave
> ships came from guinea, bearing my ancestors to this other land. . . .[2]

EVEN BEFORE THE first slaves came—bringing, perhaps, pre-Columbian explorers[3]—there was the wind: an implacable climatic, indeed, geological connection. Along its routes and during its seasonal blowing, fifteen to fifty million
Africans were imported into the New World,[4] coming to constitute a majority of
people in the Caribbean, and significant numbers in the New World.

Transference and Adaptation

Now there is a persistent, established theory which contends that the Middle
Passage destroyed the culture of these people, that it was such a catastrophic,
definitive experience that none of those transported during the period from 1540 to
1840 escaped trauma.[5] But modern research is pointing to a denial of this,[6] showing
that African culture not only crossed the Atlantic, it crossed, survived, and
creatively adapted itself to its new environment. Caribbean culture was therefore
not "pure" African, but an adaptation carried out mainly in terms of African tradition. This we can determine by looking at what anthropologists have called its
culture-focus. This concept posits that each culture has a distinguishing style or
characteristic: it may be sun-centered or acephalous, ceremonial or casual,
materialistic or contemplative. And everyone agrees that the focus of African
culture in the Caribbean was religious.

The anti-African argument claims, however, that it was *only* religion that the
slaves brought with them, and a religion already tending more to fetish and
superstition than to theology and ethics, and therefore weak and unviable. They
claim (and their twists of evidence would fill a whole paper in itself) that the slave

This essay is dedicated to John La Rose.

had no philosophy, no military organization, no social life, no family structure, no arts, no sense of personal or civic responsibility.[7]

I fundamentally disagree with this view which I consider based (and biased) on (1) mistaken notions of culture, culture change and culture transference; (2) untenable, sometimes ignorant, concepts of African culture; (3) a lack of intimacy with traditional African culture (most of those who have written on Africa have been European scholars, with both intellectual and interpersonal problems relating to Africa); and (4) an almost total ignorance of Afro-American folk culture.[8] Until sensitive *African* scholars begin to contribute to the study of New World and Caribbean folk cultures, the presence of African elements within this subculture is bound, for fairly obvious reasons, to remain obscure. How can we explain the success of the Haitian Revolution, for instance, unless we consider it a triumph of Afro-Caribbean folk arts and culture over European mercantilism? Toussaint was a slave (a coachman) and an herbalist, not an academy-drilled, socially motivated vaulter like Napoleon.

Religious Focus

The story really begins in the area of religious culture-focus already mentioned. A study of African culture[9] reveals almost without question that it is based upon religion—that, in fact, it is within the religious network that the entire culture resides. Furthermore, this entire culture is an organic whole. In traditional Africa, there is no specialization of disciplines, no dissociation of sensibilities. In other words, starting from this particular religious focus, there is no separation between religion and philosophy, religion and society, religion and art. Religion is the form or kernel or core of the culture. It is therefore not surprising that anthropologists tell us that African culture survived in the Caribbean through religion. What we should alert ourselves to is the possibility, whenever "religion" is mentioned, that a whole cultural complex is also present. Of course we have to take into account the depredations and fragmentations imposed upon African culture by the slave trade and plantation systems; but this should not alter our perception of the whole.

Emancipation

This African culture, focused upon a religious core which survived and flourished under slavery, came under very severe attack at emancipation. Under slavery, it had been possible for plantation slaves—those not immediately or always under the surveillance of the master—to continue practicing their religion and therefore their culture, or at least those elements of it that had survived under the conditions—elements signaled by things like drum, dance, *obeah*,° song, tale, and

---

  ° The African religious complex, despite its homogeneity, has certain interrelated divisions or specializations: (1) "worship"—an essentially Euro-Christian word that doesn't really describe the African situation, in which the congregation is not a passive one entering into a monolithic relationship with a superior god, but an active communit,· which celebrates in song and dance the carnation of powers/spirits (*orisha/loa*) into one or several of themselves. This is therefore a social (interpersonal and communal), artistic (formal/improvisatory choreography of movement/sound) and eschatological (possession) experience, which erodes the conventional definition/description of "worship"; (2) *rites de passage;* (3) divination; (4) healing; and (5) protection. *Obeah* (the word is used in Africa and the Carib-

herb. At emancipation, however, all this came under attack from a number of quarters.

In the first place, the missionaries were naturally against African or African-oriented religious practices among their ex-African adherents. Hence the banning of the drum (voice of god or worship: *nyame*—one of three Akan names for the Supreme Being); the gradual replacement of African foods and foodstyles (*nyam*†/*yam*) by European or creole substitutes, and the Christianization of names (*nommo*—Bantu for the Word) and ideas (*nam*). It was possible after emancipation to do this more and more effectively because there was no longer the legal restriction on missionary activity that had existed under slavery. Slowly the ex-slaves began to lose or disown the most crucial elements of their culture in the very area where it was most important and venerable. They began, in other words to go to churches and chapels rather than to beat their drums.

Second, the process of education began—first clerical, then secular, but always colonial. Depending on who owned the territory, the ex-slaves were to be molded into the British or the French or the Spanish system. They began to learn to read and write so that they were diverted from the oral tradition of their inheritance; they became literate in a language which was foreign to them, "liberated" into a culture which was not theirs. They began, in other words, to read about Versailles and cake and Lord Nelson and Robin Hood and all those frescoes which, some time ago, the Mighty Sparrow‡ de-celebrated in his calypso, "Dan Is the Man in the Van." At the same time, there was no countervailing influence to help them learn about their own tradition. This of course did not "have to" happen. It is conceivable that this education could have been truly bi-cultural, so that, who knows, we might have struggled through Asante Twi and the Zulu epics as well as French, Latin, and Anglo-Saxon. However, under the dictates of mercantilism, education had a more monolithic and materialistic aim: control of the ex-slaves for the profit of their labor.

Third, since the object of the plantocracy was to retain its wall of social and political authority in the Caribbean, it supported these two "missionary" drives with social legislation designed to prevent the former slaves from achieving very much in the community. Their voting rights were restricted, their socio-economic

---

bean) is an aspect of the last two of these subdivisions, though it has come to be regarded in the New World and in colonial Africa as sorcery and "black magic." One probable tributary to this view was the notion that a great deal of "prescientific" African medicine was (and is) at best psychological, at norm mumbo-jumbo/magical in nature. It was not recognized, in other words, that this "magic" was (is) based on a scientific knowledge and use of herbs, drugs, foods and symbolic/associational procedures (pejoratively termed *fetishistic*), as well as on a homoeopathic understanding of the material and divine nature of Man (*nam*) and the ways in which this could be affected. The principle of *obeah* is, therefore, like medical principles everywhere, the process of healing/protection through seeking out the source or explanation of the cause (*obi*/evil) of the disease or fear. This was debased by slave master/missionary/prospero into an assumption, inherited by most of us, that obeah deals *in* evil. In this way, not only has African science been discredited, but Afro-Caribbean religion has been negatively fragmented and almost (with exceptions in Haiti and Brazil) publicly destroyed. To properly understand *obeah*, therefore, we shall have to restore it to its proper place in the Afr/american communion complex: *kumina-custom-myal-obeah-fetish*.

† West African (Mende, Ashanti, etc.) and Afro-Caribbean for "food," or "to eat."

‡ The name used by Slinger Francisco, the most talented and popular calypsonion of recent times. Sparrow has dominated the calypso art form since the 1950's.

mobility curtailed, and their way of life brought under subtle but savage attack. Shango, cumfa, kaiso, tea-meeting, susu, jamette-carnival[§]—all had to go.

The situation has been very slow to change. The law banning cumfa in Surinam was only rescinded in 1971,[10] and it is not unlikely that, technically at least, laws against shango, bongo, poco,[11] and obeah are still in force in the region.[11] Recently, for instance, Dr. Eric Williams, Prime Minister of Trinidad and Tobago and author of the radical antimercantilist dissertation, *Capitalism and Slavery*,[12] remarked with sardonic disapproval that he didn't think it would be long before the obeah man would be rehabilitated in the Caribbean.[13] Such is the success of the Europhone establishment at devaluing African culture in the New World. Not surprisingly then, the teaching of African history at the University of the West Indies has been, to say the least, spasmodic. The subject's most distinguished native scholar, Walter Rodney, was cashiered from Jamaica in 1968[14] and there has been no continuity of instruction since then. African *culture* is not "taught" or even thought of at all, a fact reflected in the dearth of books, records, films, and lectures on these matters available to the public. Moreover, when an individual or group protests about this or tries to *do* something about it, a multiracial howl goes up. The protesters are accused of overemphasis on Africa (!) and asked to remember that they are Dominicans, Bahamians, or what have you, with their own distinctive (!) and locally rooted (?) cultures. In August, 1973, for instance, a Bajan cultural group, Yoruba House, commemorated Emancipation/Freedom Day by issuing a number of awards in the arts—the first such recorded in Barbados or indeed in the anglophone Caribbean. These were not awarded on the basis of annual competition/performances but in consideration of contributions to the discovery, recognition, and status of the African presence in the community. On this, the island's (then) only newspaper felt it necessary to editorialize:

Our heritage is the result of exposure to many cultures, with some having a greater influence than others. It is because of this greater influence which has been mainly of British origin in Barbados, that much of our African heritage has become submerged or even diluted to the extent that it can no longer be identified as such. . . .[15]

With Africa, then, diluted, even submerged, and certainly safely out of the way,

---

[§] *Shango:* an Afro-Caribbean form of worship, centered mainly on Shango, the Yoruba god of thunder and creativity, and most closely associated with the island of Trinidad.

Cumfa: one of the possession dance/ceremonies of the New World found under this name mainly in the Guianas. In Jamaica, it is known as *kumina*.

Kaiso: an early form/word for calypso.

Tea-meeting: a speech contest and exhibition, at which syntactical logic is increasingly abandoned or transcended. A kind of possession by the Word.

Susu: Yoruba/Caribbean word for cooperative group.

Jamette-carnival: Jamet, supposedly French Creole for *diametre* (literally, "the other half"), was a term applied in Trinidad to the underworld of prostitutes, rudies and, by extension, the black poor. The jamette-carnivals were obscured by the establishment on grounds of "obscenity" (first routes, then hours of performance were restricted, until these "ole mas'" bands could appear only in the foreday morning—*jou'vert*—of the first day), and thus became a *maroon* feature of the culture—a dark area of celebration where the folk expressed themselves without much reference to middle-class inhibitions and styles. Moko-jumbies, jonkonnus, calindas (stick-fight dancers) and nation-bands (Shango, Congo, etc.) were other features of this carnival.

[11] *Bongo:* an Afro-Caribbean dance, once connected with death ritual.

Poco: or pocomania. The name given in Jamaica to vodun/shango forms.

the article goes on to salvage from the cultural wreck the multiracial (creole) notion of "Caribbean": "not totally European, nor is it pure African." It also referred to extremists who "become fanatical in their thinking about things African" (one wonders where or when!), warns against "emotionalism" sweeping into the discussion, and finally concedes that Yoruba could play "a big part in bringing into proper perspective what we owe to the African side of our heritage." My contention is that the creation of this "proper perspective" requires more than lip service from the establishment. It requires information, and an educational program based on a revolutionized value system.

Religious Continuity

On the eve of the Morant Bay Rebellion, thirty years after emancipation, there was a "strange" movement in Jamaica which, significantly, took the form of a religious revival. Social and political unrest centered in the Baptist churches, which the slaves had always preferred, mainly because of the "African" nature of their adult baptism and the comparative freedom of their communal worship.[16] Especially militant were the Black or Native Baptist churches, started at the time of the American Revolution when loyalist colonists fled from what was to become the United States with faithful slaves or ex-slaves, some of whom (George Leile, Moses Baker) were helped or encouraged by their masters to spread the gospel of Christ on the island.[17] As a result, certain churches shifted away from a Euro-American kind of organization into congregations that were not only run by blacks, but included African religious elements into their services. In 1865, on the verge of the Rebellion (in fact a symptom and symbol of it), there was a sudden proliferation of these churches.

This was followed by an even more "startling" phenomenon—the public reappearance of *myalism*,° which had no connection whatever with Christianity. *Myal*[18] is a fragmented form of African religion, expressing, through dreams, visions, prophesying, and possession dances (*kumina*†), what the establishment called "hysteria" and later *pocomania:* "a little madness."[19] Thousands of black Jamaicans became involved in this revival which ranged from "left wing" Christian (Baptist) to Afro-Jamaican radical or anarchic (*myal*). The Rebellion itself was a militant political movement closely related to these. The leaders, mulatto George William Gordon and the black Paul Bogle, pastors of Baptist and Black Baptist churches respectively, worked in close alliance. Bogle (like Toussaint, and Sam Sharpe later) probably carried the *myal* title of "Daddy" (*Dada*) as well, although more research will have to be done to confirm this. At present we know next to nothing about him,[20] but there is evidence[21] that some of his followers took oaths and drank rum and gunpowder, leading some contemporary observers to speak of "the supernatural workings of Satanic temptation."[22] There was also an emphasis on color ("We must cleave unto the black")—all of which suggests that a radical Afro-*myal* movement underlay the more liberal/reformist creole concern with justice and land.[23] Elements similar to this were present in the ferment surrounding

---

° *Myal:* divination aspect of Afro-Caribbean religion. The term is most commonly associated with Jamaica.

† *Kumina:* Afro-Jamaican possession/dance ceremony, similar to *cumfa* in the Guianas.

Cuffee in Guyana (1763), Dessalines in Haiti (1799/1800), Bussa in Barbados (1816) and Nat Turner in the United States (1831), so that we witness again and again a chain-reaction moving the ex-African's core of religion into ever-widening areas. It is this potential for explosion and ramification that has made blackness such a radical if subterranean feature of plantation political culture; for the African "phenomenon," continuously present, like a bomb, in the New World since the abduction of the first slaves—a phenomenon subsisting in bases deep within the Zion/Ethiopian churches of the United States[24] and in the *hounforts*† of the Caribbean and South America—triggers itself into visibility at each moment of crisis in the hemisphere: 1790 in Haiti, 1860 in Jamaica, 1930 in the West Indies, and 1960 in the New World generally.

II

I cannot maintain that African continuities are as easily traced in our literature as in the social/ideological world I have so far described. This does not mean there is no African presence in Caribbean/New World writing. It simply means that, because of its almost inevitable involvement with the establishment through education, communication and sales processing (mercantilism), much of what we have come to accept as "literature" is work which ignores, or is ignorant of, its African connection and aesthetic.

Until, therefore, our definition of "culture" is re-examined in terms of its totality, not simply its Europeanity, we will fail to discover a literature of negritude and with it, a literature of local authenticity.[25] Likewise, the African presence in Caribbean literature cannot be fully or easily perceived until we redefine the term "literature" to include the nonscribal material of the folk/oral tradition, which, on examination, turns out to have a much longer history than our scribal tradition, to have been more relevent to the majority of our people, and to have had unquestionably wider provenance. In other words, while a significant corpus of "prose" and "poetry" has been created—and read—by a few persons in the major Antilles; folk song, folk tale, proverb, and chant are found *everywhere* without fear or favor and are enjoyed by all. It is from "the guitars of the people," as Nicolás Guillén recently put it, that the "*son* went to the salons of the aristocracy."[26] With this re/vision in mind, we see an African literature in the Caribbean beginning to reveal itself.

Slavery

On the eve of emancipation, at a *crise de conscience*, when the European planters in the West Indies were becoming aware of the *plural society*[27] developing around them, and conscious of the need, if they were to retain their hegemony, to destroy, subvert, or psychologically control the black majority, a few books began to appear which described slaves in terms of their own culture.[28]

The most outstanding example in English is a novel, anonymously written, called *Hamel the Obeah Man* (1827), which for the first time describes a slave,

---

† Name given in Haiti to the compound (courtyard and buildings) where vodun services are conducted.

Hamel, as a complex human being. In order to do this, the author had to give him a cultural context, and, significantly, he chose a cultural context based on his *obeah*—*obeah* seen not as a debasement but as a form of African religion of which he was a priest. Hamel was placed in ideological opposition to a white missionary. The plot of the book is, in fact, designed as a struggle between the white missionary and the African priest. Out of a personal sense of loyalty, Hamel uses his *obeah* to support righteous planter against subversive missionary. Nevertheless, Hamel's intransigent opposition to the institution of slavery is clearly established. It is suggested that, had he, rather than the missionary, fomented the slave revolt which climaxes the novel, it would have been practically uncontrollable. The book, in other words, is an antimissionary tract. But it is also a remarkable act of fiction (for its genre) in that Hamel is seen "whole," with real doubts and passions, and so provides some insight into the West Indian slave experience.[29]

After emancipation, due to the socio-cultural disengagement between black and white, there were no further works by white/creole writers, even approaching the standard of *Hamel*. Since 1900 there has been a certain re-appearance of the white writer: H. G. DeLisser (Jamaica), Alfred Mendes and Ian McDonald (Trinidad), J. B. Emtage and Geoffrey Drayton (Barbados), Phyllis Shand Allfrey and Jean Rhys (Dominica), and Christopher Nicole (Guyana), to name perhaps the most important.[30] But with the exception of DeLisser in *Jane's Career*, none of these writers has (yet) become centrally concerned with Caribbean Africans (or Indians); most of them (again with the exception of *Jane's Career*) seem romantic, while a few are the opposite—callous (Mendes in *Pitch Lake*) or just plain boorish (Emtage)—and betray what Kenneth Ramchand, using a phrase of Fanon's, has called "terrified consciousness."[31]

Indigenism/Negrismo

The above, however, is not intended in any way to exclude white West Indian writers from our literary canon. In fact, in another study,[32] I have attempted to show how the work of Roger Mais, a "white" Jamaican, could in many ways act as a model for our developing critical aesthetics. But the majority of white West Indian writers, it seems to me, are not yet prepared to allow their art to erode the boundaries set up around their minds by the physical/metaphysical plantation, and so do not yet recognize that their world has become marginal to the majority sense of local reality; or rather, that the plantation has transformed itself into other, new mercantilist forms, in which they are enslaved as surely as the descendants of their former bondsmen. It is only when this comes to them as crisis, it seems to me, that the white West Indian writers will find their voice.

The post-emancipation period, therefore, has been one of literary hiatus. Caribbean (written) literature, as truly native enterprise and expression, does not begin, in fact, until, in response to the American occupation of the Greater Antilles,[33] certain artists in Cuba and Puerto Rico began to develop distinctive literary and creative forms that have come to be called indigenism and *negrismo*. This is interesting because the populations of these two territories are predominantly ex-Spanish, rather than ex-African. Unlike those in the rest of the Caribbean, the majority in Cuba and Puerto Rico is "white" rather than "black" creole. Nevertheless, the literary expression which came out of these white creoles (and mulattoes) was black based; they recognized that the only form of expression which could be used as a protest, or an authentic *alter/native,* to American cultural imperialism, was ex-African. This is at least part of what the Cuban thinker Juan Marinello had in mind in the 1930's when he said that due to the extinction of the Amerindians and the fact that they had left "no architecture or literature," the Negro had assumed a "specific significance." "Here the Negro is marrow and root, the breath of the people, a music heard, [an] irrepressible impulse. He may, in these times of change, be the touchstone of our poetry."[34]

Crisis/Response

The best way to understand this in its fullest literary sense—one, that is, which includes the oral tradition—is to see it and the other expressions of the African presence which followed as responses to white cultural imperialism. During slavery, white cultural imposition was responded to with worksong, gospel, blues, the spiritual, *mento* (a secular Jamaican folk song form), shanto (the word in Guyana for *mento*), shango hymn, and folk tale. The post-emancipation crisis saw a certain erosion of folk tales, especially in the more urbanized areas, but it saw the entrenchment of the literature of the hounfort. Urban immigration, from the end of the nineteenth century, saw the formation of black ghettos and the emergence of a new urban folk art—the dozens, urban blues, new urban shouter churches, the Harlem Renaissance, Garveyite creative work,° Rastafari,† the Nation of Islam, and Carnival.

The crisis of American imperialism brought us Price-Mars and Hippolyte and Jacques Roumain in Haiti, José Martí and *negrismo* in the Spanish Antilles and, in a way, the international emergence of the calypso in Trinidad.[35] The crisis of European imperialism, as reflected in World War II, produced the *negritude* of the French-speaking expatriate colonials as well as a more locally based *tigritude*[36] literature in the black colonies of Africa and the Caribbean. The recent crisis of neocolonialism and indigenous disillusionment has seen the Black Power movement and its various ramifications, the explosion of urban folk in Jamaica and the United States, the re-emergence of "native" churches, a certain revitalization of calypso, and a generally increased awareness of the authenticity of folk forms. And as the Carifesta Revolution (1972) in Guyana clearly demonstrated, these Caribbean folk forms continue to be uniquely, vitally, and creatively African in form, rhythm and soul.[37]

III

There are four kinds of written African literature in the Caribbean. The first is *rhetorical.* The writer uses Africa as mask, signal, or *nomen.* He doesn't know very

° Marcus Garvey was one of the first black leaders to begin the resuscitation of self-help folk entertainment, especially in the urban ghettos.

† The Rastafari are a dynamic and distinctive ("dreadlocked") group in Jamaica, who consider themselves Africans, recognize the Emperor Haile Selassie as the Living God, and declare it their certain destiny to return to Africa (I-tiopia). As such—a kind of modern maroon group—they refuse to acknowledge the materialistic governments of Babylon. Rastafari art (including song, dance, drum, music, poetry, painting, carving, craftwork, and above all word/symbols) is revitalizing Jamaican folk culture, and their philosophy and lifestyle is already beginning to reach black communities elsewhere.

much about Africa necessarily, although he reflects a deep desire to make connection. But he is only saying the word "Africa" or invoking a dream of the Congo, Senegal, Niger, the Zulu, Nile, or Zambesi. He is not necessarily celebrating or activating the African presence. There are also elements of this romantic rhetoric within the other three categories. The second is what I call *the literature of African survival*, a literature which deals quite consciously with African survivals in Caribbean society, but without necessarily making any attempt to interpret or reconnect them with the great tradition of Africa. Third, there is what I call *the literature of African expression*, which has its root in the folk, and which attempts to adapt or transform folk material into literary experiment. Finally, there is *the literature of reconnection*, written by Caribbean (and New World) writers who have lived in Africa and are attempting to relate that experience to the New World, or who are consciously reaching out to rebridge the gap with the spiritual heartland.

Rhetorical Africa

> Tambour
> quand tu résonne,
> mon âme hurle vers l'Afrique.
> Tantôt,
> je rêve d'une brousse immense
> baignée de lune,
> où s'echevellent de suantes nudités.
> Tantôt
> à une case immonde
> où je savoure du sang dans des crânes humains.

> Drum
> when you make sound
> my soul curls back to Africa.
> Sometimes
> I dream of a great moonlit forest
> alive with leaping nudes.
> Sometimes
> there is a simple hut
> where I drink blood out of human skulls.[38]

Carl Brouard

There are many such poems in this category, among them work by Daniel Thaly of Dominica/Haiti, Pales Matos of Puerto Rico, McKay and George Campbell of Jamaica and E. M. Roach of Tobago. Perhaps the most famous, a romantic/rhetorical poem as distinct from but still connected to the primitive/rhetorical tradition of Brouard and Pales Matos, is the black American Countee Cullen's "Heritage":

> What is Africa to me:
> Copper sun or scarlet sea,
> Jungle star or jungle track,
> Strong bronzed men, or regal black
> Women from whose loins I sprang
> When the birds of Eden sang. . . .[39]

In the anglophone Caribbean, this is echoed in poems like Philip Sherlock's "Jamaican Fisherman":

> Across the sand I saw a black man stride
> To fetch his fishing gear and broken things,
> And silently that splendid body cried
> Its proud descent from ancient chiefs and kings. . . .[40]

It is this kind of concern, persistent from the earliest days of black New World expression, which finally feeds into and influences the literature of rehabilitation and reconnection:

> C'est le lent chemin de Guinée
> La mort t'y conduire. . . .[41]

Jacques Roumain

In general, however, rhetorical literature is static, wishful and willful in nature. Although it betrays a significant instinct for Africa, the instinct is based on ignorance and often, in the case of Brouard and his generation and class, on received European notions of "darkest Africa." Louise Bennett was quite right in humorously rejecting that kind of reconnection:

> Back to Africa Miss Matty?
> Yuh noh know wha yuh dah-say?
> Yuh haffe come from some weh fus,
> Before yuh go back deh?[42]

From this attraction/ignorance too, springs the sense, as in Leon Laleau[43] and Derek Walcott,[44] that the two cultures present a dichotomy and that one must choose between them. Dantès Bellegarde, a leader in the early 40's of one of Haiti's anti-Africanist groups, held that "We belong to Africa by our blood, and to France by our spirit and by a significant proportion of our blood."[45] In Andrew Salkey's novel, A Quality of Violence, the debate is expressed as follows:

We not frighten by white fowl talk or Africa or slave power! We don't belong to them things. . . . We is people who live on the land in St Thomas, not Africa. . . . We is no slave people, and there is no Africa in we blood the way you would-a like we to believe. . . .

But you wrong, Miss Mellie. Me and you and the rest-a-people in St Thomas all belong to the days that pass by when slavery was with the land. Everybody is part of slavery days, is a part of the climate-a-Africa and the feelings in the heart is Africa feelings that beating there, far down. . . .[46]

In contrast, we have the *acceptance* of this dual cultural inheritance by a poet like the Cuban mulatto Nicolás Guillén.

> We have been together from long ago
> young and old,
> blacks and whites, all mixed,
> one commanding and the other commanded,
> all mixed;
> San Berenito and another commanded,

all mixed. . .
Santa Maria and another commanded,
all mixed
all mixed

But always there is the refrain with its positive recognition of Africa:

I am yoruba, I am lucumi,
mandingo, congo, carabali. . . .[47]

The Literature of African Survival

The literature of African survival inheres most surely and securely in the folk tradition—in folk tale, folksong, proverb, and much of the litany of the *hounfort*. Here, for example, is a *marassa* (spirit twins) lament from a *vodun*° ceremony:

Marassa élo, I have no mother here who can speak for me
Marassa élo
I have left my mother in Africa
Marassa élo
I have left my family in Africa
I have no family to speak for me
I have no relations to speak for me
Marassa élo[48]

The connection between this and African elegies is obvious; as is the connection with African lamentations in "New ships," "Tano," and "Wake" from my own *Masks* and *Islands*.[49] There is also, in the hounfort, the use of language based upon what are often only fragmented phonetics of an ancestral African tongue, as in this shango hymn to Ajaja:

Ay ree ah jaja
Ay ree leh
Ah jaja wo goon
Ajaja way geh

which has been interpreted to mean

We are searching for you
Wherever you are
Show yourself
We want to see you
We are searching for you
Come let us speak to you
We call you, we speak to you
Wherever you are[50]

° *Vodun* is the largest and most public African-derived (Dahomey: *vodu*) religious form in the Caribbean, centered in Haiti. See also Shango (in Trinidad), poco (in Jamaica), santeria (in Cuba) and the candomblé or macumba (in Brazil). Often, in this text, the term "vodun" is used to apply to Afro-New World religions generally. In the culture of Dahomey, from which Haitian vodun is derived, twins are held in special reverence. In vodun, they are apotheosized as *marassa* (spirit twins).

Similarly from Jamaican *kumina* comes this poem in which *so-so* means water, and *kuwidi* means "call (*ku*) the dead (*widi*)."

> Tange lange Jeni di gal eva
> Wang lang mama o
> Di le kuwidi pange le
> So-so lange widi gal
> So-so lange mama o
>
> Dance tall Jenny gal
> Walk tall mama o
> The dead come to greet you
> Water long like the dead, gal
> Water long, mama o[51]

In "William Saves His Sweetheart," the folk imagination is again concerned with water,[52] but this time its expression is entirely in intransigent non-English or, as I prefer to call it, *nation-language*, since Africans in the New World always referred to themselves as belonging to certain *nations* (Congo, Kromantee, etc.).[53] Here there are no African word-fragments or phrases as in the hounfort, but the tonal shape of the language, its rhythm changes, structure, contours of thought and image, eruption into song/dance/movement, make it clearly recognizable as African speech-form:

an a so dem doo. dem kal de gal, an she kom. an im seh, yu nyaam mi peas tiday? him seh, nuo ma, me no heat non. Him seh, aa'right, kom, we go doun-a golli-ya. we wi' faen out. him tiek di gal an im go doun-a di golli, an when goin doun too di golli, im go op pan im laim tree, an im pick trii laim. im guo in-a fowl ness, im tiek trii eggs . . . an im staat, an haal im suod . . . an im go goun-a di golli. im pu-doun di gal in-a di lebble drai golli, an seh, *see ya! tan op deh.* mi de-go tell yu now, ef yo heat mi peas, yu de-go drounded, bot if yu nou heat ih, nottn wuon doo yu. so swie, yu bitch! swier! seh yu no heat ih, while yo nuo yu heat ih. an she lik doun wan-a di laim a-doti so, wam! an di drai golli pomp op wata, kova di gal instep. de gal sah, *mai! puo mi wan!* a-whe me deh go-do tiday? him seh, *swie! swie!* yu bitch! an im lik doun wan nedda laim so, *wam,* an di wata mount di gal to im knee. di gal seh

laad ooi! mi wilyam ooi!

ih im sweethaat im de-kal

mi wilyam ooi!
puo mi wan ooi! peas ooi!
oo, mi dearess wilyam oo
rin doun peas oi ai! a rin doun!
oo, rin doun[54]

There is also considerable metaphysical life and symbolic association contained and hidden away in some of the folk-songs and poems that have been preserved, often accidentally. Take this French creole song, for instance, "Three Leaves, Three Roots," about change and timelessness:

> Trois fé trois ci-tron oh!
> Trois fé trois ra-cine oh!
>
> Moin dit, rwo, youn jour ou wa be-soin moin!
> Trois fé trois ra-cine oh!

Moin dit oui, youn jour ou wa be-soin moin!
Gain'-yain bas-sin moin

trois ra-cine tom-bé la-dans
Quand ou wa 'bli-é

fau' ra-mas-sé chon-gé[55]

Similarly, there is a fragment of a charm, collected by the Jamaican historian, H. P. Jacobs, which reads:

Bear up, mi good tree, bear up!
Mi father always cut a tree,
The green tree falls and the dry tree stands!
Shemo-limmo! mi toto! beng! beng![56]

The paradox *dry tree stands* and *green tree falls* is yet another illustration of the levels of expression possible within the folk tradition. This fragment is especially interesting because the folk/metaphysical mind can be seen working in concert with African symbolism. For *Shemo-limmo*, which is the secret name of a bull in certain Afro-Jamaican folk stories,[57] is also connected to *lemolemo*, the Yoruba for "locomotive"; and the locomotive has become one of the guises[58] of Shango, god of thunder and creativity, in the New World.[59]

There is very little in the written "educated" tradition which offers anything approaching these insights into our collective psyche. Seldom do our writers reach beyond descriptive rhetoric when they treat "hounfort-happenings."

Most of the people on the veranda and some of those who squatted on the stones in the front yard formed a group round the three women and waited for Mother Johnson to make a statement. She asked for her bandana which she wrapped round her right forearm. She knotted it. Everybody watched her as she tucked in the loose ends and patted the bulky parts of the folds into shape.

She said: "I hope everybody see how I just tie up the bandana?" There was a chorus of muttered affirmatives. "Well," she continued, "I telling you, now, that that is the same way that somebody tie up poor, innocent Doris brain. That somebody is well beknown to all of us in St Thomas. That somebody is a selfish, class-warring, sort of house-enemy. Is a person who looking to destroy Miss T happiness and peace-a-mind." She paused for breath. She again patted the bandana, and pointing to it, she continued: "As the dead body of my husband, Dada Johnson, who everybody here did well know and like as a great prophet/'mongst us . . . I telling you, once and for all, that Miss T gal pickney, Doris, is under a spell that she can't budge from, without plenty working of the good Lawd work on her, to bring her round again."

The gathering muttered: "Oh! Jehovah! Yes, Lawd!"

Mother Johnson cleared a space on the veranda steps, and sat down.[60]

The descriptive/dramatic power of this passage is typical of the excellence of *A Quality of Violence*, but as Salkey approaches the central and most sacred experiences of the *tonelle*,° his knowledge and involvement falter, to be replaced by passages that ring more of melodramatic brass than responsive silver:

° The *tonelle* is the inner area of the hounfort. On the floor or ground are to be found the vèvè (symbols) of the gods to be welcomed, and at the center of the tonelle the *poteau-mitan:* stick, whip or ladder of god.

Dada Johnson held a cutlass high above his head, sliced the air in wide circular movements and threw it in front of the deputy. It landed blade first. The deputy dropped the white rooster, grabbed the cutlass and also made slicing movements in the air. The chanting sisters started to gyrate once more, pummelling their stomachs with clenched fists. . . .[61]

No matter how apparently violent (and not all possessions are violent), there is nothing in the choreography of Afro-Caribbean folk religion that is uncontrolled: flung *hounsis*° are softly caught; no one, except then, ever touches another, despite the complex movements and the limited space; and there is never a pulled muscle or a cricked neck.

Salkey's verbs—"grabbed," "gyrate," "pummel"—are all suddenly wrong. Or, to put it another way, the description of possession demands of the writer a choice of words, of traditions. Salkey, in the heart of the *tonelle,* opts for the Euro-rational/descriptive and therefore fails to celebrate *with* his worshippers, which in turn leads to the alienation of "In one action, they gathered up their calico gowns, stooped lower to the body of the deputy and *urinated on him.*"[62] But such is the thirst of Salkey's literary ear that fragments of litany, of powerful enigmatic metaphor soon appear and give his work a new dimension in passages like the following (which gains in power when we know that in *vodun,* and Afro-Creole religion generally, the crippled (lame) god of the crossroads, Legba, is the first to be praised in the hounfort):

The chanting sisters had stopped chanting but were still standing in front of Dada Johnson who was saying a silent prayer. The deputy had crawled under the meeting-table. Suddenly, the chanting sisters sprang back and cried out: "And Jonathan, Saul's son, had a son that was lame of his feet!" There was about five seconds' silence and the deputy crawled from under the meeting-table. He stood erect and raised his right hand towards the chanting sisters who screamed: "Him have the sacrifice in him hand! *See God dey!*" The deputy sprang around and faced Dada Johnson who bowed and snatched the white rooster out of his right hand. Dada Johnson said: "*Cock blood pour down like rain water! Cooking fowl is cloud! Cloud burst open and blood bring rain!*"[63]

The surreal images here (italicized) could hardly have been conceived outside the hounfort. And yet Salkey, like so many others caught up in the tradition of the Master, remains ambivalent in his attitude to the African presence in the Caribbean.[64] Vera Bell, in "Ancestor on the Auction Block"[65] betrays an even more direct uncertainty of response:

> Ancestor on the auction block
> Across the years your eyes seek mine
> Compelling me to look.
> I see your shackled feet
> Your *primitive* black face
> I see your humiliation
> And turn away
> Ashamed.
>
> Across the years your eyes seek mine
> Compelling me to look

° The *hounsi* are servitors, usually female, of the vodun complex. The religious leader (invariably male) of the hounfort is the *houngan,* his chief female assistant, the *mambo.*

> Is this *mean creature* that I see
> Myself?

Philip Sherlock in "Pocomania"[66] betrays this psychic dichotomy in a crucial choice of word—namely, the use of *grunt*, instead of *trump*, to describe the deep rhythmic intake/expulsion of breath which precedes possession:

> Black of night and white of gown,
> White of altar, black of trees,
> Swing de circle wide again,
> Fall an' cry, me sister, now.
> Let de spirit come again,
> Fling away de flesh an' bone
> Let de spirit have a home.
>
> Grunting low and in the dark,
> White of gown and circling dance.
> Gone today and all control,
> Here the dead are in control,
> Power of the past returns,
> Africa among the trees,
> Asia with her mysteries. . . .

Earlier in the poem, the loss of "control" under these Afro-Asian mysteries (why "Asia" isn't clear) is even more pejoratively stated:

> Black Long Mountain looking down
> Sees the shepherd and his flock
> Dance and sing and falls away
> *All the civilised today.* . . .

No wonder Fola, the young black educated sister in George Lamming's *Season of Adventure*, was afraid to enter the hounfort.[67] But what is really surprising, given the Caribbean psycho-cultural inheritance, is not really the fear/avoidance response with regard to the African presence in the New World, but the persistent attempts, at all levels, to deal with it. No writer in the plantation New World can, in fact, ignore "Africa" for long, though it is interesting to note that outside of literary *negrismo* circles, there has been more active and public interest in this area of our culture from historians, sociologists, and social anthropologists than from writers and artists generally.

Maroons°

One area of African survival is that of physical and psychological maronage. From the moment of arrival in the New World, the people of Africa were concerned with response: suicide, accommodation, escape, rebellion. Escape/rebellion often led to the setting up of African communities outside of and often in opposition to, the great Euro/creole plantations. In Surinam, for instance, the Njukka, Saramaccer and other groups, usually blanketed under the term "Bush Negroes,"

° *Maroons* is a term springing from historical maronage to connote areas of African cultural survival, or isolated resuscitation, resistant to the blandishments of the plantation.

established independencies along the rivers and waterways of the forested Guianese hinterland from the middle of the seventeenth century. In Jamaica, Maroons quickly established themselves in five independent towns in the inaccessible Blue Mountains and Cockpit country, fighting the British almost to a standstill in two highly organized guerrilla wars during the eighteenth century. There were militant Black Caribs (Afro-Amerindians) in the Windward Islands, particularly St. Vincent, and significant Afro-Maroon groups in most of the other slave islands, especially St. Domingue (Haiti). The most spectacular Maroon community, however, was that established at Palmares, in Brazil, in 1631, which was able to maintain its independence (with ambassadors, traders, etc.) for over seventy years.[68] And yet there are only two novels in English, known to me, which attempt to come to terms with even one aspect of this experience; and I suspect that the story is very much the same in the rest of the region. This, again, is a tribute to European brainwash. Many Caribbean writers don't even *know* that these communities existed and that some still exist;[69] and the few who *do* are too cut off to conjure line or metaphor from this matrix. Of the two anglophones who have attempted imaginative fiction in this field, one, Namba Roy, was himself a (Jamaican) Maroon. Unfortunately, he did not attempt, in the only novel he ever wrote,[70] more than a romantic tale of "brave warriors" and internecine conflict. Wilson Harris, on the other hand, uses in *The Secret Ladder*, the presence of an ancient black chieftain of the swamps to initiate a whole series of perceptions into the question of maronage, ancestry and filiation.

I feel I have stumbled here in the Canje [writes Fenwick, the persona through whom we perceive the interests of "progress" in this novel] on an abortive movement, the emotional and political germ of which has been used in two centuries of history. . . . What will you say when I tell you I have come across the Grand Old Man of our history. . . ?[71]

But Harris' vision is too ecumenical for it to allow him to accept too easily this celebratory gift of an ancestor.

To *misconceive* the African [Fenwick's letter continued] . . . is to misunderstand and exploit him mercilessly and oneself as well. For *there*, in this creature Poseidon, the black man with the European name, drawn out of the depths of time, is the emotional dynamic of liberation that happened a century and a quarter ago. . . . Something went tragically wrong then. Something was misunderstood and frustrated, God alone knows why and how. . . . Maybe it was all too emotional, too blinding, this freedom that has turned cruel, abortive, evasive, woolly and wild everywhere almost. . . .[72]

It is a salutary caveat, although Harris is himself guilty of misconceiving the African—certainly the Maroon. For the cruel abortion of freedom he speaks about, the over-"emotional" negritude, was and is not only a function of maronage, it was and is even more certainly the consequence of opposition to the plantation. How else can we interpret the fate and history of Haiti, the greatest and most successful Maroon polity of them all? But Harris, ambivalent like most of us, finds "West Indian [protest] politics and intellectualism" sterile,[73] so that, as with the cultural pessimists we referred to earlier, he concludes that the African slave, originator and conditional body of Caribbean militance, must/could have come here equipped with very little—with very little to offer:

One must remember that *breath* is all the black man may have possessed at a certain stage in the Americas. He had lost his tribal tongue, he had lost everything except an abrupt area of space and lung: he possessed nothing but the calamitous air of broken ties in the New World.[74]

And yet, whereas with Naipaul,[75] Patterson,[76] even Derek Walcott,[77] this nothing yields nothing, with Harris this ruin/vestige, shred of breath, vital possession of the dispossessed, becomes the survival rhythm from which transformation may proceed.

The Literature of African Expression

Limbo [is] a dance in which the participants have to move, with their bodies thrown backwards and without any aid whatsoever, under a stick which is lowered at every successfully completed passage under it, until the stick is practically touching the ground. It is said to have originated—a necessary therapy after the experience of the cramped conditions between the slave decks of the Middle Passage. Now very popular as a performing act in Caribbean night clubs.[78]

> And limbo stick is the silence in front of me
> *limbo*
>
> *limbo*
> *limbo like me* . . .
>
> long dark night is the silence in front of me
> *limbo*
> *limbo like me*
>
> stick hit sound
> and the ship like it ready
>
> stick hit sound
> and the ship like it ready
>
> *limbo*
> *limbo like me.* . . .[79]

Limbo then reflects a certain kind of gateway or threshhold to a new world and the dislocation of a chain of miles. It is—in some ways—the archetypal sea-change stemming from Old Worlds and it is legitimate, I feel, to pun on *limbo* as a kind of shared phantom *limb* which has become a subconscious variable in West Indian theatre. The emergence of formal West Indian theatre was preceded, I suggest, by that phantom limb which manifested itself on Boxing Day, when the ban on the "rowdy" bands . . . was lifted for the festive season. . . . I recall performances I witnessed as a boy in Georgetown . . . in the early 1930s. Some of the performers danced on high stilts like elongated limbs while others performed spreadeagled on the ground. In this way *limbo* spider and stilted pole of the gods were related to the drums like grassroots and branches of lightning to the sound of thunder.[80]

The power and progress of image in these quotations illustrate what I mean by transformation. In terms of literary craftsmanship, they represent a shift from rhetoric to involvement. The beginning of this is evident, for example, in the poem "Pocomania," by Philip Sherlock, which we have already considered. Note its new rhythmic emphasis:

> *Black* the stars, *hide* the sky,
> *Lift* you' shoulder, *blot* the moon

and the appearance of dialect:

> Swing de circle wide again,
> Fall an' cry, me sister, now

The most significant factor in this process, however, is its connection with the hounfort: the heart and signal of the African experience in the Caribbean/New World. We have already witnessed the operation of this in Salkey's A *Quality of Violence*, and in the *limbo* quotations, above. But the Caribbean writer who has been able to move fearlessly/innocently into this enigmatic alternative world and has therefore been able to contribute most to the literature of African expression is George Lamming. In *Season of Adventure* we watch a young girl dance toward the gods at a vodun ceremony. As she dances, we become involved, until we find that Lamming's language has become an image of the child's possession:

> The child was wide awake. . . . The dance was an instinct which her feet had learnt. . . . The women's chant was broken by applause. The child heard the voices competing in her praise. She became hysterical; wild, light as air and other than human, like the night clouding her eyes. Her voice had cried out: "Hair, hair! Give all, all, all, hair." And she clapped until there was no feeling in her hands.
> And the voices came nearer than her skin: "Dance, Liza, dance! Dance! Dance! Liza, Liza, Liza, dance! Dance, Liza, dance."[81]

The only time Lamming falters in this astonishing participation in Afro-Caribbean worship is with the word/perception *hysterical*. It is similar (and present for similar reasons) to the false notes already noted in Salkey, Bell, Brouard and Sherlock. But the faltering is only momentary. As Liza/Lamming dances to incarnation, Caribbean literature, through this encounter with the *loa*, begins its transformation into a new species of original art:[82]

> Fire of the spirits in her eyes, and no longer a child as she watched the shadows strangled by her wish for hair blazing from the summit of the bamboo pole! She trampled upon the circle of maize, exploding shapes like toys under her feet, dancing the dust away. For the gods were descending to the call of voices: "Come! Come! in O! In O spirit of water come! Come!"
> Now: gently, stage after gentle stage and feather-wise as if now orphaned of all sound, the voices were dying, second by full measure of second: then died on the gentlest of all sounds, "come, come, in O spirit of water come, come, come. . . ."[83]

Nommo

The process of transformation which Lamming so remarkably undertakes here—the art of the hounfort into the art of the novel—has its roots in a certain kind of concern for and attitude to the *word*, the atomic core of language. This is something that is very much present in all folk cultures, all pre-literate, pre-industrial societies. Within such cultures, language was and is a creative act in itself. Think of our love for the politician or the word of the preacher. Indeed, it is one of the problems of our political life how to separate the word and the meaning of the word.

The word (*nommo* or name) is held to contain secret power. Monk Lewis, who was a novelist himself, visited Jamaica (where he had some estates) in 1815/1816 and described this kind of attitude among his slaves:

The other day . . . a woman who had a child sick in the hospital, begged me to change its name for any other which might please me best: she cared not what; but she was sure that it would never do well so long as it should be called Lucia.[84]

People feel a name is so important that a change in his name could transform a person's life. In traditional society, in fact, people often try to hide their names. That is why a Nigerian, for example, has so many names. Not only is it difficult to remember them, it is difficult to know which is the name that the man regards or identifies as his. If you call the wrong name you can't damage him.[85] Rumpelstiltskin in the German fable and Shemo-limmo in the Jamaican tale above are other examples of this. In H. G. DeLisser's *Jane's Career*, there is an interesting variation in which an earthquake, a natural divine phenomenon, becomes an aspect of *nommo*:

. . . many persons talked of the recent [1907] earthquake as of *something that could hear what was said about it,* and take action accordingly. To Sampson and many others like him, the earthquake was a living, terrible force. . . .[86]

Aimé Césaire takes this a stage further with:

I would recover the secret of epic speech and towering conflagrations. I would say storm. I would say river. I would say tornado. I would say leaf. I want to pronounce tree. I want to be soaked by all the falling rains, dampened with all the dews. I would roll like frenzied blood in the slow current of the eye of the word's mad horses' newly born formations of the fire. . . .[87]

This is a kind of conjuration/divination, or rather, it comes from the same magical/miracle tradition as the conjur-man. Vibrations awake at the center of words. From the pools of their *nommo*, onomatopoeia and sound-symbols are born: *banggarang, boolooloops* and *boonoonoonoos* (Jamaica); *barrabbattabbattabba* and *bruggalungdung* (Barbados); *umklaklabulu* ("thunderclap": Zulu); *dabo-dabo* ("duck"), *munumm* ("darkness": Twi); *pampam, primprim, prampalam* (Bajan/Twi sounds of contact/movement); *patoo* ("owl": Asante/Jamaican); *felele* ("to blow in the wind, to flutter": Yoruba). In Black America it lives in the preacher/signifying tradition and the dozens, and surfaces scribally in areas of Ralph Ellison's *Invisible Man* and James Baldwin's *Go Tell It on the Mountain*. It is apparent in Ishmael Reed's *Yellow Back Radio Broke-down:*

A terrible cuss of a thousand shivs he was who wasted whole herds, made the fruit black and wormy, dried up the water holes and caused people's eyes to grow from tiny black dots into slap-jacks wherever his feet fell. . . .[88]

and in Imamu Baraka's (LeRoi Jones') "Black Art":

Poems are bullshit unless they are
teeth or trees or lemons piled
on a step. Or black ladies dying
of men leaving nickel hearts
beating them down. Fuck poems
and they are useful, wd they shoot
come at you, love what your are,
breathe like wrestlers, or shudder
strangely after pissing. We want live
words of the hip world live flesh &
coursing blood. Hearts Brains
Souls splintering fire. We want poems
like fists beating niggers out of Jocks
or dagger poems in the slimy bellies
of the owner-jews . . . .
. . . . we want "poems that kill."
Assassin poems, Poems that shoot
guns. . . . . [89]

Similarly, the Surinamese word see-er or seer Robin Ravales (Dobru) tells us

write no words
write grenades
to eradicate poverty
write no sentences
write guns
to stop injustice[90]

This concept and use of word is found throughout the entire black/African world. It is present in modern as well as traditional African literature.[91] In the Americas, it reveals itself in our love of courtroom scenes (both factual and fictional), the rhetoric of yard quarrels,[92] "word-throwings,"[93] tea-meetings and preacher/political orations.[94] The whole living tradition of the calypso[95] is based on it. But it goes deeper than this, as the metaphysical and symbolic qualities of some of the Afro-Caribbean fragments we have already discussed, indicates. Language, as we saw in the discussion of names, may be conceived as having the power to affect life. And again it is Lamming who exposes us to an interior view of the process:

The words seemed to come like the echo of other voices from outside: "is so, same so. . . ." Syllables changed their phrasing; words showed a length that had suffered by the roughness of an accent uttered in haste. Surfacing slowly . . . [they] seemed uncertain of their alliance. At every stage of awareness she could feel the change, until the rules of college speech gave way completely to the private dialect of her own tongue at home: "is same ever since, and it been the same, same so ever since. . . ."[96]

This way of using the word depends very much upon an understanding of the folk tradition out of which it comes. This folk tradition has received (not surprisingly) very little attention from scholars. There has been work by Nina Rodrigues, Renato Mendoza, Arthur Ramos and Donald Pierson in Brazil; Fernando Ortiz in Cuba; for Jamaica there has been Martha Beckwith and more recently Ivy Baxter; for Trinidad, Errol Hill and J. D. Elder. For the Caribbean generally, there has been the work of the Herskovitses and Roger Bastide.[97] But even where these studies are comprehensive, they seldom attempt to describe the sociology of nation-language. Few of them, certainly, attempt a critical/aesthetic appraisal of the word, as found in its creole context, or as illuminated in the work/thought of say, Kagame, Ogotemmêli, St. John of the Gospel, Father Placied Tempels or Jahnheinz Jahn, within the African "Great Tradition."[98]

Techniques

In addition to sound-symbols, nation-language sets up certain tunes, tones and rhythms which are characteristic of the folk tradition, and are often essential features of its expression. The overall space/patterns of this language, we might say, are controlled by a *groundation*° tendency, in which image/spirit is electrically conducted to earth like lightning or the *loa* (the gods, spirits, powers, or divine horsemen of vodun):

> Mr Frank
> my gentleman, de Lord know
> is you dat did show de way
> nourish we spirit
> when we did nothin, nothin.
> Like a fowlcock
> early pon a morning
> *jookin in de straw*
> *scratchin de rockstone*
> *nastyin up 'e beak*
> *in de muddy gutter water. . . .*[99]

Notice how, since what we *see* is in fact the speaking (seeking) voice, pause and cadence become important:

> 'e eye ball sharpen
> to catch de teeny weeny bit . . .
> before it loss away
> okra sauce slippin through de gullet
> hot, quick gone 'long for ever//
>
> An' is you dat did dey . . .[100]

Bongo Jerry's sound-system poetry is instinctively quicker—urban ghetto—but the cadence/pauses are still there, as in "Learning Rhymes":

> I want to know the truth.
> But they tell me to wait.
> Wait till when?
> Till I'm seventy.
> Or eighty and eight.
> I can/not/wait . . .
> To them truth is when you don't tell lie or when you face
> don't show it

° *Groundation* or *groundings* (verb: *to grounds*) is a term for a rap session. But since the word/idea (contributed by Rastafari) comes from the experience of religious possession, its ripples of meaning reach further than the idea of simple, secular "grounding."

Hoping that they could hide the truth and I would never
                                    know it.//
Dem cold.[101]

His poem, "Mabrak," is in itself, a brilliant example of groundation:

Mabrak:
                    NEWSFLASH!
"Babylon plans crash"
Thunder interrupt their programme to
announce:

BLACK ELECTRIC STORM
                              IS HERE
How long you feel "fair to fine
(WHITE)" would last?

How long calm in darkness
              when out of BLACK
come forth LIGHT?

[the dry tree stands and the green tree falls]

Every knee
              must bow
Every tongue
              confess
Every language
              express
                    W
                    O
                    R
                    D
                    W
                    O
                    R
                    K
                    S[102]

Again, in the ballad tradition of Sparrow's "Dan is the Man in the Van" and
"Parables" or a Jamaican ska like "Salaman A Grundy," Jerry trans/fuses weather
forecasts, ("fair to fine"), Christian liturgy ("Every knee/must bow") and
children's game-songs ("ringing rings of roses") and whatever other significant
demotic of the moment he can find (Babel-land/Babylon) into his African vision:

SILENCE BABEL TONGUES; recall and
recollect BLACK SPEECH.

Cramp all double meaning
              an' all that hiding language bar,
for that crossword speaking
              when expressing feeling

is just English language contribution to increase confusion in
              Babel-land tower—

delusion, name changing, word rearranging
              ringing rings of roses, pocket full of poses:

"SAR" instead of "RAS"[103]

Improvisation

Some time ago, I wrote an exploration into West Indian literature in which I tried to use jazz[104] as an aesthetic criterion for understanding what certain of our writers were trying to do. My assumption was that all African-influenced artists, whatever their individual styles, participated in certain modes of expression, and that understanding the patterns of one could lead to an understanding of how the work of all relates together in a mutual continuum.[105] I also found in that study that just as a cardinal element in jazz was improvisation (rhythmic and thematic), so were similar features clear in black/African literature. Bongo Jerry's "Mabrak," above, is one example of this. Nicolás Guillén's well-known "Sensemayá" is another:

> !Mayombe-bombe-mayombe!
> !Mayombe-bombe-mayombe!
> !Mayombe-bombe-mayombe!
>
> La culebra tiene los ojos de vidrio
> La culebra viene y se en reda en un palo
> Con sus ojos de vidrio, en un palo
> Con sus ojos de vidrio. . . .
>
> The snake has eyes of glass
> The snake appears and winds itself round the post
> With eyes of glass round the post
> With eyes of glass. . . .[106]

The same strong rhythmic pulse, leading to variation, is present in Césaire:

> Au bout du petit matin
> un grand galop de pollen
> un grand galop d'un petit train de petites filles
> un grand galop de colibris
> un grand galop de dagues pour défoncer la poitrine de la
>   terre[107]

and throughout the word-play in Leon Damas' *Pigments*

> Sans nom
> sans lune
> sans lune
> sans nom
> nuits sans lune
> sans nom sans nom
> ou le degout s'andre en moi. . . .[108]

and in Jamal Ali:

> Rocket up to the moon
> Living up to the moon
> Cost of living up to the moon
> Death toll sky high, twisting, up to the moon[109]

and in my own "Negus" which begins as a raindrip or drum beat and develops into cross-rhythms:

It
it
it
it is not

it
it
it
it is not

it is not
it is not
it is not enough
it is not enough to be free
of the red white and blue
of the drag, of the dragon

it is not
it is not
it is not enough
it is not enough to be free
of the whips, principalities and powers
where is your kingdom of the Word?

It is not enough
to tinkle to work on a bicycle bell
when hell
crackles and burns in the fourteen-inch screen of the Jap
of the Jap of the Japanese-constructed
United-Fruit-Company-imported
hard sell, tell tale tele-
vision set, rhinocerously knobbed, cancerously tubed. . . . [110]

Call/Response

But rhythm is not the only feature of improvisation in the literature of the "African presence. It can also involve chantwell and chorus, as in spiritual, secular soul-litany, gospel, and above all, worksong:

> Cayman ah pull man,
>   *timbakay,*
> Cayman ah pull man
>   *timbakoo,*
> Cayman ah pull man,
>   *timbakay,*
> Cayman ah pull man
>   *timbakoo.*

> "Timber Man" (Traditional Guyana)

and in *calinda* calypso:

> Sparrow: Well they playin bad,
>   They have me feelin sad;
>   Well they playin beast,
>   Why they run for police?
>   Ten criminals attack me outside of Miramar

Chorus:	*Ten to one is murder!*
Sparrow:	About ten in de night on de 5th of November
Chorus:	*Ten to one is murder*
Sparrow:	Way down Henry Street by H. E. M. Walker
Chorus:	*Ten to one is murder!*
Sparrow:	Well the leader of the gang was hot like a pepper
Chorus:	*Ten to one is murder!*
Sparrow:	And every man in de gang had a white handled razor
Chorus:	*Ten to one is murder!*
Sparrow:	They say I push de girl from Grenada
Chorus:	*Ten to one is murder!*[111]

It will be found in sermons like this Spiritual Baptist's from Silver Sands, Barbados:

I can say what troubles . . .	
have we seen . . .	*oh yea*
an' what conflicts . . .	
have we passed. . . .	*oh yeas*
There were many walls with*out* . . .	
and fears within . . .	*oh yeaa*
but God has *preserved* us by His power Divine	*oh yes*
the sun shone on our path sometimes	*oh oh!*
sometimes it was very rainy	*oh yes*
But there is no captain . . .	[humming begins]
if he only rows . . .	
near the shore	*uh!*
and still waters	*uh!*
. . . .	
we've got our glory . . .	*hello!*
we've got our shame . . .	*oh yes!*
some have said this . . .	
and some have said that . . .	
but *regardless* to what happened . . .	
we are *still* moving on!	*ah yes!*[112]

A folk-poet like the Barbadian Bruce St. John captures all this, and, significantly, the very essence of the Bajan psyche with:

Stokeley like he mad	*Da is true*
He outah touch wid de West Indies	*Da is true*

He ain't even discreet!	*Da is true*
He can't be pon we side	*Da is true*
He mussy working fuh de whites!	*Da is true*
Dem thrives pon we division	*Da is true*
So they wouldn't let 'e talk!	*Da is true*
Suppose he right though?	*Wuh da?*
Suppose he right though?	*Da is true*
	Da is true[113]

Transformation

Improvisation can also invade and erode the shape/sense of the word as in my "Mother Poem":

> Muh
> muh
> mud
> me mudda
>
> coo
> like she coo
> like she cook
> an she cumya to me pun de grounn
>
> like she lik mih
>
> like she lik me wid grease like she grease mih
> she cum to me years like de yess of a leaf
> an she issper
> she cum to me years an she purr like a puss an she essper
>
> she lisper to me dat me name what me name
> dat me name is me main an it am is me own an lion eye mane. . . .[114]

It is evident also in the "surrealism" of Césaire's:

> that two plus two makes five
> that the forest meows
> that the tree gets the chestnut out of the fire
> that the sky strokes its beard
> etcetera etcetera[115]

and in the passage in George Lamming's *The Pleasures of Exile* where a plough/slave is transformed into a plough/sword, omen of revolt:

Imagine a plough in the field. Ordinary as ever, prongs and spine unchanged, is simply there, stuck to its post beside the cane shoot. Then some hand, identical with the routine of its work, reaches to lift this familiar instrument. But the plough escapes contact. It refuses to surrender its present position. There is a change in the relation between this plough and one free hand. The crops wait and wonder what will happen next. More hands arrive to confirm the extraordinary conduct of this plough; but no one can explain the terror of those hands as they withdraw from the plough. Some new sights as well as sense of language is required to bear witness to the miracle. . . . For as those hands in unison move forward, the plough achieves a somersault which reverses its traditional posture. Its head goes into the ground, and the prongs, throat-near stand erect in the air, ten points of steel announcing danger.[116]

The Literature of Reconnection

The literature of reconnection has become an active and fairly widespread concern, particularly in the black United States, since the Black Power Revolution of the mid-sixties. Writers and jazz musicians began leaving their slave names and taking on African *nommos* and poets like Don Lee, Marvin X, and Alicia Johnson, developed a certain concern with Africa, at least as a source of inspiration/validation. Among the younger anglophone Caribbeans, Elizabeth Clarke's poem "Mudda Africa" and Tito Jemmott's "A Tale" are indicative of this new orientation.[117] But the solid work was really done before this phase, by poets like Melvin Tolson (1898-1966)[118] and Robert Hayden[119] in North America; and by Guillén, Roumain, Césaire, and Damas in the Caribbean. My own trilogy[120] is another effort in this direction.

But the example I should like to close with is Paule Marshall's novel *The Chosen Place, The Timeless People*.[121] I have developed my comments on this remarkable piece of work in the *Journal of Black Studies*.[122] The following excerpts illustrate quite unequivocally what I mean by the "literature of reconnection": a recognition of the African presence in our society not as a static quality, but as root—living, creative, and still part of the main. Take, for instance, this passage describing the famous Bathsheba coast. The people of Barbados know this coastline—wild, Atlantic, and rocky. But how many, looking down on that surf, those reefs, from Horse Hill and Hackleton, realized that there was nothing but ocean and blue between themselves and the coast of Africa—that Barbados, the most easterly of the West Indies, is in fact *the nearest to Africa*. Certainly no major Barbados writer known to me had ever made the point. Marshall, whose parents are Bajan and whose childhood was divided between Barbados and Brooklyn, saw the connection immediately:

It was the Atlantic this side of the island, a wild-eyed, marauding sea the color of slate, deep, full of dangerous currents, lined with row upon row of barrier reefs, and with a sound like that of the combined voices of the drowned raised in a loud unceasing lament—all those, the nine million and more it is said, who in their enforced exile, their Diaspora, had gone down between this point and the homeland lying out of sight to the east. This sea mourned them. Aggrieved, outraged, unappeased, it hurled itself upon each of the reefs in turn and then upon the shingle beach, sending up the spume in an angry froth which the wind took and drove in like smoke over the land.[123]

And from nature to the people who inhabit and inherit the landscape, Paule Marshall uses the word, her words, not to say "it is so," but to say, as the conjuror says, *this is how it could/should be*. So her Bajans become more than Bajans: they develop historical depth and cultural possibility—Fergusson, the cane factory mechanic, for instance:

[A vociferous] strikingly tall, lean old man, whose gangling frame appeared strung together by the veins and sinews, standing out in sharp relief beneath his dark skin. . . . His face, his neck, his clean-shaven skull, had the elongated intentionally distorted look to them of a Benin mask, or a sculpted thirteenth century Ife head. With his long, stretched limbs he could have been a Haitian Houngan man.[124]

It is Fergusson who, like an Ashanti *okyeame*, kept the memory of the ancestral dead alive with his interminable rehearsal of the tale of Cuffee Ned, the slave rebel.

Cuffee Ned becomes the ancestor of the whole village, and it is his memory and the whole African tradition which depends on it, that keeps these people inviolate under the pressures of commercialization and progress.

Then there was the Ashanti chief himself, Delbert, the shopkeeper and truck owner:

He was lying propped up on a makeshift bed amid the clutter behind the counter, a broken white leg in a cast laid up stiffly in the bed. He was huge, with massive limbs. . . . He was the chief presiding over the nightly palavering in the men's house. The bed made of packing cases was the royal palanquin. The colorful Harry Truman shirt he had on was his robe of office; the battered Panama hat . . . his chieftain's umbrella, and the bottle of white rum he held within the great curve of his hand, the palm wine with which he kept the palaver and made libation to the ancestral gods.[125]

It is rhetorical, even romantic. But Paule Marshall's *intention* is crucial, and in it she unquestionably succeeds: to transform the Afro-Bajan out of his drab, materialistic setting with meaningful correlates of custom from across the water in ancestral Africa.

Finally, at the end of the book, there is a Carnival. It is not a particularly typical Bajan happening, but Paule Marshall does not intend it to be. She links the Afro-Caribbean experience of Bajan (Chalky Mount) maroons with Trinidad carnival and Montserrat masquerades.[126] Every year the people of Bournehills put on the same mas'—the same pageant—*The Legend of Cuffee Ned*. They will not change a single iota of their metaphor. There is of course an outcry against this from other parts of the island: "Oh you poor people from the slave days, every year you doing the same thing." But Bournehills is making a point: until there is a change in the system, we will always be slaves, and until there is change, we must continue to celebrate our one, if brief, moment of rebel victory:

They had worked together!—and as if, in their eyes, this had been the greatest achievement, the thing of which they were proudest, the voices rose to a stunning crescendo that visibly jarred the blue dome of the sky. Under Cuffee, they sang, a man had not lived for himself alone, but for his neighbour also. "If we had lived selfish, we couldn't have lived at all." They half-spoke, half-sung the words. They had trusted one another, and set aside their differences and stood as one against their enemies. They had been a People! Their heads thrown back and the welded voices reaching high above New Bristol's red-faded tin roofs, they informed the sun and afternoon sky of what they, Bournehills People, had once been capable of.

Then abruptly, the voices dropped. . . . They sung then in tones drained of their former jubilance of the defeat that had eventually followed . . . in voices that would never cease to mourn . . . for this too, as painful as it was, was part of the story.[127]

REFERENCES

1. This is an edited transcript of a talk given at the Center for Multi-Racial Studies, Cave Hill, Barbados, in February, 1970; revised and extended in October and December, 1973.

2. Edward Brathwaite, *Rights of Passage*, Argo DA 101 (1968), sleevenote.

3. The most detailed examination of this possibility is the almost ignored Leo Wiener, *Africa and the Discovery of America*, 3 vols (Philadelphia: Innes and Sons, 1922). More recently, there has been

Harold G. Lawrence, "African Explorers of the New World," *The Crisis* (June-July 1962). For a useful bibliographical essay, see Floyd W. Hayes III, "The African Presence in America," *Black World*, 22, No. 9 (July 1973), pp. 4-22.

4. The latest estimates/discussion are in Philip D. Curtin, *The Atlantic Slave Trade: A Census* (Madison, Wis.: University of Wisconsin Press, 1969); Walter Rodney, *How Europe Underdeveloped Africa* (London and Dar-es-Salaam: Bogle-L'Ouverture, 1972), pp. 103-112.

5. See, for example, the work of E. Franklin Frazier in the United States, Orlando Patterson in the anglophone Caribbean. M. G. Smith's "The African Heritage in the Caribbean," *Caribbean Studies: A Symposium*, ed. Vera Rubin (Seattle: University of Washington Press, 1960), pp. 34-46, is perhaps typical.

6. See, for example, M. J. Herskovits, *The Myth of the Negro Past* (New York: Harper and Brothers, 1941) and the work of the Herskovitses generally. Then there are the works of W. R. Bascom, George E. Simpson, Alan Lomax (in cantometrics), R. F. Thompson ("African Influence on the Art of the United States"), Pierre Verger, Janheinz Jahn, and Maureen Warner (on the Yorubas in Trinidad) to name a few, and my own *The Folk Culture of the Slaves in Jamaica* (London and Port-of-Spain: New Beacon Books, 1970). A summary of work and ideas in the field appears in my Introduction to M. J. Herskovits' *Life in a Haitian Valley* [1937] (New York: Doubleday, 1971), revised in African Studies Association of the West Indies *Bulletin* No. 5 (Mona: 1972). A detailed consideration of the entire question is the subject of my *Africa in the Caribbean* (forthcoming).

7. See, for example, Orlando Patterson, *The Sociology of Slavery* (London: Macgibbon and Kee, 1967).

8. For more on this, see my review of Patterson's *Sociology* which appeared in *Race*, 9, No. 3 (1968). My own position is set out in *The Development of Creole Society in Jamaica* (Oxford: The Clarendon Press, 1971).

9. Studies of African culture are now so easily available and in such quantity that a listing here would be pointless. I would like to draw attention to the following, however: M. J. Herskovits on Dahomey; R. S. Rattray on the Ashanti; M. J. Field on the Ga; Afolabi Ojo on the Yoruba; John Mbiti, J. B. Danquah, Marcel Griaule on African religion and philosophy; and the collection edited by S. and P. Ottenberg, *Cultures and Societies of Africa* (New York: Random House, 1960).

   The question of the unity of African culture, or at least of those areas of Africa involved with or contingent upon the slave trade, is obviously one of the critical assumptions of this paper, permitting me to speak of "Africa" instead of, say, Senegal, the Gold Coast, Dahomey. For discussions on this point, see, among others, Cheikh Anta Diop, *L'Unité Culturelle de L'Afrique noire* (Paris: Présence Africaine, 1959); Melville J. Herskovits, *The Myth of the Negro Past*, esp. Ch. 3; and Alan Lomax, "Africanisms in New World Negro Music," *Research and Resources of Haiti* (New York: Research Institute for the Study of Man, 1969).

10. "Appreciation for Cumfa," *Evening Post* (Guyana), August 29, 1972.

11. See George E. Simpson (for Trinidad) in *Religious Cults of the Caribbean* (Rio Piedras, Puerto Rico: Institute of Caribbean Studies, University of Puerto Rico, 1970), pp. 82-85. Until the advent of "Papa Doc" Duvalier, vodun in Haiti also found itself under pretty regular attack from Church and State, starting with the Liberator himself, Toussaint L'Ouverture. See Simpson, pp. 254-256. The news that Guyana is to abolish its obeah laws came in November of 1973. The reverberations from Church, Press and other States (fear, ridicule, caution: when Prime Minister Forbes Burnham of Guyana visited Jamaica soon afterwards, he was met by at least one anti-obeah demonstration) indicate the revolutionary depth of the announcement.

12. Eric Williams, *Capitalism and Slavery* (Chapel Hill: University of North Carolina Press, 1944).

13. Eric Williams, *Some Historical Reflections on the Church in the Caribbean* (Port-of-Spain: Public Relations Division, Office of the Prime Minister, 1973), p. 11.

14. During this "October Crisis," the entire Jamaican mass-media apparatus came out against Rodney, Black Power and "Cave Mona" (a punning editorial pejorate for the University of the West Indies

at Mona), and clearly had little time for analysis or facts. The best and perhaps the only "Diary of Events" was therefore the students' publication, *Scope*—in the excitement, undated, but with a picture of Dr. Rodney on the cover. Rodney's own comment is in *The Groundings with My Brothers* (London: Bogle-L'Ouverture, 1969), pp. 59-67. It is interesting to note that the non-establishment newspapers that appeared as a result of this crisis carried African (*Abeng, Moko*) or Amerindian (*Tapia*) names.

15. "Yoruba and Our African Heritage," *Advocate-News* (Barbados), August 20, 1973. In addition to Yoruba House in Barbados, mention might be made here of Maureen Warner-Lewis' Omo Ajini (Children of Africa) at Mona. Mrs. Lewis has been teaching her group Yoruba songs she recorded in Trinidad during her research into the Yoruba presence there, and restoring them to life (movement and setting), using Yoruba dances she learnt while living in Nigeria. But it must be borne in mind that before Yoruba and Omo Ajini, there were several folk/survival groups, most of them ignored by the establishment.

16. Philip D. Curtin, *Two Jamaicas* (Cambridge, Mass.: Harvard University Press, 1955), esp. pp. 158-177.

17. W. H. Siebert, *The Legacy of the American Revolution* (Columbus: Ohio State University Bulletin, April 1913); Curtin, *Two Jamaicas*, pp. 32 ff.; Brathwaite, *Creole Society*, pp. 253-255 and *passim*.

18. For discussion, see Martha Beckwith, *Black Roadways* (Chapel Hill: University of North Carolina Press, 1929); Curtin, *Two Jamaicas*; and the F. G. Cassidy/R. B. Le Page, *Dictionary of Jamaican English* (Cambridge: Cambridge University Press, 1967), pp. 313-314.

19. For this and Afro-Jamaican religion generally, see J. C. Moore, "The Religion of Jamaican Negroes . . . ," Ph.D. thesis, Northwestern University (1953); Edward Seaga, "Cults in Jamaica," *Jamaica Journal*, 3, No. 2 (June 1969), pp. 3-13; and Simpson, *Religious Cults*.

20. See, for instance, Sylvia Wynter's *Jamaica's National Heroes* (Kingston: Jamaica National Trust Commission, 1971).

21. *Facts and Documents Relating to the Alleged Rebellion in Jamaica* (Anonymous) (London: 1866), pp. 12, 13, 38, 57.

22. Curtin, *Two Jamaicas*, p. 174.

23. Noelle Chutkan, "The Administration of Justice . . . as a Contributing Factor [in] the Morant Bay Riot of 1865," unpublished History Seminar paper, University of the West Indies, Mona, 1969.

24. The names of the churches are significant: First *African* Baptist Church (Savannah), *African* Baptist Church (Lexington), *Abyssinia* Baptist Church (New York), Free *African* Meeting House (Boston), etc. For full list, see St. Clair Drake, *The Redemption of Africa and Black Religion* (Chicago and Atlanta: Third World Press and Institute of the Black World, 1970), p. 26. Closely connected with these were the "Back to Africa" movements—militant under slave rebels; religious/secular with people like Paul Cuffee, Martin Delany in the U.S., Albert Thorne in Barbados, and George Alexander McGuire in Antigua, through Bishop Henry Macneil Turner, Alfred Sam, Edward Blyden, DuBois, to Marcus Garvey with the *grito*: "Africa for the Africans at home and abroad." For a discussion of these see, among others, Edwin S. Redkey, *Black Exodus* (New Haven, Conn.: Yale University Press, 1969); Vincent Bakpetu Thompson, *Africa and Unity: The Evolution of Pan Africanism* (London and Harlow: Longmans Green, 1969); and St. Clair Drake, *op. cit.* The Garvey bibliography, needless to say, is an industry in itself. In addition, there was the presence and influence of literate (slave) Africans like Phillis Wheatley, Ottobah Cugoano, and Ignatius Sancho, some of whom, like Mahammedu Sisei, Mohammed Bath, Olaudah Equiano, actually returned to Africa. See Paul Edwards' "Introduction" (p. lx) to *Equiano's Travels* (London and Ibadan: Heinemann Educational Books, 1967); Janheinz Jahn, *A History of Neo-African Literature* (1966), trans. Oliver Coburn and Ursula Lehrburger (London: Faber & Faber, 1968), p. 40. Sisei and Mohammed Bath are treated in unpublished papers by Carl Campbell, Dept. of History, University of the West Indies, Mona, 1972-1973.

25. For a development of this point, see my "Foreword" in *Savacou* 3/4 (December 1970/March 1971).

26. Nicolás Guillén, "Interview with Keith Ellis," *Jamaica Journal*, 7, Nos. 1 & 2 (March/June 1973), p. 78.

27. The concept derives from M. G. Smith's classic, *The Plural Society in the British West Indies* (Berkeley: University of California Press, 1965).

28. See, for instance, Abbé Raynal, *Histoire philosophique et politique des établissements et du commerce des européens dans les deux Indes* (1770); and Thomas Southey, *Chronological History of the West Indies* (1827). These works are examined in Elsa Goveia's *A Study on the Historiography of the British West Indies to the End of the Nineteenth Century* (Mexico: Instituto Panamericano de Geografia y Historia, 1956). On the other hand, works like the anonymous *Jonathan Corncob* (1787); J. B. Moreton, *Manners and Customs* (1790); and Edward Long, *History of Jamaica* (1774), no matter what their other qualities, were little more than travesties of black reality. See my "Creative Literature of the British West Indies During the Period of Slavery," *Savacou*, 1 (June 1970), pp. 46-73.

29. This novel, probably written by an Englishman with some knowledge of the West Indies, is discussed in detail in my "Creative Literature." The most imaginative insight into slavery from the anglophone Caribbean is perhaps James Carnegie's unpublished novella, *Wages Paid*, a long extract of which appeared in *Savacou* 3/4 (December 1970-March 1971), as "Circle."

30. DeLisser published ten novels in the period 1913-1958, including *Jane's Career* (Kingston: The Gleaner Co., 1913; London: Methuen & Co., 1914) and the well-known, *The White Witch of Rosehall* (London: Ernest Benn, 1929). Jean Rhys, who left the Caribbean c. 1912, when she was sixteen, and has never returned, has written at least six novels, only one of which deals with the Caribbean: *Wide Sargasso Sea* (London: André Deutsch, 1966). Nicole, who also makes his home outside the Caribbean, has written many novels, including a whole series of detective tales under a pseudonym. Among his books dealing with his native land are *Off-White* (London: Jarrolds, 1959) and *White Boy* (London: Hutchinson, 1966). The contribution of the other writers listed in the text is as follows: Mendes, *Pitch Lake* (1934), *Black Fauns* (1935); McDonald, *The Humming-Bird Tree* (1969); Emtage, *Brown Sugar* (1966); Drayton, *Christopher* (1959), *Zohara* (1961); Allfrey, *The Orchid House* (1953). I have not included the work of Roger Mais here, because his novels deal almost exclusively with the black proletariat and peasantry. See note 32.

31. Kenneth Ramchand, *The West Indian Novel and Its Background* (London: Faber & Faber, 1970), pp. 223-236.

32. "Jazz and the West Indian Novel," *Bim*, 44-45 (1967-1968).

33. Cuba and Puerto Rico were occupied by U.S. forces in 1898 as a consequence of the Spanish-American War. The Dominican Republic and Haiti were occupied during the First World War.

34. Juan Marinello, "Sobre una inquietud cubana," *Revista de Avance* (February 1930); and *Poética, ensayos en entusiasmo* (Madrid: 1933), p. 142, quoted and translated by G. R. Coulthard in his *Race and Colour in Caribbean Literature* (London: Oxford University Press, 1962), p. 29. Coulthard's book is an invaluable and still, after more than ten years, unique source of information about literature in the French and Spanish Caribbean.

35. The first big "hit" was a song, delivered by a white American group, the Andrews Sisters, called fittingly, "Rum and Coca-Cola."

36. "A tiger is not conscious of his stripes, he pounces." A statement, attributed to the Nigerian writer, Wole Soyinka, and indicative of a general anglophone reluctance to accept the theoretical apparatus of negritude. The term also suggests something of the post-colonial difference between French and English-speaking African writers: the former tended to be expatriate, the latter lived and worked, on the whole, in their own countries.

37. See my series of articles on Carifesta in the *Sunday Advocate News* (Barbados) (October-December 1972).

38. Carl Brouard (Haiti), "La trouée," *La Revue indigène* (October 1927), my translation.

39. Countee Cullen, "Heritage," *Color* (New York: Harper & Bros., 1925).

40. Philip Sherlock, "Jamaican Fisherman," *Ten Poems* (Georgetown, Guyana: Miniature Poets Series, edited and published by A. J. Seymour and *Kykoveral,* 1953).

41. Jacques Roumain, "Guinée," *La Revue indigène* (September 1927).

42. Louise Bennett, *Jamaica Labrish* (Kingston, Jamaica: Sangster's Book Stores, 1966), p. 214.

43.

> And this despair, equal to no other
> for taming, with words from France,
> this heart which comes to me from Senegal

Laleau, "Trahison," *Musique negre* (Port-au-Prince: Imprimerie de l'Etat, 1931) trans. Coulthard, *op. cit.,* p. 43.

44. Derek Walcott's preface to *Dream on Monkey Mountain and Other Plays* (New York: Farrar, Straus & Giroux, 1970) and his play *Dream on Monkey Mountain* are explicit explorations of this theme and "problem," memorably crystallized in his poem, "A Far Cry from Africa," *In a Green Night* (London: Jonathan Cape, 1962), p. 18.

> I who am poisoned with the blood of both,
> Where shall I turn, divided to the vein?
> I who have cursed
> The drunken officer of British rule, how choose
> Between this African and the English tongue I love?

45. Dantès Bellegarde, *Haiti et ses problèmes* (Montreal: 1941), pp. 16-17, quoted in Coulthard, *op. cit.,* pp. 73-74.

46. Andrew Salkey, *A Quality of Violence* (London: New Authors Ltd., 1959), p. 151.

47. Nicolás Guillén, "Son Numero 6," from *El son entero* (Buenos Aires: Editorial Pleamar, 1947), trans. George Irish in *Savacou* 3/4 (1970/1971), p. 112.

48. In Alfred Métraux, *Le vaudou haitien* (Paris: Gallimard, 1958), trans. Hugo Charteris as *Voodoo in Haiti* (New York: Schocken Books, 1972), pp. 152-153.

49. Edward Brathwaite, *Masks* (London: Oxford University Press, 1968), pp. 38-39, 68-69; *Islands* (London: Oxford University Press, 1969), pp. 51-53.

50. George Simpson, *The Shango Cult in Trinidad* (Rio Piedras, Puerto Rico: Institute of Caribbean Studies, University of Puerto Rico, 1965), p. 45; reprinted in his *Religious Cults of the Caribbean,* p. 40.

51. Moore, *op. cit.,* pp. 174-175, reprinted in Brathwaite, *Creole Society,* pp. 224-225, 329-331.

52. In Cuba and Brazil, Yemajaa, the Yoruba goddess of the sea, dominates ceremony and dance. In Haiti, important customs surround Agwe, the saltwater power, whose boat is annually sent drifting back to "Ibo." In folktales, *fair-maids* and *water-mammas* play important roles. In songs originating from the hounfort, we are always crossing the river, and the importance of the Baptists has already been mentioned.

53. See "Jazz and the West Indian Novel," *Bim,* 45 (1967), p. 41.

54. Adapted from R. B. Le Page and David De Camp, *Jamaican Creole* (London: Macmillan, 1960).

55. In Harold Courlander, *The Drum and the Hoe* (Berkeley and Los Angeles: University of California Press, 1960), p. 248.

56. "The Little Boy Who Avenged His Mother," in H. P. Jacobs, "An Early Dialect Verse," *Jamaican Historical Review,* 1, No. 3 (December 1948), pp. 279-281.

57. See Walter Jekyll, *Jamaican Song and Story* (1907; New York: Dover Publications, Inc., 1966).

58. For an account of some of these, see Tony Harrison, "Shango the Shaky Fairy," *London Magazine*, New Series, 10, No. 1 (April 1970), pp. 5-27.

59. The "rock-and-roll" base of black American music is another aspect of Shango, as is "boogie-woogie" (piano imitation of the train), and the innumerable spirituals and gospel songs that not only *sing* about trains, but become possessed by them. Listen, for example, to use recent examples, to Aretha Franklin's "Pullin' " (*Spirit in the Dark*: Atlantic SD 8265) or the Staple Singers' "I'll Take You There."

60. Salkey, *op. cit.*, p. 109.

61. *Ibid.*, p. 61.

62. *Ibid.*, p. 66.

63. *Ibid.*, pp. 60-61.

64. This applies not only to writers, but to Caribbean critics as well. See my commentary on this in "Caribbean Critics," *New World Quarterly*, 5, Nos. 1-2 (1969), pp. 5-15; *Critical Quarterly*, 11, No. 3 (Autumn 1969), pp. 268-276. Salkey and Sherlock particularly, however, have developed significantly during the Black Consciousness period of the 60's. Salkey's collection of stories, *Anancy's Score* (London: Bogle-L'Ouverture Publications, 1973) is an especially fine example of the new writing.

65. Vera Bell, "Ancestor on the Auction Block," *The Independence Anthology of Jamaican Literature*, ed. A. L. Hendriks and Cedric Lindo (Kingston, Jamaica: The Arts Celebration Committee of the Ministry of Development and Welfare, 1962), p. 85. For a detailed analysis of this poem, see George Lamming, "Caribbean Literature: The Black Rock of Africa," *African Forum*, 1, No. 4 (Spring 1966), pp. 32-52.

66. Philip Sherlock, "Pocomania," *Caribbean Quarterly* (Federation Anthology of Poetry), 5, No. 3 (1958), pp. 192-193.

67. George Lamming, *Season of Adventure* (London: Michael Joseph, 1960), pp. 44-50.

68. For details of the various Maroon groups see, among others, Philip J. C. Dark, *Bush Negro Art* (London: Alec Tiranti Ltd., 1954); Jean Huraul, *Africains de Guyane* (Le Haye and Paris: Editions Mouton, 1970); R. C. Dallas, *The History of the Maroons [of Jamaica]*, 2 vols., (London 1803); Sir William Young, *An Account of the Black Charaibs in the Island of St. Vincent* (London, 1795); Douglas C. Taylor, *The Black Carib of British Honduras* (New York: Wenner-Gren Foundation for Anthropological Research, 1951); Edison Carneiro, *Guerras do los Palmares* (Mexico: Fondo de Cultura Económica, 1946).

69. The Maroons of Jamaica, the Black Caribs of Honduras and the Surinam groups.

70. Namba Roy, *Black Albino* (London: New Literature Press, 1961).

71. Wilson Harris, *The Secret Ladder* (London: Faber and Faber, 1963), p. 23.

72. *Ibid.*, p. 39.

73. Wilson Harris, *History, Fable and Myth in the Caribbean and Guianas* (Georgetown, Guyana: National History and Arts Council, Ministry of Information and Culture, 1970), p. 29.

74. Harris, *History, Fable*, p. 28.

75. "History is built around achievement and creation; and nothing was created in the West Indies," V. S. Naipaul, *The Middle Passage* (London: André Deutsch, 1962), p. 29.

76. "This was a society . . . in which all forms of refinements, of art, of folkways were either absent or in a state of total disintegration," Orlando Patterson, *The Sociology of Slavery*, p. 9.

77.   those who remain fascinated,
                       in attitudes of prayer,
                       by the festering roses made from their fathers' manacles,

> or upraise their silver chalices flecked with vomit . . .
> crying, at least here
> something happened—
> they will absolve us, perhaps, if we begin again,
> from what we have always known, nothing . . .
> while the silver-hammered charger of the marsh light
> brings towards us, again and again, in beaten scrolls,
> nothing, then nothing,
> and then nothing.

From *Another Life* by Derek Walcott (New York: Farrar, Straus & Giroux, 1973), pp. 144-145.

78. Brathwaite, *Islands*, pp. ix-x.

79. *Ibid.*, p. 37.

80. Harris, *History, Fable*, pp. 9-10.

81. Lamming, *Season of Adventure*, p. 29.

82. The only other Caribbean writer who has been able to enter the hounfort in this way, it seems to me, is Alejo Carpentier in *El reino de este mundo* (Mexico: EDIAPSA, 1949). But Wilson Harris, in a remarkable passage in a public lecture, demonstrates that he too (as one would expect) is fully aware of the implosive links between *vodun* and the folk literature of the New World:

    All conventional memory is erased and yet in this trance of overlapping spheres of reflection a primordial or deeper function of memory begins to exercise itself. . . .

    That such a drama has indeed a close bearing on the language of fiction, on the language of art, seems to me incontestable. The community the writer shares with the primordial dancer is, as it were, the complementary halves of a broken stage. . . .

    "The Writer and Society," *Tradition, the Writer and Society* (London and Port-of-Spain: New Beacon Books, 1967), pp. 51-52.

83. Lamming, *Season of Adventure*, pp. 29-30.

84. M. G. Lewis, *Journal of a West Indian Proprietor* (1834; London: G. Routledge & Sons, 1929), p. 290.

85. For more on this, see Placide Tempels, *Bantu Philosophy* (1946), trans. Colin King from the 1952 French edition (Paris: Présence Africaine, 1959), pp. 69-74.

86. DeLisser, *Jane's Career*, p. 120.

87. Aimé Césaire, *Cahier d'un retour au pays natal* (1939; Paris: Présence Africaine, 1956), p. 40, my translation.

88. Ishmael Reed, *Yellow Back Radio Broke-down* (1969; New York: Bantam Books, 1972), p. 9.

89. LeRoi Jones, *Black Magic Poetry* (Indianapolis and New York: The Bobbs-Merrill Co., 1969), p. 116; which should be *heard* on *Sonny's Time Now Now* (Jihad 663), with Sonny Murray (drums) Albert Ayler (tenor sax), Don Cherry (trumpet) and Henry Grimes (bass).

90. R. Dobru, *Flowers Must Not Grow Today* (Paramaribo, Surinam: Afi-Kofi, 1973).

91. The presence and use of *nommo* is too pervasive and evident in modern African literature for us to do more than refer, among many others, to Gabriel Okara's *The Voice*, Wole Soyinka's *The Road*; the plays by Robert Serumaga (*Renga Moi*) and Duro Ladipo (for example, *Oba koso*), based closely on traditional ceremony; Camara Laye's *L'enfant noir*, the novels of Amos Tutuola and the long poems of Okot p'Bitek. For traditional African literature and thought, see, among others, William Bascom, *Ifa Divination* (Bloomington: Indiana University Press, 1969); Ruth Finnegan, *Oral Literature in Africa* (Oxford: The Clarendon Press, 1970); S. A. Babalola, *The Content and Form of Yoruba Ijala* (Oxford: The Clarendon Press, 1966); J. H. Nketia, *Funeral Dirges of the Akan People* (Achitoma, 1955); Marcel Griaule, *Dieu d'eau: entretiens avec Ogotemmêli* (Paris:

Editions du Chêne, 1948); Tempels, *Bantu Philosophy*; and Chinua Achebe "Foreword" to *A Selection of African Prose*, ed. W. H. Whiteley (Oxford: The Clarendon Press, 1964), pp. vii-x.

92. See *Minty Alley* [1936] (London and Port-of-Spain: New Beacon Books Ltd., 1971), pp. 21 and 23.

93. See DeLisser, *Jane's Career* (reprint London: Heinemann Educational Books, 1972), p. 79.

94. Listen, for example, to *Message to the Grass Roots from Malcolm X* (Afro Records, AA 1264); *Martin Luther King* (Mercury 20119). Writing *about* oratory has not been particularly successful (c.f. Marcus H. Boulware, *The Oratory of Negro Leaders* (Westport, Conn.: Negro Universities Press, 1969). Although Roger Abrahams' work on this aspect of Afro/New World folk art should be specially mentioned: "The Shaping of Folklore Traditions in the British West Indies," and "Traditions of Eloquence in Afro-American Committees," *Journal of Inter-American Studies and World Affairs*, 9, pp. 456-480 and 12, pp. 505-527.

95. In this paper I have concentrated on the religious aspects of Caribbean folk culture. There is, however, an important secular development, magnificently expressed in the Carnival and calypso of Trinidad especially. This secular aspect of our culture is as comprehensive (life-centered) as the religious art-styles being discussed. See Errol Hill, *The Trinidad Carnival* (Austin: University of Texas Press, 1972).

96. Lamming, *Season of Adventure*, p. 91.

97. From the work of the writers cited in this paragraph (themselves a selection), the following may be noted: Nina Rodrigues, *Os Africanos no Brasil* (1905; São Paulo: Cia. Editora Nacional, 1932); Renato Mendoza, *A influenca Africana portugesa do Brasil* (Rio de Janeiro: 1934); Fernando Ortiz, *Hampa Afrocubana: Los Negros Brujos* (Madrid: Editorial-America, 1906); Arthur Ramos, *O Negro Brasileiro* (Rio de Janeiro: Civilizacão Brasileira, 1934); Donald Pierson, *Negroes in Brazil* (Chicago: University of Chicago Press, 1942); Ivy Baxter, *The Arts of an Island* (Metuchen, N.J.: The Scarecrow Press, 1970); Errol Hill, *The Trinidad Carnival*; J. D. Elder, *Evolution of the Traditional Calypso of Trinidad and Tobago*. . . . (Ann Arbor, Mich.: University Microfilms, 1966, 1970); Roger Bastide, *Les Ameriques noires* (Paris: Payot, 1967).

98. See Alexis Kagame, *La philosophie bantu-rwandaise de l'être* (Brussels: 1956); Griaule, *Dieu d'eau;* Tempels, *Bantoe-Filosofie;* Jahn, *Muntu* (1958), trans. Marjorie Grene (London: Faber and Faber, 1961) and *A History of Neo-African Literature*. In the New World, studies of the African word in creole speech include Lorenzo Turner, *Africanisms in the Gullah Dialect of the Southern United States* (Chicago: University of Chicago Press, 1949); J. J. Thomas, *The Theory and Practice of Creole Grammar* [in Trinidad] (Port-of-Spain: 1869); F. G. Cassidy and R. B. Le Page, *Dictionary of Jamaican English;* F. G. Cassidy, *Jamaica Talk* (London: Macmillan, 1961); Mary Jo Willeford, "Africanisms in the Bajan Dialect," *Bim*, 46 (1968), pp. 90-97, and Fernando Ortiz, *Glosario de Afro-negrismos* (Havana: 1923). But the really illuminating studies, often providing a meaningful context for understanding the presence of the Word, are (among others), Mervyn Alleyne, "The Linguistic Continuity of Africa in the Caribbean," *Black Academy Review,* 1, No. 4 (Winter 1970), pp. 3-16; LeRoi Jones, *Blues People* (New York: Grove Press, 1972); Sylvia Wynter, "Jonkonnu in Jamaica," *Jamaica Journal,* 4, No. 2 (June 1970), pp. 34-48; and Jean Price-Mars, *Ainsi parla l'oncle* (Port-au-Prince: Imprimerie de Compiègne, 1928).

99. Monica Skeete, "To Frank Collymore on His Eightieth Birthday," *Savacou* 7/8 (January/June 1973), p. 122.

100. *Ibid;* my notation.

101. Bongo Jerry, "The Youth," *Savacou* 3/4 (December 1970/March 1971), p. 13. My notation.

102. Bongo Jerry, "Mabrak," *Savacou* 3/4, pp. 13-14.

103. *Ibid.,* p. 15.

104. Edward Brathwaite, "Jazz and the West Indian Novel."

105. I have developed my ideas on this still further in my "Introduction" to Roger Mais, *Brother Man* (1954; London: Heinemann Educational Books, forthcoming in 1974).

106. Nicolás Guillén, "*Sensemayá*" from *West Indies Ltd* (1934), in *El son entero*, pp. 60-61.

107. Césaire, *Cahier* (1956 ed.), p. 50.

108. Leon Damas, "Il est des nuits," *Pigments* (Paris: Guy Lévis Mano, 1937), p. 24.

109. Jamil Ali, "Dimensions of Confusion," *Savacou* 9/10 (forthcoming in 1974).

110. Brathwaite, *Islands*, pp. 65-66.

111. The Mighty Sparrow, "Ten to One Is Murder," transcribed in his *One Hundred and Twenty Calypsoes to Remember* (Port-of-Spain: National Recording Co., 1963), p. 37. Errol Hill in *The Trinidad Carnival*, p. 70, comments on the *calinda*-style performance as follows: "The form seems simple enough on paper, but it is highly effective and dramatic in performance. The rapid alternation from solo voice to chorus creates a feeling of tension. Sometimes the leader will anticipate the end of the chorus line and come in over it; at another time he will appear to drop behind the regular meter in starting his verse, then suddenly spring forward on a syncopated beat. He improvises not only with his lyric but also with the melody; he ornaments his short passage [s] in subtle ways, but is always constrained to return to the original tune by the insistent power of the chorus. It is as though leader and chorus complement and contradict each other simultaneously."

> Sparrow: Well I start to sweat,
>   An I soakin wet,
>   Mamma, so much threat,
>   That's a night I can never forget
>   Ten o' dem against me with fifty spectator
>
> Chorus: *Ten to one is murder!*

112. Pastor Williams and Spiritual Baptist Congregation, Silver Sands, Barbados. Transcription of cassette tape recording: October 15, 1972. We could also refer to the second preacher in the Jamaican film, *The Harder They Come*, and recordings such as the Reverend Kelsey (Brunswick OE 9256) for the United States. Examples could also be cited for Haiti, Brazil, Africa.

113. Bruce St. John, "West Indian Litany," *Savacou* 3/4 (December 1970/March 1971), p. 82.

114. Unpublished manuscript.

115. Césaire, *Cahier* (Paris: Présence Africaine, 1971 ed.), p. 72.

116. Lamming, *The Pleasures of Exile* (London: Michael Joseph, 1960), p. 121.

117. See Elizabeth Clarke, "Mudda Africa," *New Writing in the Caribbean*, ed. A. J. Seymour (Georgetown: National History and Arts Council of Guyana, 1972), p. 60-62; Tito Jemmott, "A Tale," *Savacou* 3/4, pp. 60-64.

118. Melvin Tolson, *Libretto for the Republic of Liberia* (New York: Twayne Publishers, 1953).

119. Robert Hayden, "Middle Passage," *A Ballad of Remembrance* (London: Paul Breman, 1962), pp. 60-66.

120. Brathwaite, *Rights of Passage* (1967), *Masks* (1968), *Islands* (1969), published under single cover as *The Arrivants* (London: Oxford University Press, 1973).

121. Paule Marshall, *The Chosen Place, the Timeless People* (New York: Harcourt, Brace and World, 1969).

122. Brathwaite, "West Indian History and Society in the Art of Paule Marshall's Novel," *Journal of Black Studies*, 1, No. 2 (December 1970), pp. 225-238.

123. Paule Marshall, *op. cit.*, p. 106.

124. *Ibid.*, p. 121.

125. *Ibid.*, p. 123.

126. For the close connection between the Montserrat masquerade bands and their counterparts in West Africa, see the articles by Simon Ottenberg, Phillips Stevens, Jr. and John C. Messenger in *African Arts*, 6, No. 4 (Summer 1973), pp. 32-35, 40-43, 54-57.

127. Marshall, *op cit.*, p. 287.

ROGER   BASTIDE

The Present Status of Afro-American Research in Latin America°

ALTHOUGH ENTIRE aspects of African civilization have been preserved in Latin America so clearly that no concept of "reinterpretation" is needed to discover them, it is much more difficult to do Afro-American research in South America than in North America. This is partly because miscegenation continues to occur, creating considerable ambiguity with regard to the terms "Negro" and "mulatto": Marvin Harris found no less than 492 different categories of racial identification in Brazil.[1] And how can one establish a science if its very object cannot be clearly defined? Does the term "Afro-American" include all ethnic categories where there is black blood? If not, at what point shall we limit the group we study? One must not dismiss this as a nominal difficulty, for those who claim that there is no black problem in Latin America lean heavily on this ambiguity.

Furthermore, where one cannot speak of a single ethnic identity, one cannot speak of a cultural identity either, for cultural identity will tend to shift from constituent nationality groups to the nation as a whole. In the cultural domain, in other words, the concept of syncretism corresponds to the physical concept of miscegenation. Although it might be difficult to distinguish 492 different categories, there is clearly a continuum of categories of syncretisms in Brazil, ranging from the world of the *candomblés* (where Africa is the dominant influence) to the world of peasant folklore (where Portugal dominates). I will not play this little game. But I understand why Latin American Africanology stresses syncretism as if it were the fundamental problem, and why it cannot go beyond a mechanical concept of syncretism as a simple tally sheet of cultural traits of different racial origin—a concept long obsolete in contemporary anthropology.

The second difficulty follows. If syncretism is the basic phenomenon, and if cultural identity shifts from blacks and mulattos to the nation as a whole, one will find African cultural traits in whites as well as European cultural traits in the descendants of Africans. Gilberto Freyre stressed that, as a result of this cultural transfer from blacks to whites through the black wet-nurse and the colored mistress, one now finds as much of Africa in one race as in the other.[2] One can understand that these conditions of interracial cultural mobility present difficulties for the researcher. When asked why he didn't publish a book on Brazil, Herskovits

° Central America and most of the Antilles belong to Latin America. Contemporary anthropology, however, tends to single out one special area—the Caribbean—which it enlarges constantly so that today it includes Colombia, Equador, and the Guianas. This means that my article can deal only with the rest of South America, a problem since, with the exception of Brazil, we have at our disposal only a few studies on Afro-Americans from these countries, and many of them are old, as are those on Argentina.

answered that he would first have to do some research in Portugal, so that he would not mistake the origins of cultural traits he had patiently inventoried among blacks. Perhaps these difficulties explain why, in Brazil, after a brilliant period of research and publication ranging from the end of World War I to the beginning of World War II, interest in Afro-American studies abruptly ceased, and is being resumed only now.

At the beginning of World War II, these studies were characterized, first, by the radical separation of disciplines. In all of Latin America, the black was the object of historical studies based on archive documents and conducted, with a few exceptions, such as the work of Gilberto Freyre, according to the traditional methods of classical history, those which call for descriptions of events in their chronological order. On the other hand, sociology was almost nonexistent, and the ideology of "racial democracy" which took its place prevented all objective research into the nature of the relationships between the descendants of masters and slaves.

These studies were characterized, secondly, by a lack of research continuity and a consequent failure to accumulate knowledge. After having gathered a great deal of new data in the field, each scientist simply repeated the same facts from one book to another as if he had forever depleted his area of interest, instead of continuing to explore, year after year, to fill in the gaps.

Finally, the theories used to systematize the observations were exogenous. Instead of springing from the data, they were imposed from the outside, borrowed first from Europe, then from the United States, as were, for example, the theories of Levy-Bruhl's prelogical mentality and Arthur Ramos' Freudian psychoanalysis. Afro-Brazilian descriptions were like simple illustrations of reference systems born elsewhere; often, furthermore, they were behind the times in terms of the evolution of the science. Nevertheless, at the time there was a great fervor for Afro-American research in Brazil (although interest did not develop until later in other Latin American countries from Uruguay to Colombia and Venezuela). It was as if Brazil, in the wake of "modernist" literary movements which had sought to discover Brazilian originality and break the umbilical cord to Europe, suddenly became aware of the value of cultural traits which had come from Africa. From 1934 to 1938, important Congresses, at Récife, at Bahia, and in the State of Minas, gathered writers and scientists to lay the foundations for a distinctive Africanology and to find channels of communication among the opposing disciplines represented, ranging from history to folklore, from mythology to psychiatric epidemiology.

But there was already opposition to this first attempt at defining Afro-American research. Black values were stressed, but this was done by whites for the benefit of whites. Certain critics, such as Sergio Buarque de Holanda, denounced the racism of these works which, by emphasizing what was different and exotic about the Negro, placed him in a kind of cultural ghetto, so as not to have to deal with his fundamental problems—those of integration and improvement in his social, educational, and professional status. The Afro-Brazilian civilization was treated as a source of aesthetic enjoyment for whites, who remained outsiders, and manipulated in order to create a cultural nationalism which might compensate blacks for the whites' simultaneous push to maintain the country's colonial economy. Blacks, however, were beginning to become aware of their marginal positions and of the insidious racism of such Afro-Brazilian research. At the end of this period, this awareness took on a political aspect (*A Frente Negra*) not subject to our analysis. The current resurfaced after the Second World War, but this time with a political nature strong enough to rescue cultural matters from analysis by white Africanists.

The transition from the work of these congresses to the present type of Afro-Brazilian research is marked by Herskovits' visit to Bahia, and the research on racial relations in Brazil funded by UNESCO. Herskovits broke in a definitive way with the old interpretations, which placed trance at the center of the *candomblé* and saw it as a pathological phenomenon. By proclaiming that trance was an institutional phenomenon, Herskovits opened new roads by detaching research from old bases which had not left it free to innovate. He suggested to Brazilian scientists some completely neglected fields of analysis which should be approached, like the social organization and economic intra-structures of Afro-Brazilian cults. In short, he gave new life to Afro-Brazilian research.[3] At the same time, he trained a new generation of researchers and assigned them to new geographical areas of study: Ruy Coelho to Honduras, for example, and Octavio da Costa Eduardo to Maranhao. To René Ribeiro, who was working in Récife, which was already under study, he suggested new approaches. If I may mention myself, I made an analogous effort with my students in São Paulo to open new explorations which seemed more promising to me than the old ones.[4] René Ribeiro's work proves that this renewal has been fruitful (although Octavio da Costa Eduardo and Ruy Coelho have abandoned the field of Afro-American research). The change, however, does not constitute a total break with the old methods, in that the theories through which the researcher observes and explores the facts are always exogenous conceptual systems applied to new groupings—based, in this case, on the functionalism brought from the United States by Herskovits. And no one can deny that this functionalism has made possible important breakthroughs: the discovery of the dual system of adaptation in Afro-Brazilian cults in relation to their own members and to the black society; and of the ways blacks achieve balance, catharsis, and resolution of tensions and consequent social integration into their environment. On the other hand, Herskovits risked locking Afro-Brazilian data into an international system of explanation which, like all international systems, will one day be rejected as a distortion of reality (North American functionalism is now under criticism for this reason by both structuralists and Marxists). Few years will pass in Brazil before blacks become aware of their need to create an Afro-Brazilian science themselves, based on their own experience, and to reject calls for exogenous theories which falsify the true significance of phenomena—calls for what the black sociologist Guerreiro Ramos has so appropriately called "consular sociology."

In 1950-1951, at the request of UNESCO, Alfred Metraux organized a group of research projects on racial relations in Brazil. They were directed in the north and center of the country by Charles Wagley, Thales de Azevedo, and Luis A. Costa Pinto in collaboration with H. W. Hutchinson, Marvin Harris and Ben Zimmerman; in the state of São Paulo, where successful industrialization posed problems of social relations in new terms, by Florestan Fernandes and myself in collaboration with sociologist Oracy Nogueira, psychologists Virginia Leone Bicudo and Aniela Meyer Ginsborg, and the leaders of black associations of São Paulo. This research has resulted in a series of publications;[5] it is sufficient here to note the lesson their work offers in terms of the rejuvenation of methods and theories. The northern group affected only a partial revolution; it moved from cultural anthropology to social anthropology, but remained, even when dealing with history, within the realm of an Anglo-Saxon-type anthropology in which the synchronic outweighed the diachronic. The southern group, on the other hand, started a total revolution: the transition from anthropology to sociology as the only discipline capable of elucidating, in depth, the Afro-Brazilian data. Its particular brand of sociology was imbued with history, put together not by the old methods of factual analysis, but by a new method inspired by Marxism—the dialectic. This is why, in the North, once the research requested by UNESCO was accomplished, interest diminished and research stopped, whereas in the South, a new school appeared, contested but still successful, which I will call the São Paulo School, with Florestan Fernandes, Fernando Henrique Cardoso and Octavio Ianni.

UNESCO's contribution did not end with this research. After the war was over, black intellectuals who had become aware of their problems recreated their old Defense Associations, but now the socialist humanist inspiration prevailed over the old reversed racist inspiration and they were of a predominantly political nature. They also created new groups, such as the Experimental Black Theater of Abdias do Nascimento, in order to rejuvenate their strategies of change with new ideologies and practices. They felt confirmed in their claims by the first results of the UNESCO research. This research revealed, first, that interpreting the Brazilian racial situation in terms of the North American racial situation, as suggested by Pierson in *Negroes in Brazil* (1942), obscured the true meaning of that situation, for, although alienation, dependence, and discrimination take forms different and less manifest in Brazil than in the United States, they are nevertheless just as operative.[6] In the second place, the group in the south criticized certain stereotypes such as the idea that Brazil has the distinction of not having any prejudices, il-luminated myths such as that concerning social democracy, and elucidated ideologies such as that regarding the progressive whitening of the population.

In an article criticizing all the theories proposed from the time of Nina Rodrigues and Gilberto Freyre to the present, Guerreiro Ramos initiated black dis-cussion of blacks; he rejects, as equally distorted by ethnocentrism, all prior white discussion, whether delivered by foreigners, whom he sees as incapable of decoding the Brazilian message, or by nationals, who, he says, falsify the facts by trying to fit them into conceptual systems from abroad.[7]

One more Afro-Brazilian Study Congress was organized, much like the prewar congresses, but by blacks, although interested whites were invited to attend. It took place in Rio, in 1950, in a climate of optimism inspired by the UNESCO research. One has only to compare the texts published by this congress with those from previous congresses to perceive the almost complete change in approach affected between 1945 and 1955.[8]

The change was not a total one, however, for empirical descriptions continued to be widespread in all of South America after the Second World War, especially in the area of folklore. A National Commission on Folklore in Rio de Janeiro, and federal commissions in each Brazilian state gather facts on folklore, disseminate them in specialized, more or less short-lived journals (of which there are several—in Rio, in the south, and in São Paulo) and maintain folklore by presenting large musical or choreographic demonstrations. Of course we are talking about Brazilian folklore, but, since blacks play an important part in the folklore, they are very important in the overall scheme. We shall not deal with this abundant literature here. We do not scorn it, however. On the contrary, a theory cannot decode a cultural or sociological message unless facts have been gathered with objectivity, scientific honesty, and patience, then inventoried as completely as possible. This empirical research on folklore is not of interest here, however, precisely because it does not offer decoding rules and hence it does not contribute to our "knowledge" of the Afro-American. The research remains, in fact, somewhere between aesthetics and science—between ideology (research draws attention to the originality of the Brazilian culture at a time when urbanization and industrialization are "debrazilianizing" it) and praxis (by fossilizing folklore, research kills it while trying to save it, tearing it away from the spontaneity of life, which is unceasing becoming). Although this study deals with new theoretical approaches, not with strictly empirical research, this folklorization of black culture in Latin America constitutes a sociological fact which can become, in and of itself, an object of science. It seemed so important to me on a recent research trip in Brazil, that I plan to dedicate an entire chapter to it in my next book.[9]

Cultural Anthropology

When one is dealing with cultural traits transferred from Africa to the New World, empirical research invariably leads to comparative research. The comparative method was used from the start, of course, by such specialists in Afro-Brazilian religions as Nina Rodrigues and Arthur Ramos, but only by means of books. Due to lack of funding and interest, researchers could compare data from their field observations in Brazil only with published descriptions of African religions much too general for effective comparison. Finally, Pierre Verger, by constantly moving between the city of Salvador (Bahia) and the old Slave Coast (Togo, Dahomey, Nigeria), established a comparative method based on double field research on cultural, mythical and ritualistic traits.[10] His book on this research is illustrated with magnificent mirror photographs on facing pages, showing, for example, the same ceremony as interpreted in Africa and in Brazil. The work had a slight bomb-shell effect, since Brazilian specialists had tended, more and more, to insist upon acculturation, syncretism, and change, and thus to describe the *candomblé* as more Brazilian than African. Verger demonstrated irrefutably that Afro-Brazilian religion was a continuation of African religion whose extraordinary faithfulness extended even to the most minute details of the ceremonials—including sequence, duration, and even, here and there, the manipulations of the sacred as it was lived and spoken.

But precisely because the Afro-Brazilian religion was rooted in African thought, though undoubtedly in a mutilated form, a new vision was possible, different from that of the old researchers who, even when their descriptions were empirically exact, gave the impression that Afro-Brazilian religion was a system of superstitions rather than a coherent philosophy of man's fate and the cosmos. My first encounter with the world of the *candomblés*, in 1944, led me to write that there was an "extremely rich and subtle philosophy" behind this religion, which, though different from our own, was as valid intellectually as that of Plato or Spinoza. I persuaded young researchers to explore these new paths, promising them many discoveries. I myself made a first attempt at describing this philosophy with relation to African epistemology and the structure of the logical processes of African thought.[11] Clearly, however, even if I entered the *candomblé* as a member and not just as an observer, the law of the secret's maturation, which dominates any initiatory religion, would still keep me too much of an outsider to do more than introduce a certain black vision of the world. Only a priest of the cult, high up in the hierarchy, could provide the kind of text I hoped for. Thus I attach great importance to the work of Deoscoredes M. dos Santos, *West African Sacred Art and Ritual in Brazil* (1967), and of his wife, Juana Elbein dos Santos, *Le Nagô et la Mort* (1972) and to the works they collaborated on, such as *Esù Bara Léroye*. Unfortunately, even now these texts, which reveal all the richness of esoteric Afro-Brazilian thought, are available only in mimeographed form and in relatively short supply; they are unable to find Brazilian publishers, as if the white society, willing as it is to accept the *candomblé* as folklore or artistic spectacle, feels its intellectual security threatened by the competition, on an equal basis, of a philosophy other than its own—a philosophy I shall call *négritude*, meaning true *négritude*, not that *négritude* which is nothing more than a political ideology.[12]

Nonetheless, cultural anthropology must not become hypnotized by the world of the *candomblé*, or by its fidelity to an ancestral culture. Afro-Brazilian religions are living religions which, in order to survive, have adapted to the new socio-economic structures of Brazil and other metamorphoses, giving birth to new forms—first *macumba*, and above all, *Umbanda spiritualism*. For approximately half a century, the analysis and interpretation of the new religions which have been appearing and multiplying everywhere in the world has been gaining importance in anthropology. A whole series of categories has been suggested for classifying and understanding them: prophetism, millenarianism, nativism, vitalism, religious movements of oppressed people, and salvationistic religions. Earlier, however, we denounced the easy method which consists of applying exogenous reference systems to original facts, and, as Rainer Flasche points out, none of the suggested categories can be applied to *macumba* or *Umbanda*.[13] Hence the interest of his study for comparison with similar religious movements.

Curiously, despite the fact that *Umbanda spiritualism* has millions of followers, and poses a problem for the missionary activities of the Catholic Church so great that it produces almost daily polemics in the newspapers, it has, to my knowledge, given rise to only one scientific publication in Brazil, the excellent work of Procopio de Camargo,[14] though it has aroused impassioned interest abroad (among such scholars as Flasche, H. H. Figge, E. Pressel, Mombelli, and myself).[15] I am not interested, here, in enumerating the various interpretations of this religion and its functions in the society as a whole—interpretations which are contradictory and range from those which see the religion as one of black protest to those which see it as a religion of national integration. Paradoxical as it may seem, we believe that these interpretations, are all true, for *Umbanda* is the meeting place of racial groups—whites, Indian half-breeds, blacks, European migrants, even Japanese—each of which plays a unique part. What interests us here is the diversity of approaches and perspectives through which these phenomena are grasped and judged: the sociological approach (To what extent does spiritualism reflect the transition from folklore to urban society?); the psychological approach (To what extent do the phenomena of possession or dissociation of the personality constitute defense mechanisms against the stresses of urban society?); the political approach (To what extent is *Umbanda* a revolutionary alternative or the expression of a black counterworld?); the phenomenological approach (What is the nature of African religiosity as it is expressed in *Umbanda* and to what extent is it identical with that expressed in Brazilian peasant Catholicism?); and what I call the Weberian approach because it attempts to define what Max Weber called the "social ethic" of the religion and to observe the effects of this living ethic on social facts.

Of course, whether one takes a diachronic or a synchronic perspective, there are other approaches. From a diachronic point of view, black culture in Brazil appears, not as a frozen culture, but as a dynamic one, capable of constant innovations and original creations, each of which removes it a little further from Africa, but is nonetheless authentically Negro. This could lead either to a theory of discontinuous continuity—the only one, in my opinion, which takes into account Afro-American blackness—or to an undoubtedly interesting analysis of the Afro-Brazilian imagination in the process of constructing an "other society," although following Steger's expression, the utopia here is built on the past rather than oriented toward the future. From a synchronic perspective, one could study *Umbanda* by means of the structuralist theory: *Umbanda* offers a structure for the integration of contradictory elements, because it reflects and unites all the contradictions of a society in transition—a society economically, ethnically, and racially heterogeneous, and searching for its identity, an identity which must turn out to include oppositions in dialectical relationships to each other.

Although *Umbanda* is the most original of the "new" religions springing up in South America, it is not the only one. Batuque of the Para, born from the encounter of African *vodun* and of Amerindian *pagelance,* was studied by Seth and Ruth Leacock using life histories and case analyses with an eye to the motivations and psychology of its members,[16] but it is only of local interest. More important is the cult of *Maria Lionza* in Venezuela, of Indian origin, which is becoming more and more Africanized through contact with national and immigrant (Cuban) blacks and has given rise, in the past few years, to interesting descriptions and sociological reflections by Angelina Pollak-Eltz.[17] Clearly, a comparison of all these Afro-Latin-American religious innovations, perhaps including the rural messianic phenomena in South America (although blacks have a very secondary role there, if any)[18] could contribute to our knowledge of what a "new religion" is.

History

Is it not possible that the history of blacks in Latin America might be enriched by using the methods and orientation of cultural anthropology, by applying the perspectives we have just enumerated to the past, for example? This idea inspired one of Acosta Saignes' recent books on Venezuela, which, though concerned with events, particularly slave revolts, aims above all to reconstitute black *culture* as it existed under slavery: work techniques, diet, methods of healing the sick, matrimonial and sexual relationships, etc.[19] This could be related to an earlier work by Gilberto Freyre, *Maîtres et Esclaves*, which related descriptions of social history and the slave's everyday life more to the ecology and geography of the big plantation than to classical cultural anthropology. It could also be related to certain current attempts by black intellectuals, both in Anglo-Saxon America and in Latin America, to provide themselves with an ethnohistory separate from that which whites write for them. We would then have a continuum extending from the culture of the slavery system as a whole, at least in Portuguese countries (G. Freyre), through the culture of the slave under this system (Acosta Saignes), to ethnohistory as a foundation on which the American Negro can build his racial identity.

Social Anthropology

I would like to return now to the São Paulo School which arose from the new orientation resulting from the UNESCO inquiry. Although Florestan Fernandes, Henrique Cardoso and O. Ianni[20] differ from one another in the handling of method and the use of Marxist dialectics, this discussion will confine itself to what is common among them.

The first notion they emphasize is that of "totality." Contrary to what happens in cultural anthropology, facts are always considered on a macroscopic level, in all their historical-sociological and structural-functional aspects, and in terms of their connection and reciprocity. The black can be understood only in terms of his interactions with whites within a certain mode of organizing productive labor. The functionalists, of course, also give special status to the notion of "whole" or of system. One cannot, however, as the functionalists believe, arrive at the concrete from purely empirical research, for what defines the concrete is the pattern of affinities among empirical relationships, a pattern not defined by simple experience, but arrived at by the reasoning process. Furthermore, whereas functionalist theorists can understand social change only as a malfunction of the system, the São Paulo school authors see it as part of a continuum because they hold that social systems are not closed, but open, engaged in a process of dynamic evolution guided by human praxis. The dynamic aspects of the system of racial relations constituted the basis for the research of the São Paulo team in the states of Santa Catarina, the Parana, and the Rio Grande do Sul. The idea of "totality" is expanded to the point where what happens in Brazil can be understood only in terms of what happens in the rest of the world, and where the evolution and ultimate suppression of slavery are seen as mere manifestations of a broad dialectical movement from commercial and protected capitalism toward industrial and competitive capitalism.

The second major notion of the São Paulo school is that of praxis or human creativity. Since what interests our authors is flux and motion, their approach to the problems of blacks in Brazil is essentially historical. What distinguishes their approach from the classical historical one, or even from a historical approach emphasizing economic determinism, is that they attempt to observe history "in the making," step by step. The important thing, in other words, is not so much the historical situation itself, but the way various social participants perceive it. Their awareness alone gives meaning to things and guides their activity; indeed, "dialectics," as I understand it, is basically nothing more than this incessant exchange between creative man and the weight of socio-economic determinisms. Still another element removes this approach from that of linear, classical history: although events move from a *before* toward an *after*, our authors use the *after* to elucidate the *before*. When slavery was at its height, the ideology of the masters permeated the whole system and obscured its internal contradictions; when the system ceased to function satisfactorily, however, the crisis enabled observers to measure its uniqueness and to understand the meaning of the facts. The importance ascribed by our three authors to crises and internal conflicts is fundamental to their commitment since praxis is clearly favored by periods of competition. Florestan Fernandes, for example, defended the transition from accommodation to conflict, pointing out that conflict presents a chance for democratization of racial relations, whereas accommodation leads to the passive capitulation of blacks to whites.

In my opinion, the great value of this dialectical approach has been to debunk a good deal of data previously considered empirically established. These authors have shown that certain notions once held as factual—"racial democracy" in Latin America, the "progressive whitening or Aryanization" of the Brazilian population through the mixing of blood and of values,[21] and even the "luso-tropicalism" which Gilberto Freyre presents as a new "science" and not as a philosophy or aesthetic vision of colonization[22]—are nothing more than ideologies or myths evolving further with each crisis. They reveal that such notions are based on re-elaborations of a mental logic designed to insure the continuity, despite historical disruptions, of the social domination of one race by another. "Racial democracy," according to Ianni, is linked to the "metamorphosis" of the "slave" into the "Negro" and the "mulatto," a metamorphosis which began at the time of the emancipation crisis and marked the transition from slavery to the suppression of servile labor. "Luso-tropicalism" began with the contemporary crisis in which Brazil is being transformed from a traditional and very rural country to an urbanized and industrialized one.

There are, however, gaps in this approach. It entirely omits any study of black culture. If black culture were mentioned, even in parentheses, this would not be very grave, for the expert has every right to limit the object of his studies (despite his contradictory wish to study concrete "totalities"). More often than not, however, these authors deny black culture. They state, for example, that the Latin American world was so shaped by and for the white man, that the black man never had any say in how he should live, preserve his cultural heritage, or exert a creative cultural influence; and that the black, lacking the tools to create a coherent image of himself, is forced to understand himself in terms of the counterimage which the white man has of him. I agree that blacks remained on the fringe of historical events and the social processes of the industrial revolution. But does one have the right to carry this general observation of social anthropology into the area of culture?[23] I also agree that black culture is controlled by the white man, used by him for his own profit, and manipulated by the governing class; J. B. Borges Pereira's little pioneering book on the Negro, broadcast on São Paulo radio, proves it well, (see note 20), and the "folkorization" imposed by whites on Afro-Brazilian culture is a case in point. If, however, Afro-Brazilian culture can be manipulated, it must exist. And it is unfortunate that the São Paulo School did not try to integrate it into its own anthropological perspective. I tried to do this myself a few years ago by studying African religions in Brazil from the perspective of social anthropology rather than of cultural anthropology—by studying them, that is, in terms of their dialectical ties to the transformation of economic and social infra-structures.

Toward a New Vision of Afro-Latin-American Cultures

Three main conclusions can be drawn from this paper. First, even if empirical research dominates in terms of quantity, only theoretical research can draw the meaning of things, revealing what is hidden in the evidence. Secondly, during the last two or three decades, profound changes have occurred in the fields people choose to study; we have moved, for example, from a genetic cultural anthropology engaged in researching origins, to a structural-functionalist cultural anthropology. However, and this is my third conclusion, researchers too often used foreign theories, emanating from Europe or the United States, rather than theories based on their own analyses, thereby running the risk of neglecting the most original aspects of Afro-Latin-American data. The only exceptions to this rule were Guerreiro Ramos' affirmation of a black sociology based on the black Brazilian's awareness of himself and of his fate, and Deoscoredes dos Santos' revelation of an original cosmology and psychology, based on oral traditions transmitted from one generation to another by the priests of the *candomblés*.

Except in the immediate prewar period dominated by Arthur Ramos and giving rise to three Congresses on Afro-Brazilian Studies,[24] and the immediate post-war period (when UNESCO revolutionized the preoccupations of researchers), scholars interested in blacks have not been very numerous in Brazil. They are even less numerous in other South American countries. This is because, until very recently, Afro-Brazilian research was limited to members of the university community; except in the realm of folklore, with its contests and prizes, no other institution actively supported it. Thus, the only incentive for participating in such research has been the publication of a thesis. However, since Janio Quadros' short-lived Presidency of Brazil, and especially since the army assumed power, Brazilian politics has become a politics of reconciliation and solidarity with the new African states. This policy can bear fruit only if the government values Brazil's black people and their cultural contributions. A whole series of research institutions has sprung from this change. Previously, the only one was the Joaquim Nabuco Institute of Récife; although it was set up to encourage economic and social development of the northeast, thanks to Freyre and Ribeiro, it made an important contribution to Afro-Brazilian research. Among the new institutions are the Center for Afro-Oriental Studies—first affiliated with the University of Bahia but now under the authority of the Ministry of Foreign Affairs—with its journal *Afro-Asia*, which has published important articles by people like Vivaldo da Costa Lima and Rolf Reichert; and the Centers for African Studies at the Universities of Rio de Janeiro and of São Paulo, with their post-graduate courses and seminars. During my recent trip I observed with great satisfaction that well-prepared young researchers in Afro-Brazilian affairs were getting ready to relieve the old researchers. Funding for future research projects, however, is still a problem; one can only seek money from foundations which have more general goals, such as the *Fundacao de Amparo á Pesquisa do Estado de São Paulo*.

At present, it is difficult to foresee the future direction of Afro-Latin-American studies or to predict what kind of position the black intellectuals gathering in the universities will occupy. Clearly, however, social anthropology will be the springboard for tomorrow's research because it has shown that the Afro-Brazilian can only be understood within the network which ties him to the society as a whole, and thus that Brazilian society must be studied as a pluralistic one from now on, rather than as a series of individual segments, including a very separate black segment. But to analyze the pluralistic society, future researchers must overstep social anthropology by including cultural anthropology, for it is cultural values which mediate among individuals and among social groups, and constitute the basis for the interaction networks and the semantic fields which give social groups their meaning. Fortunately for Brazil, these researchers must also discover new concepts, ones which will enable Brazil to free herself from old categories, such as those of "caste" and "social class," which, though still useful, have now almost depleted their heuristic fruitfulness. I shall limit myself to one example, the one I have studied in most depth. One cannot understand Afro-Brazilian religions in isolation from other religions which fulfill analogous functions within the same social strata, such as folk Catholicism or the Pentacostal movement. One must lump them all together on the market of beliefs and look at them through an economic model, in isolation from other forms of power.[25] Seen from this point of view, Afro-Brazilian religions are a manifestation of the search for a power effective against the forms of power monopolized by the whites, and thus are best seen in terms of a political model.

I could make analogous statements concerning other areas, such as black folklore or the structure of the black family. The important thing is to find new methods of analysis which can elucidate phenomena which have thus far been slighted because they were dealt with only in terms of limited perspectives, and of categories dating from the beginning of the twentieth century. Then it will become clear that black culture is not, as it appears, frozen into a system of defense mechanisms too rigid for change, but a living culture, capable of constant creation, keeping in step with the rhythms of change in the global society, of which it is not a marginal but a dialectical element.

REFERENCES

1. Marvin Harris, "Referential Ambiguity in the Calculus of Brazilian Racial Identity," *Afro-American Anthropology*, ed. Norman E. Whitten, Jr. and J. F. Szwed (New York: The Free Press, 1970), pp. 75-86.

2. Gilberto Freyre, *Casa Grande e Senzala* (Rio de Janeiro: J. Olympio, 5th ed., 1946).

3. Melville J. Herkovits, *Pesquisas Etnologicas na Bahia* (Bahia: Publicaçõe de Museu da Bahia, 1943).

4. Roger Bastide, *Metodologia Afro-Brasileira*, I, *O metodo liquistico* (São Paulo: Revista do Arquivo Municipal da São Paulo, 1939); II, *O metodo psicanalitico* (*idem*, 1943); III, *Estudos Afro-brasileiros* (*idem*, 1944).

5. UNESCO-Anhembi, *Relacoẽs raciais entre Negros e Brancos em São Paulo* (São Paulo: Anhembi, 1955); L. A. da Costa Pinto, *O negro ao Rio de Janeiro* (Rio de Janeiro: Companhia Editora Nacional, 1953); C. Wagley, ed., *Races et Classes dans le Brésil rural* (UNESCO); Thales de Azevedo, *Les élites de couleur dans une ville brésilienne* (UNESCO, 1953); Réne Ribeiro, *Religião e Relacões raciais* (Rio de Janeiro: Ministerion de Educaçāo e Cultura, 1956).

6. In this article we are not going to deal with Van den Berghe and his dichotomy between the two racial situations, paternalistic and competitive, since—although we have brought Van den Berghe into the study of racial relations in Brazil in terms of stereotypes, norms and interracial behavior in São Paulo (*American Sociological Review*, 22, No. 6 [1957])—Van den Berghe's work evolves outside South America. The Brazilian example would be relevant to show that the two derived types belong to one and the same transformation group.

7. Guerreiro Ramos, "O problema do negro na sociologia brasileira," *Cadernos do Noso Tempo*, 2 (1954), pp. 207-215.

8. Abdias do Nascimento, ed., *O Negro Rebelde* (Rio de Janeiro: Ed. G. R. D., 1968).

9. *The African Religions in Brazil During the Industrial Era* (Paris: Flammarion, forthcoming).

10. Pierre Verger, *Notes sur les cultes des Orisa et Vodun à Bahia, la Baie de tous les Saints au Brésil et à l'ancienne Côte des esclaves en Afrique* (Dakar: IFAN, 1957).

11. The book in which I called young researchers to a new approach to the world of the *candomblé* appeared, in Portuguese, under the title of *Imagenes do Nordeste misto en branco e preto* (Rio de Janeiro: 1945). The book where I present the Afro-Brazilian conception of man and the cosmos appeared in French under the title of *Le Candomblé de Bahia, rite nagô* (The Hague: Mouton, 1958).

12. Blackness, as a political ideology, is the black's answer to the white's challenge. However, precisely because it is, the "answer" is determined *a priori* by the structure of the challenge; in other words, it is "colonized" by the way the white man has put the terms which serve as its stimulus. On the other hand, true blackness does not encumber itself with polemics, it is an existential affirmation.

13. Rainer Flasche, *Geschichteund Typologie afrikanisches Religiosität in Brasilien* (Marburg an der Lahn: Marburger Studien zur Afrika und Asien Kunde, 1973).

14. Candido Procopio de Camargo, *Aspectos sociologicos del espiritismo en São Paulo* (Friburg: Feres, 1961).

15. R. Bastide, *Religions Africaines au Brésil* (Paris: Presses Universitaires, 1960), Ch. IV; Hanns-Albert Steger, "Revolutionäre Hintergründe der Kreolischen Synkretismus," *Int. Jahrbuch für Religionsoziologie* (Koln: Bd. VI, 1970); L. Weingertner, *Umbanda-Synkretische Kulte in Brasilien* (Erlander: Evangelical Lutheran Mission, 1969); Savino Mombelli, *Umbanda, Fede e Civiltà*, 9-10 (1971); Rainer Flasche, *op. cit.*; Esther Pressel, "Umbanda in São Paulo: Religious Innovation in a Developing Society," *Religion, Altered States of Consciousness and Social Change*, ed. E. Bourguignon (Columbus, Ohio: Ohio State University Press, 1973), pp. 264-318; Horst H. Figge, *Geisterkuit, Besessenheit, und Magie in der Umbanda Religion Bresiliens* (München: Alber Freiburg, 1973).

16. Seth and Ruth Leacock, *Spirits of the Deep* (New York: American Museum of Natural History, 1971).

17. Angelina Pollak-Eltz, *Cultos Afroamericanos* (Caracas: Univ. Catol. Andres Bello, 1972).

18. As those studied by Maria-Isaura P. de Queiroz, for example, in *Images messianiques du Brésil* (Cuernavaca, Mexico: *Sondeos*, No. 87, 1973).

19. Miguel Acosta Saignes, *Vida de los esclavos negros en Venezuela* (Caracas: Hesperides, 1967).

20. Florestan Fernandes, *A integração do negro à sociedade de classes* (São Paulo: Thesis, 1964); *O Negro no mundo dos brancos* (São Paulo: Difusão Européia do Livro, 1973); Fernando Henrique Cardoso, *Capitalismo e Escravidão* (São Paulo: Difusão Européia do Livro, 1962); Oactavio Ianni, *As metamorfoses do escravo* (São Paulo: Difusão Européia do Livro, 1962). The last comer to Afro-Brazilian research in São Paulo, Joao Bastista Borges Pereira, can be linked to this São Paulo School, even though his early Marxism has been abandoned—*Côr, professão e mobilidade* (São Paulo: Bibl. Pioneira, 1967).

21. We are speaking of Latin America in general, because Mexican sociologists have taken up, for the Indian, what the São Paulo School had already established for the black, through similar analyses, showing, for example, that the Indian does not define himself "culturally" but rather by dialectical opposition to the *Ladino*, while the progressive *ladinization* of the Indian was more a myth to hide the genocide of the Indian than an effort to move him toward modern civilization.

22. G. Freyre, *O mundo que o português criou* (Rio de Janeiro: J. Olympio, 1940); *Aventura e rotina* (Lisboa: Livros do Brasil): G. Freyre's luso-tropicalism is not of direct concern to this article since he wishes to define a science of the adaptation of the white man to tropical life, but it is of indirect concern insofar as the idea of racial democracy is a part of the Portuguese mentality.

23. The problem is discussed, in part, in the book edited by Jürgen Gräbener, *Klassengeselschaft und Rassismus*, dedicated to the problem of Negro marginalism (Düsseldorf: Bertelsmann Universitätsverlag, 1971); See the texts by F. Fernandes and R. Bastide.

24. We should add the magnificent collection of data from the Mission Mario de Andrade in the northeast and in Amazonia, funded by the São Paulo Prefecture. This data was published after the death of Mario Andrade, through the care of one of his disciples, Oneyda Alvarenga, in the collections of the Municipal Record Library of São Paulo. The loss of Mario de Andrade unfortunately deprived us of the interpretation which could have been given to these facts.

25. Jean Ziegler, *Le Pouvoir africain* (Paris: Ed. du Seuil, 1971).

J. F. ADE. AJAYI
E. J. ALAGOA

Black Africa: The Historians' Perspective

MAN MAKES HISTORY, in a fashion, and history also makes man. As with other men, the historical experience of the African over the centuries has had a profound effect on his self-image as well as on his perception of the external world. Perhaps more than other men, the African in precolonial times developed a strong historical tradition, and his perception of himself and his world came to depend very much on his view of the past. European colonialism, brief as it was, produced a traumatic effect largely because it tried to impose on the African a gross distortion of this historical tradition.

It is clear from the historical research of the past two or three decades that Black Africa has a long and variegated history. Before the Europeans burst in on this world, there were many other conquerors and agents of change both from within and from beyond the continent. The story of change over the centuries—gradual and rapid, peaceful and violent, local and widespread, superficial and fundamental—is being pieced together.

It is significant, however, that the African viewed this past as remarkably stable and continuous. The African historical tradition accepted the factor of change, of course. There were stories of migrations and wars, of the origins and extinction of peoples, of the founding and breaking up of cities and states. But migrations, change, and renewal were regarded as part of the continuous flow of history. There was a past, a present, and a future, but they were linked inextricably together. The past to a large extent determined the present, as the present would determine the future.

The historical tradition was a central part of a religion and philosophy that stressed continuity and stability as essential factors in a healthy relationship between man and nature, between man and the gods, between members of one community, and between communities. Historical myths explained the origin of these relationships, and thus regulated them. Ancestral cults demonstrated in ritual the continued relevance of the past and of the laws and institutions established in the past. Within the historical tradition, these laws and institutions provided the only valid bases for present laws and institutions. King lists and genealogies provided the valid charters for ruling dynasties. The most far-reaching change in the present was justifiable as a return to the precedents of the past. Indeed, change was not acceptable unless it could be thus related to the past.

The historical tradition did not attempt to detail so much as to understand the historical experience, to draw attention to salient features of the past that were regarded as significant and of continuing relevance. It was not interested in chronological explanations of cause and effect. Its approach was often philosophical, employing myth, allegory and symbolism.[1] Thus, when the Igala of central Nigeria gathered at the graves of their kings in the royal cemetery called *Ojaina*, only twenty-three graves were individually identified, though the number of kings spanning the history of the kingdom was obviously larger. Twenty-two graves represented rulers of the present dynasty, while a single grave served collectively to represent the graves of all remote past rulers. In ritual functions, only nine graves were used, eight of the most recent to validate the current dynastic structure in which the crown rotated among four lineages, and a ninth to represent all those not individually named.[2]

This functionalism, this readiness to use the past in the present, did not imply that the present was only a copy of the past. On the contrary, the recent past was often disapproved of and seen as brutish, while the remote past of the founding ancestors was generally seen as wonderful and much to be preferred to the present. It was in fact because the ancestors were seen as wiser and better that the rules they laid down for the government of society were accepted without much dispute. The founding ancestors were remembered as god-like or close to the gods in their life, and were often translated into gods at their death.[3] Accounts of their doings often transcended prosaic historical narrative into poems and songs, such as those the *griots* of Mali used to declaim on the harp.

Yet in spite of this conceptualization of a prosaic recent past and a glorious remote past, a sense of continuity was maintained. The living identified themselves with the founding ancestors, and each man's self-confidence derived largely from his pride in them. He faced odds and tribulations in the knowledge that they continued to care about what happened to him. The youth were taught to know and revere their ancestors. The elders, who were seen to be drawing closer to the ancestors, were regarded as potential recruits to their ranks and deemed to possess similar power to influence the actions and fortunes of future generations.

This historical tradition emphasized the solidarity and uniqueness of each community. It was the source of strength that made the African so resilient. It ensured his ability to absorb and refashion foreign influences in the light of his total historical experience. Ethiopia evolved its own brand of Christianity and utilized biblical lore to build up a tradition of the Solomonid descent of the dynasty much like the traditions of origin of so many other African kingdoms. Similarly, West African Islam developed along lines consistent with reverence for ancestors, the solidarity of the lineage, and the continuity of its historical traditions.[4]

The Colonial Experience

Having conquered through the technological superiority of their armaments, Europeans sought to maintain control over Africans not only through technology, but also through moral and psychological defeatism. Their view of Africa grew out of the traders' accounts and fables of the slave trade era compounded by the missionary propaganda and the racial theories of the nineteenth century.[5] They asserted that there was no African history because the African ancestors had done nothing worthy of historical attention, and that while others had been making history, Africans had been passive recipients or mere spectators of the march of human development. They claimed that the colonial era represented new departures and new initiatives with no continuities with the precolonial African historical experience.[6] They tried to ignore, if not abolish, the African historical tradition, to cut the African away from his past, and to deny that the past was relevant to his present or future. In this way they struck at the core of the religion that gave him self-confidence and the philosophy that helped him maintain a balanced relationship with his internal and external impulses. This attempt to cut the African adrift from his historical experience and in effect to undermine his basic humanity was the most upsetting feature of European colonialism.

Needless to say, in retrospect it appears that the impact of this experience has been exaggerated, and that wide areas never felt the full impact of European colonialism. Nevertheless, an initial feeling of shock, disorientation, and loss of identity were widespread. Those who came most directly under the influence of European ideas reacted in a variety of ways, but generally with the object of finding a sustaining religion and philosophy. Some tried to reaffirm their faith in the old religion, but found the old deities rather impotent against the new forces unleashed by the white man. Many turned toward Islam as a world religion that could rival the European's, but was better adapted than Christianity to the African historical experience. Others rushed to accept the white man's religion, to learn his new ways and the secrets of his technology. Before long, however, it was obvious that Africans were interpreting the new religion in terms of the old, and that the old religion continued to be the source of their values and philosophy of life.[7]

Basic to these forms of readjustment, to this "politics of survival,"[8] was the effort to rehabilitate African history and reestablish the relevance of the African historical experience. Essentially, Africans and Europeans entered into an intellectual struggle for the control of the African mind. Since the European was already in charge physically, and had established the machinery for intellectual control as well, the struggle had to be carried out in the European medium and on terms acceptable to the European. For the disoriented African to reestablish his identity, he had not merely to satisfy himself that he had a relevant past, he had also to convince his captors and mentors of this. He had to demonstrate the continuity of African history and the relevance of the precolonial experience to the predicament of Black Africans not merely in philosophical and symbolic myths as of old, but in terms of a Western historiography based on chronological explanations of cause and effect.

It is significant that there were always some in the Western world who did not readily accept the facile theory of European moral and psychological superiority over the African. Some of these were Africans of the diaspora who, for their own survival, asserted through publications such as the *Journal of Negro History* that there had to be an African past that was relevant. There were also radicals in the European world who found a vigor in African art and cosmologies that they found lacking in the depressed Europe of the First World War.[9] But these early assertions of the existence of African history lacked content and utterly failed to convince those who had to be convinced of the relevance of the African's historical experience.

The data needed for a rehabilitation of African history had to come from within

Africa, first in the recordings of oral tradition, ancient lore, customs, and laws, compiled by patriotic amateurs imbued with a sense of the importance of these evidences of past cultural resilience.[10] Although these were often recorded with much apologia, and an explicit acceptance of the moral superiority of the white man and his culture, they provided data that others could use. The European rulers too began to draw attention to a few fragments of Arabic chronicles and early Portuguese accounts about Africa. More important still, even as they asserted their own superiority and denied the existence of African history, many European administrators, missionaries, traders, and anthropologists recorded oral traditions and other ethnographic data. The Intelligence Reports of the colonial period, for example, are much sought after by historians. An essential feature of such writings, however, was that they painted a static picture of African society; they interpreted the continuity of African historical traditions as a total absence of historical development. Where the evidence of such development was clear, they attributed it to external agents like the Arabs, or European traders, or imaginary "Hamitic" influences.[11]

Attempts to reinterpret this data began with anticolonial propaganda by African nationalists[12] in alliance with Africans of the diaspora and radical Europeans, but they carried no great conviction. However, two important themes began to emerge even during the colonial period which have had much influence on later developments. The first was a correction of the idea that Africans had no large-scale political organizations in the past. Nationalist propagandists pointed to evidence of major empires, particularly in the Sudanic regions of black Africa. In the tradition of the golden remote past of heroic ancestors, such works as *African Glory* and *African Empires of the Past*[13] emerged, based on recordings of epic poems of the *griots* of the Western Sudan and other local historians, archaeological evidence of such great ruins as at Zimbabwe, and fragments of Arabic literature. There was little direct information available about who built the empires and in what circumstances, or about their internal structures, weaknesses, and achievements. There were, for the most part, only eulogies, which did little to convince either educated Africans or Europeans that there was a direct relationship among the history of those empires, the historical experience of Africans, and their predicament in the colonial situation. Yet the point was made that the African claim to independence had a possible basis in the history of precolonial kingdoms and empires. This put a premium on political history per se, and it was accorded the highest priority in the program to reestablish the relevance of the African historical experience.

The second theme was a denial of the European idea that African society was small scale and fragmented, comprised of various elements which were at one another's throats in a chaotic struggle that not only explained their backwardness and lack of historical development, but also justified European colonialism. Nationalist propagandists asserted that, in spite of frequent wars and apparent fragmentation, there was a basic unity of all African cultures; that these cultures had long historical roots reaching back to a common source in Ancient Egypt and Merowe; and that the Europeans were trying to balkanize African society through the imposition of arbitrary colonial boundaries. This theme, which has been taken up by several scholars,[14] has still not won much of a following, but it established the necessity, in the rehabilitation of the African experience, of emphasizing the long historical perspective and of thinking in terms of the entire continent rather than of the uniqueness of individual African cultures.

The Politics of Decolonization

The Second World War marked a significant watershed in the process of reestablishing the relevance of the African historical experience. Until then, professionally trained historians had been little involved, either in Africa or in the Western world, in the debate between colonial and anticolonial propagandists. The most notable group of scholars involved in the debate had been anthropologists championing on the one hand the static, functionalist view of African society, or struggling on the other to establish the idea that African cultures shared a basic unity and historical development. However, the increased vigor of the movement toward political independence brought with it a rapid expansion of education and the establishment of new universities in Africa. The universities raised the issue of what history should be taught to African students, and began to involve professional historians in the politics of decolonization.

Hitherto, on the assumption that Africans had no history, schools had taught courses in British Imperial history; similarly, the new universities devised syllabuses on European activities in Africa, taking as their basic text, Harry Johnston's *Colonization of Africa by Alien Races*. The typical doctoral thesis of students trying to understand what was happening in Africa was to study in detail British, French, Belgian, German or Italian policy *toward* some part of Africa. The minutes of officials in the colonial offices seemed to explain all that needed knowing about Africa. Later, emphasis shifted to the personalities and policies of the European officials—the men on the spot. Goldie became the "Maker of Nigeria" and Lugard the "Founder of Modern Nigeria."[15] There were studies of the conquest of African peoples; the drawing of boundaries; the emancipation of slaves; the building of ports, railways, and new urban centers; the raising of colonial armies and police; and the economic policies of the governments. However, all these were viewed not as factors in the lives of African peoples—in which case one would have asked how they affected Africans and what Africans thought of them—but as extensions of the colonial will. Africans were featured in the accounts only as "natives," and the "native policies" of different colonial governments were compared and sharply contrasted. The assumption was that policies were carried out more or less as described by the colonial officials writing up their reports and worrying about their next promotions. Africans remained nameless chiefs or miseducated agitators who represented no one but themselves, and raised irrelevant noises of protest at various aspects of colonial native and economic policies.

Since anticolonial propaganda had failed to establish the high standards and foreign acceptability so essential to the politics of decolonization, the new nationalist governments emerging in Africa were willing to invest funds in a more scholarly approach to African history. The immediate task of the professional historians was to translate the political slogans of the time—"Négritude" and the "African Personality"—into scholarly historical works: to make Africans the *dramatis personae* of African history, to view African history from within on a continental basis, to examine the roots and historical development of African cultures, and to base their writing on material and methodologies acceptable by the standards of historiography in the Western world.

Two factors were important in this new development. The first was the initiative of African scholars such as Dr. K. O. Dike and Dr. S. O. Biobaku,[16] who were trained as professional historians in the traditions of the Western world and anxious to promote a scholarly study of the African past. The second was the series of international conferences on African history and archaeology, beginning with the meetings in the School of Oriental and African Studies in London in the 1950's.[17] These emphasized the importance of nonwritten sources of African history and the need for interdisciplinary cooperation in collecting and evaluating them. The initiative of African scholars encouraged African governments to invest money in interdisciplinary research projects and generally to encourage the scholarly study of African history as educationally, socially and politically desirable. Centers and Institutes of African Studies also developed in various parts of Europe and the Americas, initially with significant emphasis on studies of the African past. Historical research on Africa blossomed in the late 1950's and early 1960's.[18] There was systematic collection not only of oral material,[19] but also of manuscripts in European, Arabic, Kiswahili, Hausa and other African languages.[20] These, as well as previously exploited colonial and missionary records, were reviewed in the light of fresh historical insights.

These researches and the interdisciplinary cooperation promised to yield much fruit. Systematic projects in archaeology replaced reliance on accidental finds. Archaeology offered the best prospect for a long perspective of the African past. The processes of radio-carbon dating promised to solve some of the problems of chronology in African history.[21] The important discoveries of the Leakey family in the Olduvai Gorge vastly extended the information provided by the earlier discoveries of Australopithecine in South Africa, and placed Africa in the position of the cradle of humanity. The evidence of the artifact and fossil is difficult to deny, and archaeology has already gone some way to establish that Africa in antiquity was by no means a laggard in human development.[22] Archaeology, however, is expensive and the scientific interpretation needed to transform archaeological finds into historical data has been slow.

Similarly, linguistic classification as an index of relationships on a broad historical canvas and as a source of leads on the directions of human migration; glottochronology and lexicostatistics as a means of calculating chronologies for the separation between languages or dialects of the same language; proto-language reconstruction as a method for determining the historical relationships between dialects of the same language complex[23]—all have opened up new vistas for African history, even if conclusive results have not been as readily forthcoming as anticipated.

Cooperation with the social sciences[24] has provided historians with much of their methodology for handling oral material. Many historians have also learnt the value of models as research tools, although they would insist that models are no substitutes for historical inquiry, since models "set out the necessary rather than the sufficient conditions for the developments which they seek to explain."[25]

History for Self-Government

These efforts at interdisciplinary research succeeded in getting African history accepted as a valid intellectual discipline in the universities. It was accepted that Africans had a past worthy of historical attention and that there was enough evidence, written and unwritten, to write African history which revolved around the lives of Africans.[26] Initially, attention was focused on the well-documented periods of the last stages of precolonial African history and the colonial era. There was also a dominant interest in political history which demonstrated the African's ability at political organization, diplomacy, and statecraft, including the management of wars both between African combatants and against European invaders.

However, as the African states began to face the challenges of independence, decolonization came to require more than a strategy for bargaining with former European rulers. It came to involve the more positive objectives of establishing national integration and mass involvement in national life, new philosophies to achieve more rapid social and economic development, less dependence on the Western world, and a greater capacity for self-reliance and self-direction. The concept of African history worked out in the era of decolonization proved inadequate. Although it enabled the African politician to hold up his head with pride vis à vis the rest of the world, it did not equip him with the understanding and sense of values necessary for reshaping his own society.

As early as the International Conference on African History held at Dar-es-Salaam in 1965, issues began to be raised about the continuity of African history and its role in African development, including some affirmation that "it is only the African people who through an interpretation and safe-guarding of their history can say what they were, what they are and what they want to be."[27]

The challenges of self-government have thus raised again the relevance of the total historical experience of black Africans. No doubt, the colonial period has left its mark. The African historical tradition has been demythologized. African history is no longer only of local significance to each African people, but has a universal importance as an aspect of human history. Thus, African historians now work within a new system. Nevertheless, the role of history within African society remains essentially the same: to provide a sense of continuity, and to explain to each person and to each people where they fit into the scheme of things. A man's self-perception is vital to what he does and his self-perception is still largely the result of his view of history. If African history is to provide the African with this self-perception, and thus to play an effective role in independent Africa, it has to correct the distortion and bridge the gap created by the colonial experience in the African historical tradition. African history must evolve its own identity independent of Western historiography, the shackles of outside acceptability notwithstanding.

In the last decade, there have been developments in various directions. The needs of schools and universities have encouraged the historical synthesis of peoples within state-boundaries which are not always the most significant ones historically. Sometimes there has been insistence that Africans should dominate not merely among the chief characters in written African history but also among the historians themselves, even in such international cooperative projects as the UNESCO General History of Africa.[28]

The most significant developments, however, have been those involving the subject matter of African history. Attempts at national histories have shown how important it is that historians cover the more recent parts of the twentieth century as well as the earlier periods before the nineteenth century. Even more, they have shown how much of the African past cannot be covered if historians are preoccupied with large kingdoms and empires. There is an increasing interest in the histories of small-scale societies. This in itself draws attention to the importance of nonpolitical kinds of history. Interest in the history of such societies focuses not on political organization and war, but on problems of origin and migrations, on social and economic institutions as factors of change and development, and on religion as a source of values and ideas in a society.[29]

It is in an emphasis on social and economic history that African historiography can show the relationship between the concerns of historians and the preoccupations of modern African states.[30] Similarly, it is through an emphasis on cultural, religious[31] and intellectual history that the continuity of African history and the relevance of the total historical experience of black Africans to their present predicament can be explored. We are far from definitive conclusions, but we are clearer as to what our role and preoccupations ought to be.

REFERENCES

1. Cf. Bolaji Idowu, *Olodumare: God in Yoruba Belief* (London: 1962); Jack Goody, *The Myth of the Bagre* (Oxford: 1973); Marcel Griaule, *Conversations with Ogotemmeli* (London: 1965).

2. J. S. Boston, *The Igala Kingdom* (Ibadan: 1968); "Oral Tradition and the History of Igala," *Journal of African History*, 10, No. 1 (1969), pp. 29-43.

3. There is some controversy concerning the status of the ancestors, as to whether they were worshipped as gods or merely regarded as "dead elders" worthy of the respect due to elders and to the dead. In many parts of Africa the rituals for the ancestors are indistinguishable from those for the gods. See Igor Kopytoff, "Ancestors as Elders in Africa," *Africa*, 41, No. 2 (1971), pp. 129-142; James L. Brain, "Ancestors as Elders in Africa—Further Thoughts," *Africa*, 63, No. 2 (1973), pp. 122-133.

4. K. O. Dike and J. F. Ade. Ajayi, "African Historiography," *International Encyclopaedia of the Social Sciences*, 6 (1968), pp. 394-400.

5. P. D. Curtin, *The Image of Africa, British Ideas and Action, 1780-1850* (Madison, Wis.: University of Wisconsin Press 1964).

6. J. F. Ade. Ajayi, "Colonialism: An Episode in African History," *Colonialism in Africa, 1870-1960*, Vol. I of *The History and Politics of Colonialism, 1870-1914*, ed. L. H. Gann and Peter Duignan (Cambridge: Cambridge University Press, 1969), pp. 497-509.

7. J. F. Ade. Ajayi and M. Crowder, "West Africa 1919-1939: The Colonial Situation," *History of West Africa*, ed. Ajayi and Crowder, 2 (London: Longmans, 1974).

8. J. F. Ade. Ajayi, "The Continuity of African Institutions Under Colonialism," *Emerging Themes of African History*, ed. T. O. Ranger, Proceedings of the International Congress of African Historians (Dar-es-Salaam: 1965), pp. 189-200.

9. D. C. Gordon, *Self-Determination and History in the Third World* (Princeton: Princeton University

Press, 1971), pp. 105-108; Joseph Ki-Zerbo, *Histoire de l'Afrique noire, d'Heir à Demain* (Paris: 1972), pp. 478-479.

10. See S. A. Kiwanuka, *History of Buganda from the Foundation to 1900* (London: Longmans, 1971); Apolo Kagwa, *Ebika Bya Buganda* (1912), and *Bassekabaka Be Buganda* (London: 1927); S. Johnson, *History of the Yorubas* (London: 1921—completed in 1897); J. U. Egharevba, *A Short History of Benin* (Lagos: 1934—first published in Edo); Rupert East, trans., *Akiga's Story: The Tiv Tribe as Seen by One of Its Members* (London: 1965—first published in 1939); William A. Moore, *History of Itsekiri* (London: 1970—first edition 1936). Also T. Hodgkin, *Nigerian Perspectives* (London: 1960), p. 9, citing early chronicles, such as Ahmad Ib Fartua of Borno and al-Hajji Sa'id, *History of Sokoto*.

11. C. G. Seligman, *Races of Africa* (London: 1930).

12. For example, E. W. Blyden, *West Africa Before Europe* (London: 1905); J. C. Casely-Hayford, *Ethiopia Unbound: Studies in Racial Emancipation* (London: 1911); Nnamdi Azikiwe, *Renascent Africa* (Lagos: 1937).

13. J. C. de Graft-Johson, *African Glory* (New York: 1954); *African Empires of the Past* (Paris: Présence Africaine, 1957).

14. For example, J. O. Lucas, *The Religion of the Yorubas* (Lagos: 1948); and *Religions in West Africa and Ancient Egypt* (Apapa: 1970); Cheik Anta Diop, *L'Unité culturelle de l'Afrique Noire* (1959), *Nations nègre et culture* (Paris, Présence Africaine, 1954 & 1968), and *Antériorité des civilisations nègre: mythe ou vérité historique* (Paris: Présence Africaine, 1967).

15. J. E. Flint, *Sir George Goldie and the Making of Nigeria* (London: 1960); M. Perham, *Lugard, The Maker of Modern Nigeria*, Vol. II of *The Years of Authority, 1898-1945* (London: 1960).

16. K. O. Dike, *Trade and Politics in the Niger Delta, 1830-1895* (London: 1956); and S. O. Biobaku, *The Egba and Their Neighbours* (London: 1957). Dike later directed the Benin Historical Research Scheme and Biobaku the Yoruba Historical Research Scheme.

17. In 1953, 1957, 1961. See *Journal of African History*, 3, No. 2 (1962). Also papers of the Northwestern University symposium of 1962, published in C. Gabel and N. R. Bennet, eds., *Reconstructing African Culture History* (Boston: 1967); J. Vansina, R. Mauny, L. V. Thomas, eds., *The Historian in Tropical Africa*, studies presented at the fourth International African Seminar at the University of Dakar, Senegal, 1961 (London: 1964); Daryll Forde, "Tropical African Studies; A Report on the Conference Organised by the International African Institute in Conjunction with the University of Ibadan, 5-11 April, 1964," *Africa*, 35, No. 1 (1965), pp. 30-97; Lalage Brown and Michael Crowder, eds., *The Proceedings of the First International Congress of Africanists, Accra, December 1962* (London: Longmans, 1964).

18. The development was most noticeable in English-speaking Africa. There have, however, been notable works also on French-speaking Africa—for example: Abbe Alexis Kagame, *L'histoire des armées-bovines dans l'ancien Rwanda* (1961), and *Un abrégé de l'ethno-Histoire du Rwanda* (Butare: 1972); Abdullahi Ly, *La formation de l'economie sucriere et le développement du marché d'esclaves africains dans les iles françaises d'Amérique au XVII* (Paris: Présence Africaine, 1957); *La Compagnie du Sénégal de 1673 à 1696* (Paris: Présence Africaine, 1958); D. T. Niane & J. Suret-Canale, *Histoire de l'Afrique Occidentale* (Paris: Présence Africaine, 1961); D. T. Niane, *Sundiata, An Epic of Old Mali*, trans. G. D. Pickett (London: Longmans, 1965).

19. See, for example, J. Vansina, "Recording the Oral History of the Bakuba," *Journal of African History*, 1, No. 1 (1960), pp. 45-53; *De la tradition orale*, Annales du Musée Royal de l'Afrique Centrale, No. 36 (Tervuren: 1961), translated as *Oral Tradition: A Study in Historical Methodology* (Chicago: 1965); "The Use of Oral Tradition in African Culture History," *Reconstructing African Culture History*, ed. Gabel & Bennet (1967), pp. 55-82; "The Use of Ethnographic Data as Sources for History," *Emerging Themes*, ed. T. O. Ranger (1968), pp. 97-124; Jan Vansina, "Once Upon a Time: Oral Traditions as History in Africa," *Daedalus* (Spring 1971), pp. 442-468.

20. For an account of the situation in 1960, see Philip D. Curtin, "The Archives of Tropical Africa: A Reconnaissance," *Journal of African History*, 1, No. 1 (1960), pp. 129-147.

21. See proceedings of an international conference on African Chronology, 1966, in *Journal of African History*, 11, No. 2 (1970); D. P. Henige, "Oral Tradition and Chronology," *Journal of African History*, 12, No. 3 (1971), pp. 371-389; Brian M. Fagan, "Radiocarbon Dates for Sub-Saharan Africa (from c. 1000 B.C.)," *Journal of African History*, 2, No. 1 (1961), pp. 137-139; 4, No. 1 (1963), pp. 127-128; 6, No. 1 (1965), pp. 107-116; 8, No. 3 (1967), pp. 513-527; 10, No. 1 (1969), pp. 149-169; Frank Willett, "A Survey of Recent Results in the Radiocarbon Chronology of Western and Northern Africa," *Journal of African History*, 12, No. 3 (1971), pp. 339-370; J. E. G. Sutton, "New Radiocarbon Dates for Eastern and Southern Africa," 13, No. 1 (1972), pp. 177-187; cf. W. F. Libby, *Radiocarbon Dating* (Chicago: University of Chicago Press, 1952); Thurstan Shaw, "Radiocarbon Dates from Nigeria," *Journal Hist. Soc. Nigeria*, 3, No. 4 (1967), pp. 743-751.

22. Mary D. Leakey, *Olduvai Gorge: Excavations in Beds I and II, 1960-1963* (Cambridge: 1971); L. S. B. Leakey, *Adam's Ancestors: The Evolution of Man and His Culture* (New York: 1960). See also numbers of *Azania*, the archaeological journal of the British Institute of East Africa.

23. J. Greenberg, *Studies in African Linguistic Classification* (New Haven: Yale University Press, 1949-1950), reprinted in *Languages of Africa* (Mouton: 1966); also "Linguistic Evidence Regarding Bantu Origins," *Journal of African History*, 13, No. 2 (1972), pp. 189-216; M. Guthrie, "Bantu Origins; A Tentative Hypothesis," *Journal of African Languages*, 1 (1962), pp. 9-21; Robert G. Armstrong, "The Use of Linguistic and Ethnographic Data in the Study of Idoma and Yoruba History," *The Historian in Tropical Africa*, J. Vansina, *et al.*, pp. 127-144; "Glottochronology and African Linguistics," *Journal of African History*, 3, No. 2 (1962), pp. 283-290; D. H. Hymes, "Lexicostatistics So Far," *Current Anthropology*, 1 (1960), pp. 3-44; Kay Williamson, "Some Food Plant Names in the Niger Delta," *International Journal of American Linguistics*, 36, No. 2 (1970), pp. 156-167. Prof. Williamson has also been engaged in reconstructing proto-Ijo.

24. Some West African examples are M. G. Smith, *Government in Zazzau* (London: 1960); G. I. Jones, *The Trading States of the Oil Rivers* (London: 1963); I. M. Lewis, ed., *History and Social Anthropology* (London: 1968); D. Forde and P. M. Kaberry, eds., *West African Kingdoms in the Nineteenth Century* (London: 1967); P. C. Lloyd, *The Political Development of Yoruba Kingdoms in the Eighteenth and Nineteenth Centuries* (London: 1971); R. Horton, "From Fishing Village to City-State: A Social History of New Calabar," *Man in Africa*, eds. Douglas and Kaberry (London: 1969).

25. R. C. C. Law, "Anthropological Models in Yoruba History," *Africa*, 43, No. 1 (1973), pp. 18-26.

26. A. T. Porter, "History," *Africa in the Wider World, the Interrelationship of Area and Comparative Studies*, eds. D. Brokensha and M. Crowder (London: 1967), pp. 85-103.

27. T. O. Ranger, ed., *Emerging Themes of African History*, Proceedings of the International Congress of African Historians held at University College, Dar-es-Salaam, October, 1965 (London: 1968).

28. The following editors have been chosen:
    Vol. 1 *Methodology & Prehistory:* J. Ki-Zerbo, Ouagadougou.
    Vol. 2 *The Classical Period* (pre-7th Century): Mouktar, Cairo.
    Vol. 3 *Africa in 7th to 12th Century:* Mohammed El-Fasi, Morocco, and I. Hrbek, Czechoslovakia.
    Vol. 4 *Africa from 12th to 15th Century:* D. T. Niane, Guinea.
    Vol. 5 *Africa from 15th to 18th Century:* Bethwell Ogot, Kenya.
    Vol. 6 *Africa 1800 to 1880* (eve of colonial period): (?), Nigeria
    Vol. 7 *Africa under Foreign Rule, 1880-1950's:* A. A. Boahen, Ghana.
    Vol. 8 *Independent Africa:* A. Mazrui, Uganda.

29. See, for example, B. A. Ogot, *History of the Southern Luo, Migration and Settlement 1500-1900* (Nairobi: 1967); B. A. Ogot and J. A. Kieran, *Zamani, a Survey of East African History* (Nairobi: 1968); I. N. Kimambo and A. J. Temu: *A History of Tanzania* (Nairobi: 1969).

30. J. F. Ade. Ajayi, "History in a Developing Society," *Proceedings of the Second Congress of Africanists* (Paris: Présence Africaine, 1972), pp. 131-141.

31. T. O. Ranger and I. Kimambo, eds., *The Historical Study of African Religion* (London: 1972).

PER WÄSTBERG

Themes in African Literature Today

AFRICAN LITERATURE is *contemporary*. With few exceptions, its authors are alive *now*. Its special characteristic is that it constitutes a document of the present. The arrival of the white man is the first precise historical event in Africa, for it is the white man who brought with him the modern concept of time which changed the whole African view of existence.

African literature comes from West Africa, East Africa, South Africa and its suburb Rhodesia. These literatures are, quite naturally, different from each other. But they have in common the fact that they are written by young and middle-aged authors, most of them born after 1930. In an anthology such as *African Writing Today* (ed. Ezekiel Mphahlele, 1967), with very few exceptions the contributors are just under forty-five years of age. This literature, which has shown a sudden vitality and an equally sudden maturity during the last twenty years, is the principal work material for those African literary researchers who study African literature at their own universities.

Someone who sets out to write a history of African literature finds himself in a paradoxical situation. The dead African authors have at most a historical role, and are not nearly as significant in African literature as earlier European authors are for European literature. Thus, for example, there are a few novels and chronicles that meant something for the development of African literature and the creation of literary self-feeling, but that no longer have great interest: Bakari Diallo's *Force Bonté* (Senegal, 1926), Thomas Mofolo's *Chaka* (South Africa, 1931), Ousmane Socé's *Karim* (Senegal, 1935), Paul Hazoumé's *Doguicimi* (Dahomey, 1938).

The authors alive today, on the other hand, step right into the history of literature, although no one knows how long they will remain there. Some may survive simply because they are able to stimulate poets whose names we do not yet know; every year seems to bring new faces and new channels.

African literature means different things to different people. Some consider it a new world literature, a new genre with new messages. Others regard it as a political document, characterized by the protest against colonialism's downgrading of the blacks. For some it is simply an appendage to English and French literature. In any case, African literature does not create masterpieces in the fastidious Western sense of the word. The interest lies in what the works deal with and not so much in what they constitute as poetry or form. African literature is didactic and instructive; it is a handicraft more often than an art. Even the well-known novelist, Chinua Achebe (born 1930 in Nigeria), is something of an anthropological reconstructor who uses the past to examine the present, hoping to create a new kind of literature.

African fiction is, for the most part, less complicated than the methods of critical analysis it is exposed to. Such a statement is not a form of paternalism; it simply refers to the youth of the literature and its lack of an established tradition. It is well to realize that the new literature is being produced in countries that are as poor as Sweden was in the eighteenth century. Tribal animosity, rule by an elite, nationalistic conformity, and illiteracy prevail. With these, one finds the worst Hollywood movies, the worst weekly magazines, and the most sensationalist press of the capitals of the Western world. It is a mixed culture with a colorful and painful life on the surface that has been compared with the England of Hogarth and Defoe; one finds in it the beginnings of realism and of artistic journalism.

Perhaps one is most fair to African literature if one sees it as a documentary literature: testimony that is intended to be useful. The sense of political obligation is shared by almost all writers. In fact, a parallel development may be seen in almost all areas of cultural activity in Africa. The historian works to unmask the barbarism of colonial conquest and to resurrect the chiefs who resisted it. The ethnographer polemicizes against those who doubt Africa's ability to bring about a civilization. The theologian discovers intricate metaphysical phenomena in the various forms of animism, and sees how these are often closely related to Christianity.

I will be using the term "African literature" to cover fictional works by black authors from countries south of the Sahara. I have ignored Arab North Africa and the Sudan, Amharic Ethiopia, and even the important white authors who are still able to work in South Africa (Nadine Gordimer, Alan Paton, and the dramatist Athol Fugard). These last-named authors have their place in the history of English literature, even if their insight into the conflicts of that part of the world will perhaps one day carry them over to the history of African literature.

It is well to remember that many countries in Africa do not meet UNESCO's minimum requirements for information and access to media—ten copies of daily newspapers, five radios, two cinemas and two television sets per one hundred inhabitants. The population of Africa lacks the simplest means of informing itself on what is happening at home, not to speak of what is happening in other countries. Given these situations, it is not at all strange that Africa is making history more quickly than it makes literature.

From the end of the eighteenth century, when eight African slaves narrated their sufferings, until 1970, approximately one thousand authors have written works of fiction, drama, and poetry. Half of these come from West Africa, and a third come from South Africa. Nearly half the authors write in a European language. Ninety-five percent made their literary debut after 1920. By 1970 these one thousand writers had published 1,745 volumes. Thirty percent of these are collections of short stories or narratives; 22 percent are novels and another 22 percent collections of poetry; 21 percent are drama (dramatic works); and 5 percent are autobiographies. As is obvious, there is a certain internal equality among the three principal modes of literature, but in specific parts of Africa one does not necessarily find this balance. In West Africa, for example, where many repertoire groups link up to an old tradition of drama, 26 percent of all literature is in the form of dramatic works. The novel, on the other hand, dominates in South Africa, accounting for 32 percent of the total. In East Africa, poetry with 45 percent greatly overshadows all other literary forms. In some parts of Africa—Central Africa, for example—there is scarcely any literature at all; it accounts for only 2 percent of the literature published in black Africa. Socially progressive states such as Tanzania and Zambia have virtually no literature of any kind. Because of illiteracy, many works of fiction are never printed, but instead are transmitted on the radio in the form of short stories, satirical essays and epic poems.

Fifty-seven percent of the books written in a European language are written in English, 34 percent in French, and 6 percent in Portuguese. Three-fourths of these books come from West Africa. Poetry, short stories, and novels, together with autobiographies, have a fourth of their respective production in European languages. However, one does not find the same proportions *within* the different languages. Half of all books printed in Portuguese are poetry, but only 12 percent of books printed in English come under the same category. Twice as many poetry books are published in French as in English; with respect to drama, it is just the opposite. The number of novels is almost the same in English as in French—this, despite the fact that almost 60 percent of all Africans live in English-speaking areas and only 30 percent in French-speaking areas.

The number of African languages is usually estimated to be approximately 800. Works of fiction have been published in 47 of these as the original language. Almost all of these 47 languages are spoken within former English territories. With the exception of Madagascar—a historical exception—there is no literature in an African language within the old French colonial empire. The French school system commenced French in the first year of school and forbad the children from learning their own language.

Six languages answer for over half of the fiction printed in African languages: South Sotho, Xhosa, Zulu, North Sotho—all in South Africa—and Yoruba in Nigeria and Twi in Ghana. In South Africa, 83 percent of African fiction is written in African languages. This reflects the policy of the white government of encouraging the tribal languages and of preventing a basic study of English in order to exclude Africans from political and economic power. In East Africa barely half the literature is written in Swahili, the other principal language being Malagasy. Swahili is the official language of Tanzania and the *lingua franca* in the surrounding states, while Malagasy is the official language of Madagascar. In West Africa, where most of the literature with a serious intention originates, only 17 percent of the books are in an African language.

While it is hazardous to generalize, one may say that books written in an African language generally have less literary importance than those written in a European language. Most of the African-language books are principally narrative; many have a historical theme; some are bloodcurdling or sentimental; almost all are moral and didactic. There are exceptions, of course, and these can generally be studied in English translation.[1]

An author seldom writes in his first language and his work is seldom published in his home country. Publishing houses have begun to appear—mainly in Kenya, Nigeria and Cameroon—but they do not distribute books very widely. Indigenous literary journals, usually tied to the universities, are published sporadically. The rule is that valuable African literature is published in Paris and London where it attracts more notice from the press than it does in its own locale. Pocket editions of some of the literature have reached the smaller places in Africa, but only in limited numbers. Heinemann's *African Writers Series* (London), now up to approximately 150 volumes, has made an important contribution. The authors write for a whole continent, but at least 80 percent of its inhabitants can neither read nor write. In consequence, as far as one knows, there is still no author who writes full time. He is a teacher, a civil servant, a scientist, a diplomat, a journalist, or a shop assistant. It is difficult for him to communicate with those he would most like to influence and, involuntarily, he ends up in an elite position. I speak of the author as "he," for female authors are still rare.

In a lecture held in Stockholm in 1967,[2] Wole Soyinka, probably Africa's most outstanding author, traced the development of the typical African poet. First he witnessed the rebellion against colonialism and the expulsion of tyranny in country after country, beginning when Ghana achieved its independence in 1957. In the period of victory and stabilization which followed, he identified with nationalism and, accommodating himself to the demands of the moment, let himself become part of the machinery of the state. By so doing, he postponed the personal reflection on experience so necessary to him as an author; he did not want to deny his society, but he could temporarily deny himself. Furthermore, although he took his place in the new state as a privileged person, no one deemed his special knowledge as a poet relevant.

Only ten years after independence was achieved in Ghana, Soyinka described the mood among writers as one of prevailing disillusionment, a mood which no doubt persists today. The complex realities of government had been taken over by politicians. Distracted by attention and flattery from the non-African world, the writer looked back nostalgically at history and at what he imagined as idyllic tribal life. Even if he didn't yield to material rewards, he fell into a class situation, as a member of the educated elite, opposed to his view of national duty and threatening to his source of inspiration. The fact that he wrote in a European language cut him off from the people he wished to speak for.

When he awakened from his intoxication with metaphysics and began to express his view of society, the politicians who had taken his place put him in prison. Or they allowed him to go into exile, or even to sit in a dark suit in the United Nations or UNESCO. Soyinka himself was in prison in Nigeria between 1967 and 1969 because he tried to prevent the civil war. Camara Laye, Guinea's most outstanding poet, lost his citizenship in 1966 when he published the novel *Dramouss*. Mongo Beti, in whose novels one finds the most penetrating criticism of French colonialism, went to France himself as a voluntary exile when Cameroon became free.

Authors are divided in their attitudes toward this problem. Some, the traditionalists, speak in favor of returning to traditional African values. They distrust politically inspired literature and want to build a new writing, especially a new poetry, on the foundations of the oral tradition. This attitude goes back in part to the *négritude* school which wanted to create an alternative to Western technology and belief in progress. Its proponents demand a social and intellectual reappraisal and rejection of the European individualism expressed in the myths surrounding Robinson Crusoe, martyrs, ascetics, and individual heroes. Traditional African literature, they argue, incorporates the individual with the group, and leaves no room for egotism or egocentricity. In African philosophy the theme of loneliness is unknown and there is no counterpart to the Western tradition of man in revolt against his situation in life. Instead, man and matter, dead as well as alive, are coordinated powers which are part of *ntu*, being itself.

The other attitude emphasizes the author's responsibility to work for the freedom of the individual—that same freedom he earlier defended against colonialism. It is advanced by Wole Soyinka and Chinua Achebe, among others, both of whom nevertheless incorporate traditional elements into their work. For Achebe the foremost duty of the author is to maintain his freedom of thought even against his own countrymen. According to Soyinka, the author must not content himself with chronicling society's customs and experiences. He must also play the part of bard and oracle; he must see more clearly and exactly than other people; he must be a visionary, a warning voice, and a builder of the future.

II

The novel is the only literary form which is not connected with patterns of expression in traditional Africa. The term, "African novels," refers mainly to novels written in English or French in West Africa and Cameroon. In most of them, the narrative is restrained and nonexperimental, and character takes second place to situation and plot. An individual's emotional conflicts are seldom a central element. Nowhere in African literature, for example, do we find a gripping description of love or a great tragedy.

African prose could be arranged around such headings as these: the decadence of society (Ayi Kwei Armah), the synthesis of folklore and realism (Amos Tutuola), humor and irony as weapons of revolt (Mongo Beti and Ferdinand Oyono), existential humanism (Cheikh Hamidou-Kane), the morality of absurdity (Olympe Bhêly-Quénum and Gabriel Okara), and apocalyptic mercy (Camara Laye). In terms of subject matter, it deals with the glory of "untouched" Africa before the arrival of the white man, with the colonial past, with the cultural divisions which arise when only a select few are allowed to go to school, and with the ways in which contemporary Africa stifles the artist. They are concerned with the divisions caused by the imposition of Western rationalism which has, for example, set up a puritanical work ethic and replaced a collective attitude with individualism. And, finally, they treat the profound generation gap which has arisen as a result of the conflicting ways of life in country and city both before and after independence—a problem dramatized by events like the Mau-Mau revolt in Kenya reported in the writings of James Ngugi.

In addition to novels dealing with autobiography,[3] history with contemporary parallels,[4] satire with a moral to it,[5] and psychology,[6] there is a group of symbolic, philosophical novels[7] distinctly different from those we are accustomed to in Western literature. Olympe Bhêly-Quénum's *Le chant du lac,* for example, a folktale with built-in social criticism, portrays a village in the grip of animism and supernatural powers. Symbolically, the author presents Africa as a battlefield for the powers of enlightenment and terror. In *Le regard du roi,* Camara Laye creates

a unique situation: a European seeking assimilation with Africa to get rid of his individualistic upbringing. Once he discovers the continent's jealously guarded
secret, he cannot depart. Laye's almost inaccessibly mysterious many-leveled novel
presents Africa as a way of life which cannot be defined by socio-anthropologists.
In Cheikh Hamidou Kane's classically simple *L'aventure ambiguë*, a tragedy of
faithfulness and treachery, the conflict between Islam and Western materialism
leads the hero to suicide after he has returned to his tribal village from the Latin
Quarter, the home of rationalism.

The best novelists are a category unto themselves. Among them are Sembene
Ousmane, born in 1923 in Senegal; Mongo Beti, born in 1932 in Cameroon; and,
above all, Chinua Achebe, born in 1930 in Nigeria.[8] Ousmane is a Marxist, a
former docker and trade unionist active in Marseille and Dakar, and a pioneering
director of full-length film in Africa (*Le Mandat*). *Les bouts de bois de Dieu* (1960)
is representative of his seven books. It deals with the 1947 strike of the workers
along the Dakar-Niger railway. Ousmane outlines their daily routine—going to
work, buying food at the market, collecting their pay, and fetching water in
buckets—which they see as governed by uncontrollable and indifferent powers.
Forced to choose between capitulation and the uncertainty of striking, the workers
strike, trusting their feeling of solidarity. The strike unites ethnic groups,
generations, and sexes, and creates a new awareness in the workers of the spiritual
condition imposed on them by the white man's rule. Ousmane is capable, as few
African novelists are, of commanding a wide social panorama without diminishing
his sympathetic focus on the suffering and intricate condition of the individual.
Ousmane deals with the collective society again in *Vehi-Ciosane* (1967), where he
portrays the poet—the traditional village bard—as "the voice of conscience and
truth which the collective society needs to stay together."

Mongo Beti's four picaresque social satires—all written in the 1950's—deal with
an individual's attempt to defend his integrity in a society, be it colonial or tribal,
which takes no notice of him. Beti reflects the recent rapid changes of thought
about Africa as a political, psychological, and moral entity. His main theme is the
difficulty of adaptation in a world where it is uncertain just what one should adapt
oneself to. Beti's own hesitations and inability even to hint at solutions to the
dilemmas he presents make it seem that he questions whether real freedom is possible in Africa under current social conditions.

For him there is no Good, no Evil, no clear-cut solution, and the city is the symbol of this. His main characters are youngsters left to fend for themselves in a
world more often indifferent than hostile. Like the new Africa, however, they are
proud, tired of humiliation, and reluctant to reveal that, despite their impatiences,
they hesitate on the threshold. The novels end in an atmosphere of pain and uncertain breaking up.

Beti is obsessed by the city, which he sees as a symbol for moral uncertainty. In
his literary debut, *Ville Cruelle* (1954), the city is not only the background for his
heroes' uncertainties, it is the very personification of their own qualities. It is a
battlefield of souls, and a meetingplace of the conflicts of the time. Beti's views are
most clearly revealed in his second and best novel, *Le pauvre Christ de Bomba*
(1956). On a two-week sightseeing tour through the Tala province of Cameroon,
the white missionary Drumont and his faithful black Denis wake up to reality. By

the end of the third week—and the book—the Bomba mission Drumont has built up no longer exists, and Drumont is leaving Africa, realizing that his life's work has been based on a misunderstanding so great that he has become an accomplice to the colonial oppressors. Similarly, in *Mission terminée* (1957) the hero finds that, as he works at his life's task, it takes on a new and different significance which prevents him from carrying it out as he had planned.

The African novel at the time of independence (1957-1962) is characterized for the most part by straightforward realism. It deals with the detail of contemporary life: with festivals and rites, with demands of striking polygamists for family allowances, with the "been-to's" who are sent to universities in England and France and return, according to Lenrie Peters of Gambia, like "the wind-swept seedlings of another age."

> There at the edge of town
> Just by the burial ground
> Stands the house without a shadow
> Lived in by new skeletons.

The new skeletons are the public administration officials housed in the buildings previously occupied by colonial civil servants.

After independence, novels often went to extremes of satire and criticism, closing the door on a deeper investigation of human motives. In 1967, Soyinka wrote a satirical drama, *Kongi's Harvest*, about the arrogance of an African dictator. In his novel, *The Interpreters* (1965), however, he takes up the emotional experiences of creative people who feel shut in by the limitations of their society. They dissociate themselves from bureaucracy, opportunism, and the pursuit of influence, and turn against the depravity of big city life in Lagos and the pleasure-seeking middle class. They are forced to create their own moral and aesthetic values, ones which will allow them to utilize their personal resources. Soyinka runs the risk of falling into loneliness, into an internal exile. Nevertheless, he is one of exceptionally few authors who can show the excesses of African nationalism when it goes against personal freedom, as well as the excesses of conservative tribalism, without putting himself on either side. No one is safe from criticism in his writings.

Perhaps the first task to confront African authors was that of revaluing Africa's past and creating a history in which real people lived in real situations. An author needs a background—a past to refer to—as well as a future when his work will become, for a new generation, part of the resonant tone of the past.

In 1958 Chinua Achebe began that process in English-speaking Africa with the novel, *Things Fall Apart*. Achebe's clear desire to teach his people to understand themselves better by becoming conscious of their historical background reveals how deeply the idea of the author as teacher is rooted in his readers: a novel is seen as a school book, among other things—preferably with exercises at the end.

The novel is an instrument of self-discovery for Achebe as well as for many of his contemporaries. The African defines his identity and finds his historical roots by writing. This function of the novel is particularly important for the post-colonial authors whose upbringing in a European culture has tempted them to look down upon traditional values. Thus it is hardly surprising that the autobiographical novel dominates modern African literature. Even more important, however, than its role in evaluating past experiences is its potential for analyzing possibilities for future action: the need to understand one's present identity is followed by a need to define what one can be or do.

Achebe's artistic purpose is to help African society regain its faith in itself and to eradicate the unfortunate attitudes it acquired during years of negation. His subject is the tragic consequences of Africa's meeting with Europe: African society was in repose when white society broke right into it, producing a crisis in African identity. Nevertheless, Achebe warns against seeing the precolonial past as "a long idyll in technicolor."

Achebe himself has pointed out that his first three novels reconstruct the situation of people like himself, whose grandfathers resisted the European influence, but whose fathers went over to the side of the conquerer. Achebe is obsessed in all of his work by fellow-travelers and collaborators. *Things Fall Apart* (1958) portrays a world which is being consumed from the inside by superstition and from the outside by the assault of the West. Okonkwo, defender of tribal values, sacrifices his personal life for his sense of communal duty, and is driven to suicide. Nwoye, on the other hand, puts personal feelings and relationships before social responsibility. His movement away from tribal values sets the stage for those of Achebe's generation to be brought up in a Western manner. Ironically, in portraying the depth and beauty of the Ibo culture, Achebe uses tools he has gained only as a result of its destruction.

He gives a particularly good picture in this book of the way Christian missionairies worked in Africa. Whereas in Sweden, they first converted Olof Skotkönung and by so doing converted his followers, in Africa, they began with the restless, the very young, and those who had been cast out according to tribal law: mothers of twins, rogues, and rebels. Thus the missionaries created a new center of power within the tribe, split its unity, and brought about its disintegration.

No Longer at Ease (1960) deals with what happens when the universe of tribal powers has been broken up. Public morality is a front like a clean white collar, and there is a profound gap between what is said to happen and what actually happens. Obi, the hero, finds himself unable to unite his communal responsibilities with his personal life. He is as anxious to appear liberated from the traditions of the tribe as his grandfather Okonkwo was to defend them. He remains uneasy with his individualistic values, however, for they do not satisfy his need to identify with the past.

Unlike the Western novel where the characters are often responsible for what happens to them, the characters in *Arrow of God* serve as arrows which gods shoot at each other. A fatalistic choir of old proverbs translated directly from Ibo provides background for the antics of two rival tribal gods and the Christian god. Achebe is filled with wrath over the fact that Ibo society was ravaged by foreigners who believed that they brought the light of civilization, but who—unlike Ezeulu, the chief priest of the village—could not see the darkness within themselves. The tragedy of the novel is the inability of some Africans as well as Englishmen to experience the life of the *other* as real, or to understand the decisive difference between their ways of life.

In Achebe's writing, man is captured in a vision, a profession, or a social situation, and never gets free. In *A Man of the People* (1966), Odili Samalu tells his story in an effort to defend himself. Despite his good intentions and his efforts to follow up his ideal, however, it is clear that he is caught up in self-deceit and hypocrisy. He is tragically innocent and unconscious of his double bookkeeping. At a time when most people saw Nigeria as the stronghold of democracy in Africa, Achebe foresaw the coming disintegration, the betrayal of the leaders, the Biafra war. Politics in Africa is deadly serious even when it lends itself to description in comical turns of phrase. People die. There was even an element of the old-fashioned tragic epic in the Congo struggle around 1961. Like the capricious gods in the *Iliad*, Westerners flew in and out, always sure of themselves, manipulating strings in a war fought by ordinary people.

Achebe and Mongo Beti deal with many of the same subjects, but whereas Beti writes in self-contained episodes; Achebe's situations are more open-ended. Caught on a seemingly predestined course, his characters do not fully realize what is happening to them. Furthermore, Beti takes a comic stance while Achebe regards his conflicts as essentially tragic. Achebe, however, also has a gift for comedy. There is a certain dualism in Achebe's style; he vacillates between the tragic pastoral and the urban farce. He puts this to good use, however. By associating this comic imagination with the new and urban and his gift for tragedy with the old and pastoral, he is able to do justice to both sides of the most intransigent of conflicts facing Africans—that between the city and the countryside, between the rational and the intuitive.

III

African literature has two roots: one in the European tradition, and one in the African. Often the former decides its structure, the latter its content. The oral tradition of literature springs, of course, from the African root, and will continue to live as long as illiteracy is widespread. For a long time it was deemed interesting mainly because its contents shed light on the study of African society; in other words, the information it made available was considered more important than its form. It is easy to dismiss oral literature as folklore—to deny its aesthetic intentions, and to see it as radically divorced from written literature.

In the 1950's and 1960's a new interest in oral literature arose, mainly because African scientists, working closely with their own languages, drew attention to the important community roles played by poet, singer, and story-teller. Oral literature is performed literature. It lives in the moment it is formed by an actor or story-teller. Print cannot record it adequately; a film with a soundtrack captures much more. For example, when a song of tribute to a dead person is performed, the words are often only one of several elements. The voice of the singer and its overtones, the sobbing, the changing facial expressions, the movements, and the melody are not mere ornaments but integral parts of the work. Furthermore, there is no authentic version of a piece of oral literature: neither the words nor the narrative fall into any set structure. Each story-teller has his own style, and it may be very different from that of the person who taught him the story. Even the arrangement of a story is often changed. New elements can be added which relate to the immediate surroundings of the performance; references can be made to the characteristics of the listeners or to the appearance of objects brought in by civilization. The public, for its part, often assists with choruses, refrains, or spontaneous singing.

Since 1964, the Oxford Library of African Literature has published more than ten volumes of recorded oral literature from recent decades. They include a heroic epic of the cattle-tendering Bahima people of southwest Uganda, taken down and translated from the Runyankore language, by H. F. Morris. It is a series of enormous poems of praise in intricate meter, filled with metaphor, alliteration, and sometimes startling contrasts. After a passage of apparently timeless enlightment, for example, we find this description of the coronation of an Ankole king.

> The letters were sent out by the Dispatcher of
>   Warriors
> The typing was done by Mashunja. . . .
>
> The motor-cars spent the night in the valleys
>   making a noise;
> The police drums prevented the local ones from
>   being heard. . . .

One of the most reckless stories among the Oxford Library selections ends when the hero, helped by friendly ants, turtles, and snakes, settles down with his lovely wife:

> They lived happily together.
> He had several sons and daughters
> Who grew up and helped in
> Raising the standard of education
> In the country.

This passage led Chinua Achebe to comment, "If anyone thinks the last sentence is a naive anticlimax he cannot know much about Africa today."

There is less difference between oral and written literature than one might think.[9] Witches and talkative animals perform in both. We meet moral exhortations in both. The anonymous reciters and poets of our day have a substantial share of artistic ability. And, of course, many writers draw on the oral tradition for material.

One hears the spoken voice in everything Amos Tutuola writes. Born in 1920 in Nigeria and uneducated, he comes from the Yoruba tribe, and tells about the world which school-hungry young Africans are trying to escape. Due mainly to his ungrammatical and drastic English and his untroubled use of naive wording, he is regarded in Europe as especially African, and for that very reason is belittled in his native country.

What is exceptional in Tutuola is his ability to organize oral narrative material in a literary manner. He provides a middle link in the development from a purely oral narrative tradition to a sophisticated literature. The books he writes are not novels. His characters are not related to one another and they do not live in a society; they are alone with their vision, their imagination, and their terror. Tutuola's prose epics about man's wandering through existence follow patterns similar to that in *Pilgrim's Progress*. In his literary debut, *The Palmwine Drinkard* (1952), the Drinkard joins up with the eternal heroes of the myth. Tutuola describes the fantastic with implacable exactness, but beneath the grotesque and the monstrous, his pattern is clear: the Drinkard must complete his upbringing with a picaresque voyage to the City of the Dead, and to the center of the world where knowledge is. This book and *Ajaiyi and His Inherited Property* (1967), an extremely unhappy folk saga told in the style of a more childish Dante, are Tutuola's least fragmentary creations.

IV

The drama has roots deep in the oral tradition. In many tribal societies, a play is performed in order to celebrate a good harvest, a success in battle, or the exploits of heroes. Within a circle of fires after the working day is over, dance, mime, and music with a dramatic narrative for several voices are produced for spectators, often more consciously than an outsider might suspect. The task of the performing artist is to keep the lines open to ancestors and gods who are neither completely good nor completely evil but simply powerful. The purpose of the various rituals of the Yoruba people is to lessen the fear of death by letting the spirits of their ancestors appear dramatically among the people. The actors' masks represent contact with the other world. Mortal and immortal meet in the person of the dancer: when he goes into ecstasy, the spirit of the ancestor reveals itself through him.

Dramatic production thrives, especially in West Africa, and in many places there are both state theaters and experimental theater workshops. Theater is the medium through which authors reach the most people, including those who cannot read or write.[10] It is also the place where they can best unify the experimental and the traditional, for the blend is one which fascinates their large and inexperienced public.[11] John Pepper Clark's dramas,[12] for example, explore the view of the Ijaw people that man is the carrier of two destinies—one personal or genetic and one created by the tribe and its ancestors. Clark uses Ijaw philosophy to free his gift of creativity without sacrificing his fellowship with his tribe and his past.

Wole Soyinka is Africa's most outstanding dramatist as well as a poet and novelist. His collection of poems, *Iandre* (1967), is a Nigerian myth about how the people call Ogun, god of creation, iron, and war, down from his mountain and ask him to help in a war. Ogun, who has drawn himself back after completing his creation, shows himself once again, is blinded by blood, and kills friend and foe without distinction. Soyinka's theme is that violent powers must be bound—electricity to earth, industry to civilization, aggression to work, and man to woman. Ogun also appears in the novel, *The Interpreters*, this time as symbol for the artist—destroyer of traditions and creator of the new. The characters here are deeply rooted in Yoruba's deities and their behavior—not unlike the way Joyce's characters are rooted in folklore in *Ulysses*. A European reader should remember that Soyinka's characters and likewise many auto mechanics and bus drivers in Nigeria literally believe in Ogun. During the festival of Ogun, homage is paid to him by people like blacksmiths, bicycle repairmen, and plumbers, for he is the special protector of those who work with iron.

Wole Soyinka's ten dramas—including *Five Plays* (1964), *The Road* (1965), *Kongi's Harvest* (1967), and *Madmen and Specialists* (1972)—take place in the present, in independent Nigeria with its corrupt city life on the one hand and its backwardness and superstition on the other. His framework is a civilization trying to find new values but lacking the will to destroy its traditional inheritance. By utilizing ritual, mime, dance and music, Soyinka gives his public a sense of continuity between the past and the present. *The Road,* for example, written in a Nigerian-English dialect, deals with how people continually discover new symbols in order to give meaning to their lives. In this case the "road" is seen as Ogun himself, the victims of accidents as his victims.

Human sacrifice is an important theme in Soyinka's writing, as is martyrdom, particularly the self-chosen death. The professor in *The Road* wants to become acquainted with his own death without dying, but his desire to go beyond the borders of knowledge brings about his death. Similar things happen in *The Strong Breed* (1963), *A Dance of the Forests* (1963), and the novel, *The Interpreters* (1965). In each, someone chooses death, or, in Soyinka's words, "grants his own death" in order to become acquainted with his nature and to defy passive annihilation.

V

The majority of African poetry is written in French, and intimately involves the French concept of *négritude*, which has been defined in various ways. The term occurred in debates as early as the beginning of the 1930's; it was used in 1939 by Aimé Césaire, the West Indian pioneer of modern black poetry, in his explosive long poem, *Cahier d'un retour au pays natal:*

> Ma négritude n'est ni une tour ni une cathédrale
> elle plonge dans la chair rouge du sol.

It was brought to life when the journal *Présence Africaine,* started in 1947, declared war on the culture of the colonists and objected to the habit of regarding the world from a strictly European point of view, especially considering the bankruptcy of Western civilization after World War II.

There is a certain vagueness surrounding the term *négritude*, due, to some extent, to the fact that its two dimensions are partially in conflict with one another. It demands, for example, both rediscovery and political reorientation. The journey of rediscovery, however, leads the seeker to a static African concept of society, while political reorientation implies progress in the Western sense. This conflict is reflected in the respective creation myths of Europe and Africa. In European religions, a god creates man and the universe from the outside. In many African faiths, on the other hand, the first man is discovered already complete: he is found in a fishing net, he appears in a plant, or he is brought down by a bird. He seems to have existed through all eternity. Thus, in the terms of African myths, progress may do violence to that which already has a completed form.

In 1948, Léopold Sédar Senghor, born in 1906 in Senegal, published his *Anthologie de la nouvelle poésie nègre et malgache de langue française;* a black Orpheus, maintained Jean Paul Sartre in a famous introduction, had begun to sing in French. Not only is Senghor the President of his country, he is regarded by many as Africa's most outstanding poet and, along with Césaire, as the foremost theoretician and exemplifier of négritude. In connection with Placide Tempels and Alexis Kagame, among others, Senghor states[13] that, at a deeper level than the linguistic and developmental differences among various parts of Africa, all Africans share a sphere of experience, a culture, and an authentic African way of regarding the world. In contrast to European culture—which is distinguished by a coldness of feeling, materialism, and objective intelligence—African culture approaches reality through the senses. Négritude, however, is less a rejection of Europe than an affirmation of Africa's uniqueness. It is "the presence of life," "man's fellowship with other people and in that way fellowship with everything that exists, from a stone to God." Out of this fellowship arises a knowledge which expresses itself, not in algebra but in image and rhythm.

In his poetry, which is at one and the same time romantic and socially conscious, Senghor envisions the pre-industrial period—when conversation and intercourse were more important than invention and business competition—as a kind of paradise. In his portrayal, Africa before the deluge of white men was filled with the wisdom of elders and the playing of children. In his first collections, *Chants d'ombre* (1945) and *Hosties noires* (1948), he contrasts the Africa of secure rites with Europe in the captivity of war. His later poems—*Ethiopiques* (1956) and *Nocturnes* (1961)—are elongated invocatory ballads designed to be recited to instrumental accompaniment.

Senghor's rhetoric and innocent pseudoracism can be irritating. Négritude has at least two dimensions—that of rediscovery and that of political reorientation. A younger and more radical generation of poets takes issue with Senghor's anthropological mystical idea of négritude. For Mario de Andrade and other poets involved in the struggle for freedom, for example, négritude is a battlecry which erases humiliation. According to them, its day will be past once a feeling of self has taken root, for then Africans can take their place among other socialist peoples of the world. Others reject négritude altogether. Yambo Ouologuem compares it to a statue of a hundred myths, a marketplace of fanciful concepts where traders in ideologies list their imaginations on a stock exchange. Ezekiel Mphahlele feels that, despite its important historical role in arousing protest, négritude itself contains a subtle form of segregation and paternalism. Like Frantz Fanon, he feels that West African intellectuals are wasting their time making pilgrimages to the source while blood runs in the southern Africa of white racist regimes.

African poetry in a European language is a new phenomenon. At the end of World War II, not even Senghor and Birago Diop, the veterans of French-speaking lyric poetry, had yet published a book. The exception was Jean-Joseph Rabéarivelo of Madagascar (1903-37). He was isolated from the rest of the literature on his own continent, from African concerns and négritude. In contact with the tradition of French symbolism, he pictured man as close to suicidal despair, as unreachable and anonymous—so alone that he cannot even give birth to new loneliness. Rabéarivelo's seven collections of poems, published in one volume (*Poèmes*, 1960), placed him alongside Senghor as the most outstanding of African lyric poets.[14]

African poetry in English first achieved prominence in the 1960's, and derived from a broader social spectrum than that in French.[15] Christopher Okigbo, who was born in 1932 and died in battle in 1968 fighting for Biafra, is one of many prophetic poets. He himself lived on the razor edge of existence and his poetry is enigmatic and loaded with anguish. In *Heavensgate* and *Limits* (both 1962), and in his posthumously published poems, he anticipates approaching catastrophies and interprets them as parables of African history.

Okot p'Bitek, born in 1931 in Uganda, has developed a poetic language of his own, in which structure, metaphor, and reference points all emanate from the Acoli language. Bitek is a regenerator. In *Song of Prisoner* and *Song of Malaya,* published in one volume in 1971, he reveals a powerful sympathy for political prisoners and prostitutes. In *Song of Lawino* (1966), a long and bitter burlesque, rich in shades of meaning, a traditional village woman scorns and deprecates her husband Ocol who has been hooked by a modern city woman. She satirizes his cultural snobbery and complains that Western sophistication has robbed him of his vitality:

> For all our young men
> Were finished in the forest
> Their manhood was finished
> In the classrooms.
> Their testicles
> Were smashed
> With large books!

In 1967, Bitek wrote a reply for Ocol, *Song of Ocol,* in which male and female and the two cultures once again confront each other.

In South Africa, political reality is so overwhelming that authors, to the extent that they can speak at all, are obsessed with it. *South African Writing Today*[16] includes four white and five black authors who "May not be published or quoted in South Africa." Many writers have gone into exile. What African literature still exists, panting and on the border of extinction, derives its strength from the big city and the contemporary environment. For example, Oswald Joseph Mtshali, born in 1940, a university graduate forced by apartheid laws to work as a delivery boy in Johannesburg, has broken through the forces of silence within South African poetry with *Sounds of a Cowhide Drum* (1971). Africa's poetry reflects a historical situation. In the captive countries—and in others as well—most people feel that poetry, by involving the people, will contribute to the struggle for freedom. A great deal of poetry, written for this purpose, is intended to function collectively—to be recited at meetings, for example.

The writers of the Portuguese colonies seem even more conscious than those elsewhere that they are giving voice to previously unarticulated feelings of the masses. Poets here are politically active. They write about the slavery of the people and the will to rebel. Many are or have been in prison, and the most important liberation movements in Angola and Mozambique number poets among their leaders.[17] Needless to say, the pages of their songs of rebellion and poems of lamentation are filled with wrath and pain.

Africa has obtained a voice. Its manifold effect, however, is still stronger than that of the individual voices. It is, of course, extremely risky to speculate about what may endure among the works of authors still only halfway through their careers. Regardless of our aesthetic judgments, however, as the collective testimony of a continent in the process of dynamic transformation, the literature as a whole is certainly adequate: witness the development not only of Senghor, Achebe, and Soyinka, but also of the fertile literary undergrowth manifested by market booklets in gigantic editions such as the so-called Onitsha literature in Nigeria with its authors who readily style themselves Masters of Life (M.L.) instead of Masters of Arts. What we have been able to observe from 1950 to 1970 is, after all, an unusual phenomenon—the literary awakening of an entire continent.

REFERENCES

1. B. W. Vilakazis, *Inkondlo kaZulu* (Johannesburg: 1935), translated into English as *Zulu Horizons* (Cape Town: 1962); A. C. Jordan's novel written in Xhosa, *Ingqumbo Yeminyanya* (Lovedale, South Africa: 1940) translated into English as *Wrath of the Ancestors;* D. O. Fagunwa's five narrative adventures in Yoruba which have been printed in hundreds of thousands of copies, one of them translated into English by Wole Soyinka as *The Forest of a Thousand Daemons* (1968).

2. Wole Soyinka, "The Writer in a Modern African State," *The Writer in Modern Africa*, ed. Per Wästberg (New York: 1969).

3. Camara Laye, *L'enfant noir* (Guinea: 1953); Bernard Dadié, *Climbié* (Ivory Coast: 1956); Aké Loba, *Kocoumbo* (Ivory Coast: 1960); Peter Abrahams, *Tell Freedom* (South Africa: 1954); Ezekiel Mphahlele, *The Wanderers* (1970); and Ayi Kwei Armah, *Fragments* (1970).

4. Peter Abrahams, *Wild Conquest* (South Africa: 1950); Djibril Niané, *Soundjata* (Guinea: 1961); Nazi Boni, *Crépuscule des temps anciens* (Upper Volta: 1962); Yambo Ouologuem, *Le devoir de violence* (Mali: 1968); and Ahmadou Kourouma, *Les soleils des indépendances.*

5. See Abdoulaye Sadji of Senegal, who died in 1961: *Nini* (1954) and *Maimouna* (1958); the many novels of T. M. Aluko and Cyprian Ekwensis about the corrupt, glamorous city life in Nigeria; and the novels of Mongo Beti from Cameroon.

6. Peter Abrahams, *A Path of Thunder* (South Africa: 1948); Olympe Bhêly-Quénum, *Un piège sans fin* (Dahomey: 1960); and James Ngugi, *A Grain of Wheat* (Kenya: 1967).

7. Olympe Bhêly-Quénum, *Le chant du lac* (Dahomey: 1960); Camara Laye, *Le regard du roi* (Guinea: 1954); Cheikh Hamidou-Kane, *L'aventure ambiguë* (Senegal: 1961). Gabriel Okara's *The Voice* (Nigeria: 1963) is a rare experiment in language, utilizing direct translations from the Ijaw language. Its contents, however, are representative: Hamlet, a young intellectual with lofty principles fights against the evil powers in a static society.

8. See also the work of Ferdinand Oyono, born in 1929 in Cameroon; Ayi Kwei Armah of Ghana; and Kofi Awoonor. Ferdinand Oyono published three satirical novels describing the way Africans made themselves into a distorted picture of white men until bitter experience taught them how their masters really were. The best is *Le vieux nègre et la médaille* (1956). Oyono describes Africans beginning to understand that they do not have to take Europeans and their social order so terribly seriously. But he offers no positive alternative. After independence he became an ambassador and stopped publishing books.

   In Ayi Kwei Armah's *The Beautiful Ones Are Not Yet Born* (1968), two men desire an aesthetic and ethical life, but are paralyzed by the corruption of the new Ghana. One envisages eternal values such as Justice, Truth, Equality and Beauty, but flees from people. The other is "Everyman": he has a family and must work in the darkness of human conditions where all values are vulgarized and only money and power entice. "The Beautiful Ones" is a misspelled advertisement on a bus, but the real beauty and the right people are not yet born. Armah's pessimism contains a utopian hope, noticable also in *Fragments* (1970), an autobiographical novel of a return to Ghana which leaves the hero disillusioned, nauseated, and aware of the impossibility of being an artist in Africa today. The novel contains descriptions of physical love which are unusual in African writing.

   The poet Kofi Awoonor's novel, *This Earth, My Brother* (1970), which contains elements of both autobiography and allegory, is composed of dream-like inner monologues mixed with kaleidoscopic pictures of a society which finally drives the hero to despair. The woman of the sea who entices him down to her grotto is also Africa. But here the hero's death does not have to be interpreted pessimistically, for to give oneself up to the sea is a cleansing ritual of the Ewe tribe, one which reconciles man with himself.

9. Birago Diop (born in 1906 in Senegal) has used the sagas he heard in the Wolof language of his youth. His three collections are regarded as minor classics: *Contes d'Amadou Koumba* (1947), *Les nouveaux contes d'Amadou Koumba* (1958), and *Contes et Lavanes* (1963).

10. See Duro Lapidou, *Three Yoruba Plays,* folk operas with librettoes available in English (Nigeria: 1964).

11. Among talented dramatists are Ama Ata Aidoo and Efua Sutherland from Ghana: Robert Serumaga from Uganda, and Sarif Easmon from Sierra Leone. But as yet their production is limited and our perspective on it is entirely too short to permit us to judge it with any validity.

12. *Song of a Goat* (1961) and *The Raft* (1964).

13. See *Liberté I: Négritude et humanisme* (1964).

14. The most remarkable of the new lyric poets in French, but also the most difficult to approach is Tchicaya U Tam'si, born in 1931 in the Congo (Brazzaville). He has written seven collections of poems—among them *Epitomé* (1962).

15. See Wole Soyinka; Gabriel Okara; and John Pepper Clark's *A Reed in the Tide* (1965).

16. Peter Abrahams; Lewis Nkosi who wrote the essays *Home and Exile* (1966); and Alex la Guma who has written three novels about the lives of coloreds in Cape Town, and a description of prison, *The Stone Country* (1967).

17. Agostinho Neto and Mario de Andrade in MPLA and Marcelino dos Santos in Frelimo.

J. H. KWABENA NKETIA

The Musical Heritage of Africa

THE DOMINANT ROLE that music plays in the lives of African peoples has long been noted by observers. Writing about the peoples of the Western Sudan, Ibn Butlan, an Arab writer of the thirteenth century, observed, "Dancing and beating time are engrained in their nature. They say were the Negro to fall from Heaven, he would beat time in falling."[1] Accounts of Africa by Western observers from the fifteenth century to the present also make abundant references to music, for, as Hickens observes, the African "is born, named, initiated into manhood, warriored, armed, housed, betrothed, wedded and buried to music."[2]

In the African heritage, music is an art that pervades social life and is believed to be vital for sustaining community life. Just as the cry of the newborn baby gives the first concrete indication that it is alive, so music is considered an expression of "being." A community that does not have a vigorous musical life is often described as "dead," for to make music is to be alive. Through music, an African people expresses its inner life and its determination to remain alive even under conditions of extreme hardship and suffering. Hence participation in music as a social activity is generally encouraged and, in certain contexts, music-making by all and sundry is accepted as part of the normal way of life. For this reason the processes of socialization or enculturation in music are so intense that music-making—a learned behavior—appears to the casual observer to be an inherited trait.

The African experience in music can best be observed within the framework of community life, for music is conceived of not only as a mode of artistic expression but also as a social activity. It offers the individual aesthetic experience as well as a sense of belonging. During performances, these experiences are shared with the entire community. Because music is regarded as a social activity in Subsaharan Africa, performances generally take place on "social" occasions—occasions, that is, when any group comes together for recreation or communal labor, the performance of rites and ceremonies, the worship of divinities, or the celebration of festivals. Traditional African music, therefore, is performed in a variety of social settings and not in concert halls. The performance itself usually takes into account not only the aims and purposes of an occasion, but also the needs of those who take part in the actual music making. This arrangement makes it unnecessary to set up special institutions for the promotion of music in community life.

In actual performances, music tends to be part of a complex of events in which various artistic expressions are integrated. Music may be linked not only to the dance but also to various forms of visual display conceived as elements in dramatic

151

communication or as foci for aesthetic appreciation. A great deal of emphasis is laid on the use of speech as an essential element in musical communication. Verbal texts may be spoken, sung or chanted. Recitations, declamations and lyrics may be performed to the accompaniment of music. Instrumental sounds may be used as speech surrogates, that is to say they may be organized in such a way as to reflect the intonation and rhythms of specific texts.[3] The languages of societies that use speech surrogates are generally tone languages—languages in which tone is phonemic and may be used for distinguishing meaning. The following pairs of words in the Akan language, for example, are distinguished solely by tone.

bogya	[_ ‾]	firefly
bogya	[‾ -]	relative
papa	[- -]	goodness
papa	[_ _]	fan
dadɛ	[_‾‾]	iron
dadɛ	[‾--]	name of a tree

In addition to distinguishing meaning, tones may be used for making grammatical distinctions or for expressing the syntactical relationship between words. Hence in such languages the tones of words, phrases, and sentences tend to be fixed. Any instrument that can reproduce these and the rhythm of speech texts, therefore, can be used as a speech surrogate. Wooden slit drums, drums with parchment heads, double bells, flutes and trumpets are the most widely used. Texts reproduced in this manner may be played to convey messages. They may also be played against a musical ground or ostinato provided by other instruments. They can also be superimposed on the music or played as interludes between performances.

Unlike the situation in Western cultures, music designed for action is emphasized much more than music designed for contemplation, although the latter may be heard during rituals and ceremonies when it is desired to set a particular mood, or during breaks in a dance performance. Such music is also played by performers like the shepherd boy, the lonely traveler, or the individual communing with his god in seclusion. A greater premium, however, is put on music that stimulates an active rather than a passive response.

With regard to the specific functions performed by music, the traditions of Africa have a lot in common with those of other cultures. Music may be organized as an activity concurrent with others, as a terminating activity, or as a free activity. There are work songs, recreational songs, cradle songs, religious songs, healing songs, and incidental music of all kinds.

In addition to these universal types, societies in Africa lay particular emphasis on the use of music for generating social action and for expressing social relationships within the context of performance. Music may be used as a vehicle for expressing or recording a people's history—their dynasties, migrations, hardships and sufferings, defeats and victories. It may be performed as a tribute to a ruler, to an individual who is the focus of a social ceremony, or to a deceased person; it may be performed as an offering or service to a divinity. Above all it is used as a vehicle for making statements likely to provoke action—for registering protests or for criticizing people.

Music may even be institutionalized as a means of criticizing people. In the

Brong Ahafo region of Ghana, for example, songs of insult form part of the worship of the god Ntoa who has ordained that once a year, at a special festival lasting a whole week, his worshippers should sing to get rid of all the ill-feeling that they have been harboring during the year. Thus the festival is the time for organized expression of public opinion, for open criticism of those in authority, and for insulting individuals who may have misbehaved or offended others. All this, however, must be expressed in a specific social context and only through the medium of song. Spoken insults and criticisms are not the acceptable modes of behavior. Moreover, anyone who has something to say must do so within a performing group by taking the solo lead or by getting the whole group to take up and sing what he wants to express. If anyone offended by a singing group wishes to hit back, he must do so in song with another performing group. In other words, statements originating from individuals must come out as collective expressions. The rules stipulate that during the entire period of the festival, no one can be taken to court or even questioned afterwards for singing songs of insult. However this license ends with the festival. Thereafter anyone who sings songs of insult openly rather than in a discreet allusive manner does so at his own risk.

Another form of social behavior which is institutionalized is praise singing. In some areas of the savannah belt of West Africa, such as Senegal, Gambia, Guinea, Mali and Northern Nigeria, there are professional praise singers who are also chroniclers and bards. They recount the reigns of kings if they are court functionaries, family genealogies and histories if they are attached to individual households.[4] Song as a form of social behavior includes boasting songs such as *ibiririmbo* songs of the Hutu of Zaire,[5] songs of contest such as the halo songs of the Ewe of Ghana, and judicial songs sung by people contesting cases.

Because of the use that music is put to in African societies, its meaning is not restricted to the intrinsic values of music but may include extramusical values as well. Hence it is not always enough to hear music or to pay attention only to its formal features. One must also evaluate it in terms of the other meanings associated with it.

There is an Ashanti expression used when someone hears something but does not appear to understand it, or when he looks somewhat unconvinced. It says, "It is like singing to the White man." The person hears what goes on and seems to give it polite attention, but he is not moved because he really does not understand it. The Ashanti used to make musical jokes in such situations, even on important state occasions. There is a piece played by the *kete* drum ensemble of the royal court, entitled Yɛde brɛbrɛ bɛkum Adinkra, which means, "Slowly but surely we shall kill Adinkra." Adinkra was an enemy of the Ashanti who proved rather difficult to vanquish but was eventually captured in a battle. When the Ashanti succumbed to the British after seven battles taking place over a period of about seventy-five years, this was the piece that, in their characteristic humor, they chose to play for the representative of the British crown whenever he came on state visit. This remained the musical convention throughout the colonial period. As the governor went round beaming and shaking hands with each of the chiefs who met on the durbar ground to receive him, one by one their *kete* drum ensembles would strike up the tune, "Slowly but surely we shall kill Adinkra." Like the earlier travelers and administrators who wrote about African music, he would hear the piece without understanding it.

Performing Groups and Their Music

Songs are used not only for generating social action but also for the related purpose of expressing group identity and solidarity. The recreational life of a community depends very much on the existence of voluntary associations and bands of musicians, and court life is much enriched by the variety of performers in a ruler's regular entourage. Performing groups of all kinds are found in African societies. There are groups organized solely for the performance of recreational music, professional groups or bands, and groups attached to a patron or ruler. Some are voluntary associations or clubs which include a core of music "specialists" who have a more than average command of musical skills and repertoire; a number of officers, patrons or leaders; and a majority who join in the chorus. Membership in such a club confers certain privileges, such as the right to have the group perform at one's funeral or at the funeral of a close relative. (It does not matter whether funeral music is sad or gay, for the group is enjoying it with the deceased for the last time and paying him tribute in this manner.) Participation in music is not always wholly voluntary. In some contexts, it is an obligation imposed by membership in a social group which functions also as a performing group. Performing roles are distributed and every member is expected to play his part. It is his obligation to attend performances and to make financial contributions when required to do so.

Social groups which are not specifically musical perform special music designed for their leisure activities or for the ceremonies, rites, and other activities which their communities expect them to undertake. Such a social group may be defined by descent: it may be a matrilineage, a patrilineage, or a clan. Or it may be defined by age or sex. There are musical types to be performed by children in connection with their recreational activities or rites; others to be performed by women in connection with religious rites and ceremonies and with their roles in war and peace. Similarly, for male groups, such as warrior or heroic associations, hunters' clubs, and craft guilds there is special music. Generally the music performed by each type of social group is distinct from that of others, and its music is one of the things that give a group its identity. The music of warrior organizations is different from that of hunters or of music clubs which specialize in different forms of recreational music.

The link of music with different occasions gives rise to the creation of a wide variety of musical types. Naturally, since they are contributed over the years by different individuals, the items that constitute such musical types reflect different degrees of sophistication in the use of musical materials. On any given occasion, a group performs as many items as it can recall, including those that have immediate appeal because of their relevance to the particular situation. The structure of musical items generally reflects the different performing roles that members of a social group can assume. There are simple parts that everybody can perform, as well as complex parts for specialists. There are minor instrumental parts which can be picked up quickly by most people as well as ones that require the attention of experts. Songs are divided into sections for cantor and chorus in order to facilitate group participation. Pieces are usually of moderate length, since everything has to be learned by word of mouth or by ear. Repetition and improvised variations are used to sustain performances of given pieces for the required duration. Other common techniques include the ostinato and the hocket.

Children's songs do not, of course, show the same degree of formal complexity as those performed by adults. Nor is the music of the court on the same level as music in the public domain. Songs intended for processions, or for group action rather than for contemplation, or for keeping people alert during a story-telling session do not have the same sort of form as praise or narrative songs. Likewise, formal organization is more sophisticated where music is performed solely by specialists or where specialists have scope for improvisation—where, for example, music is performed by solo instrumentalists, by solo singers performing alone or with a supporting chorus, or by court musicians. However, the repertoire even of sophisticated musicians may include quite a few items that are fairly simple in form. Thus African music can only be fully understood and evaluated when social determinants of form and structure are taken into account.

Musical Resources

The music of African societies is based on four, five, six, or seven tone scales.[6] A great deal of emphasis is laid on vocal music, since singing allows for active participation by all members of a social group.

Handclapping, stamping and improvised sound-producing objects, as well as regular musical instruments, are widely used to accompany singing, or, in some contexts, in their own right. Instruments include a large variety of idiophones; rattles of all kinds, such as container rattles of gourd or wicker, seed shell rattles, beaded rattles, strung rattles, and the sistrum; and all sorts of struck and concussion instruments, such as percussion sticks, bells, wooden slit drums or gongs, and stamping tubes. All these are used principally as rhythm instruments, for there is a strong preference for music that has a rhythm section which gives a steady, forward drive to it.

In addition to such rhythm instruments, however, there are two tuned idiophones in common use: the *mbira* or *sansa* (also referred to as a hand piano, finger piano, or thumb piano) and the xylophone. These may be played as solo instruments, in ensembles along with a rhythm section, or as an accompaniment to singing.

African societies are, of course, very rich in membranophones (drums with parchment heads). They are made in all sorts of shapes and sizes and used for conveying signals and imitating speech as well as for playing music. The African concept of music allows for the creation of pure rhythmic music on drums with or without the addition of idiophones. In some contexts, however, the drums are also used to provide the rhythm section of an instrumental or vocal ensemble.

Aerophones found in African communities include varieties of vertical and transverse flutes either made out of materials with a natural bore or carved out of wood. There are single reed pipes as well as the double reed instruments found mainly in Islamized areas. Trumpets are carved out of wood or, in a few cases, made out of metal or sections of gourd. Animal horns and elephant tusks are also treated and used as musical instruments. Some aerophones are used as "talking" instruments in much the same way as drums are, while others are used as musical instruments to be played for solos or in ensembles. An aerophone ensemble may be homogeneous in composition or it may have a rhythm section of drums, or of drums and idiophones.

There is an equally wide variety of chordophones, including bowed and plucked lutes, arched lutes, harp lutes, arched harps, lyres, and zithers. It is customary to use these for accompanying vocal music.

Varieties of African Music

Although the aggregate of African musical resources is very large, each ethnic group tends to limit itself to the materials it considers adequate for communicating its own personal and social values. The weight of tradition and the community orientation of organized performances tend to constrain radical changes. Innovations in style do occur, especially in recreational music, but these are never radical except where there has been contact with other cultures, particularly with non-African cultures that have taken root in Africa.

Similarly, those who make creative additions to repertoire tend to use models within the tradition or something close to them, for in music organized as a form of community experience, the directness of the message and the immediacy of the response are essential. The choice of musical materials may also be limited by environmental factors—by a people's life style as farmers, sedentary pastoralists, or nomads, or by their peculiar historical circumstances. Hence, in the final analysis, what counts is how well a piece of music communicates to the social group.

Such limits and the cultural autonomy expressed by ethnic groups in the past have led to considerable divergencies in certain details of musical practice. In the area of tonal organization, for example, African societies tend to specialize in the use of one or two scales as the basis for all their music. When groups base their scales on different divisions of the octave as well as on different intervallic values, they create the impression on the sensuous level of distinct musical cultures. A music based on a five-tone scale does not sound the same as one based on a seven-tone scale even if it employs similar melodic and rhythmic procedures. The difference sounds even greater between a piece of music based on the hemitonic pentatonic (five-tone scale with half steps) and another based on some sort of equidistant scale.

There are closely related variations in the textures of vocal music. Some ethnic groups sing mainly in unison or in octaves, with sporadic fifths and fourths; others sing in parallel thirds, fourths, or fifths, depending largely on the scale and the prevailing concept of "consonant" intervals. Some use complex vocal and instrumental polyphony, while others keep to very simple forms. Similarly, ideals of voice show considerable variation. Some prefer an open quality of voice; others a somewhat tense quality. Individual ethnic styles are characterized by the presence or absence of slight pulsation, the use of tongue flutter, yodeling, or slight nasality. Futhermore, differences in language tend to color singing styles because phonetic features of speech may be reflected in the melody itself or in the style of performance. Since over 700 distinct (though historically related) languages are spoken in Subsaharan Africa, it is often difficult for a group to understand the verbal basis for the music of its neighbors.

Variations in tuning are found, sometimes even within the same ethnic group.

Apart from the tonal differences in the music of individual ethnic groups, there are differences in the selection and use of musical instruments. In spite of the importance attached to drums, some societies either do not possess drums or do not emphasize them nearly as much in their music as one would expect. Varieties of chordophones have a restricted distribution. Arched harps and lyres are concentrated in Eastern Africa, while trough zithers, tube zithers and bar zithers are more common in Eastern and Central Africa than in West Africa. The savannah belt of West Africa, on the other hand, is relatively rich in lutes.

Even where the same types of instrument are used, differences are found in design and construction and sometimes in the degree of sophistication of performing techniques. The *mbira* (*sansa* or hand piano) for example, may have as few as five keys or as many as forty-three. Some such instruments have a single manual of keys while others have two or three ranks. In this connection, the mbiras of Zambia and Rhodesia appear to be more sophisticated than those of other areas. Similarly, although the musical bow is widespread in Africa, those of Southern Africa are more sophisticated than those found elsewhere. All of this points to a need for recognizing that there are different *varieties* of African music based on the distinct usages of ethnic groups—the Yoruba variety, the Wolof variety, the Tutsi variety, the Sukuma variety, and so on. Each variety is a valid African musical expression incorporating the historical and cultural preferences of an ethnic group.

In addition, however, each variety shares certain characteristics with other varieties which make it distinctively African. Structurally, for example, most varieties use large intervals rather than microtones as formative elements of pitch systems; "prosodic" features of speech, such as on and off glides or rising attack and falling release for markers; changes in pitch values and tone qualities for sporadic effects; and buzzing devices to increase the ratio of noise to pitch. Other stable elements of form and structure are the use of sectional structures, the interplay of fixed and free forms, and other procedures relating to the construction of melody, rhythm and multipart textures.

It is these common elements of structure and musical procedure that tend to persist in situations of culture contact when the ethnic bonds that support indigenous traditions are broken, and new musical values are acquired. This is evident in the musical cultures of the African Diaspora which, torn from their African roots, have nevertheless created music that reflects not only their new cultural environment and its pressures and challenges, but also certain aspects of musical procedure characteristic of the African musical tradition. It is also evident to some extent in the music of African musicians in cities who, separated from their indigenous musical cultures by the forces of acculturation and urbanization, are making a new effort to draw on the resources of their traditional music.[7] On stylistic grounds, therefore, the concept of "varieties of African music" can be applied not only to the traditional African music identified with ethnic groups in Africa, but also to nontribal "contemporary" varieties of African music and to much of the so-called "African-derived" music of the New World. Such an application emphasizes the commonality of the black experience in music.

Documentation of African Music

Against the foregoing background we can now look briefly at some of the problems engaging the attention of those interested in African musical studies. The musical traditions of Africa, as we have seen, are practiced and perpetuated by oral tradition, and this has repercussions on its modes of organization for performance. With the exception of Ethiopia, whose church has a kind of notation for biblical cantillations, African societies have not developed written systems of notation. The foremost concern of all scholars, therefore, has been to record and document African music in all its varieties in order to provide materials for creative work and for listening, as well as data for systematic study.

There is some urgency about this task because of the rapid social changes taking place in Africa today. The efforts of collectors like Hugh Tracey, Charles Duvelle and Tolia Nikiprowetsky have been considerably enlarged by other field collectors and scholars. UNESCO is giving active support to this aspect of African musical studies through its series of anthologies of musical sources. A discography of African music on long-playing records compiled by Alan Merriam has 390 entries.[8] These do not include the extensive recordings of Bantu music made by Hugh Tracey for the International Library of African Music. Because of the enormous size of the African continent and the rather large number of ethnic groups, there are still many gaps in the available recordings. Inadequate documentation and uncertainty about the bases of selection, particularly with regard to the norms of the societies whose music is recorded, pose problems for the scholar, and the need for field studies of African music in its social context continues to be felt.

Students of African music are also concerned with the study of musical instruments in danger of falling into disuse because of the alluring splendor of the products of Western industry. As we have seen, the variety of pitch systems and the lack of interethnic group norms make this area of African music particularly vulnerable and susceptible to change. The Western guitar is fast usurping the place of traditional chordophones, while Western wind instruments are gaining roots everywhere as the instrumental medium for popular music. Interest in the study of African musical instruments has been stimulated by the existence of European museum collections and, in the past, by colonial museums in Africa. The field poses a number of problems that continue to fascinate scholars, such as those involving scales and tuning systems, and the contribution that musical instruments can make to the study of cultural history.[9]

Just as students of African music as a whole feel the need for field recordings, so students of musical instruments feel the need to go beyond the purely descriptive or ethnological to detailed investigations into performing techniques, musical styles and repertoire. Studies of the music of individual instruments are being done—particularly of drums, xylophones and *mbiras* (hand pianos)—which are grappling with problems of suitable notation as well as with analysis of style and the theoretical basis of the procedures followed by African musicians. Similar studies are being done in vocal music, particularly with respect to vocal techniques, tonal organization, and the analysis of song texts.

As would be expected, a number of methodological questions have arisen as scholars address themselves more and more to the problem of meaning in African music. They are taking a new interest in biographical studies of African musicians as a source of insights into the African experience in music. They are also applying the methods of cognitive anthropology to the study of forms of musical knowledge, especially of musical terms in African languages.[10] Acculturation in music has been of particular interest, especially with respect to the influence of Arabic and Western musical cultures on African traditions. Studies of the historical interaction among African societies that led to the borrowing of musical instruments and other resources are being pursued.[11]

Because of the large number of varieties of African music, scholars are stressing the need for comparative studies on the patterns of variation and their geographical distribution. Their hope is that such studies will lead, ultimately, to the proper classification of the varieties of African music into style clusters. The extension of such comparative studies to the music of the African Diaspora is beginning to receive active consideration by scholars in Africa.[12]

There is increasing concern for the use of a multidisciplinary approach in the study of African music, since music used for generating social action and at the same time for recreational enjoyment cannot be understood in isolation from its social context. Apart from the initial problem of "tuning in" to unfamiliar sound materials, to relate to African music, one must appreciate not only its forms, structure, and modes of expression, but also any pragmatic or extramusical meaning embodied in it or associated with it by tradition. Since the symbols of extramusical meanings are not universal but culturally defined, what a piece conveys beyond its sensuous or surface structure can only be grasped by those acquainted with its background, and may be missed not only by an outsider but also by members of a community who lack certain background knowledge.

For arriving at the kind of knowledge which aids understanding and appreciation of the role of music in community life, the best techniques of investigation proceed from the musical event to its wider social and cultural context, thereby enabling us not only to analyze and describe the modes of expression cultivated in each society but also to isolate the significant social and cultural factors that shape and determine these.

It is important also that we do not allow the traditional compartmentalization of the arts in academic institutions to blind us to the need for looking at African music as part of larger events. Our understanding of musical performances in community life can be greatly enhanced by a knowledge of related arts and the way music is integrated with them. Examination of the nexus between music and dance, music and drama, music and verbal art, and music and visual art might enable us to isolate the determinants of structure in such complexes, or the range of complementary information that their juxtaposition provides over and above the purely aesthetic.

Obviously, for example, our analysis of features of African rhythm should proceed from a deep awareness of movement and the dance, on which, to a large extent, it is based. To appreciate African music, one must develop a feeling for movement in order to relate internally to the propulsive effect of recurrent patterns. To be able to perform this music, one must develop a sense of periodicity, an ability to repeat a phrase, rhythm pattern, motif or even a single note at the same point of entry within cycles of a given time span.

The link of musical performances with the drama of ritual and with ceremonial occasions similarly influences the organization and use of repertoire as well as the selection of instrumental sounds. Music and verbal art are also linked. In many parts of Subsaharan Africa without indigenous traditions of writing, literature occurs as a verbal art form; it is spoken or recited, chanted or sung, or transmitted by a surrogating medium such as a drum, a trumpet, or a double bell. Music closely linked to verbal art is influenced in certain details of its structure by linguistic factors, including the markers of prosody.

In conclusion I would like to emphasize that the study of African music in terms of the African experience is of particular interest to us in Africa at this critical time in our history when we are building new nations out of ethnic groups that practice their own varieties of African music, a time when opportunities for learning this music in the community through the processes of socialization are dwindling because of the social changes taking place.

The building of cultural bridges to enable citizens of new nations to develop greater tolerance and understanding for the music of different ethnic groups is an urgent task. Interest must be generated in different African traditions so that they can be accepted as a common heritage irrespective of their ethnic origins. Closely related to this is the problem of building up a new audience for this heritage through properly planned music education programs for children and the adults of tomorrow.

There can be no doubt that scholarly studies can play a part in providing information on music and a theoretical basis for its appreciation. Properly selected and programmed sound recordings can also play a part in all this by helping listeners to develop new listening habits and to broaden their musical horizons. What we need even more than this, however, is for music to continue to be promoted as a form of community experience, for there is no better way of preserving music than by keeping it alive through regular performances. African governments are responding to this need as well as to the need for scholarly research into African music and related arts.

REFERENCES

1. Helen Hause, "Terms for Musical Instruments in the Sudanic Languages of West Africa: A Lexicographical Enquiry," *Journal of American Oriental Society,* Supplement 7 (January-March 1948).

2. William Hickens, "Music, a Triumph of African Art," *Art and Archaeology,* 33, No. 1 (January-February 1932), p. 37.

3. J. H. Kwabena Nketia, "Surrogate Languages of Africa," *Current Trends in Linguistics* (The Hague: Mouton, 1971), pp. 699-732.

4. Michael G. Smith, "The Social Functions and Meaning of Hausa Praise Singing," *Africa,* 27, No. 1 (1957), pp. 26-44.

5. Alan P. Merriam, "African Music," *Continuity and Change in African Cultures,* ed. Bascom & Herskovits (Evanston: Northwestern University Press, 1958), pp. 49-86.

6. J. H. Kwabena Nketia, "The Musical Languages of Subsaharan Africa," *African Music* (Paris: La Revue Musicale, 1972), pp. 7-49.

7. Ben A. Aning, "Varieties of African Music and Musical Types," *The Black Perspective in Music,* 1, No. 1 (Spring 1973), p. 21.

8. Alan P. Merriam: *African Music on L. P.; An Annotated Discography* (Evanston: Northwestern

University Press, 1970).

9. Klaus P. Wachsmann, ed., *Essays on Music and History* (Evanston: Northwestern University Press, 1971). The most outstanding contribution to this area has been made by Klaus Wachsmann following the lead of Sachs and Hornbostel in the general field of organology and the pioneering work of Percival Kirby on the *Musical Instruments of the Native Races of South Africa.*

10. David Ames and Anthony King, *Glossary of Hausa Music and Its Social Context* (Evanston: Northwestern University Press, 1971).

11. Klaus Wachsmann, ed., *Essays on Music and History in Africa* (Evanston: Northwestern University Press, 1971); J. H. Kwabena Nketia, "Sources of Historical Data on the Musical Cultures of Africa," *African Music* (Paris: La Revue Musicale, 1972), pp. 43-49.

12. J. H. Kwabena Nketia, "The Study of African and Afro-American Music," *The Black Perspective in Music,* 1, No. 1 (1973), pp. 7-15.

BENJAMIN QUARLES

Black History Unbound

UNTIL RECENT TIMES the role of the Afro-American in our national life was thought to be hardly worth considering. An intellectual "white flight" held sway; most writers in the social sciences and the humanities, whatever their individual specialties, assumed that they knew as much about blacks as they needed to know or as their readers cared to learn. With this static image, the black was considered something of an intruder, if not indeed an outsider. In many quarters he was regarded as an exotic, an offshoot, hardly "a peece of the Continent, a part of the maine." Certainly he was underplayed in American history and letters.

This situation has undergone considerable change in the past two decades. The stepped-up civil rights movement following the Supreme Court's public school desegregation decision in 1954 heightened black consciousness and sparked the demand for black power, thereby creating a larger audience for black expression in its various forms. The popularization of black history in the mass-circulation monthly, *Ebony,* particularly in the writings of its senior editor, Lerone Bennett, Jr., left a deep imprint on hundreds of thousands of readers hitherto unresponsive to the call of the past. Of considerable influence, too, in raising the level of black consciousness was the emergence of more than a score of black nations below the Sahara, whose newly acquired independence was at once a symbol and a reminder of a rich precolonial African heritage too long in limbo.

The colleges and universities have assumed a major role in this contemporary example of the present recreating the past. In predominantly white colleges, the proliferation of black studies owes much to pressures from black students, often supported by fellow students and faculty. The marked increase in the number of blacks attending these colleges in the sixties, combined with their search for personal identity and group solidarity, led to their demand for courses relating to the black experience, a demand often heading the list designated as "non-negotiable." Black colleges had long operated precursor programs in black studies, but in the sixties they considerably increased their offerings.

Although such black-oriented programs, quite unlike other college offerings, made their way into the curriculum as a result of student pressures, the colleges soon realized that the newly introduced disciplines were worthy of inclusion. Black history might well have healing in its wings, but it also had an intrinsic importance much broader than its therapeutic value.

Black studies, despite their tender years, can no longer be regarded as a controversial academic innovation, though coming-of-age ceremonies would certainly be premature at this "growing pains" stage. It is impossible for American society to be properly appraised if blacks are left out of the picture. "We cannot," writes Columbia historian Walter Metzger, "understand America without the help of those studies now called 'black.'" John W. Blassingame of Yale concurs, pointing out that "no American can truly understand his own society and culture without a knowledge of the roles Negroes have played in them." The black looms large in American letters, writes Jean Fagan Yellin: "His dark figure is ubiquitous in our fiction; the American imagination was as obsessed in the nineteenth century by the black as it is today." Since Jamestown, black-white relationships have been a central attribute of our national culture. The experiences of blacks and whites, though profoundly different, have always been intertwined and complementary, even symbiotic on occasion, however much whites may have monopolized the process and substance of power. Hence American studies, properly perceived, must be viewed through a multiracial lens.

The role of blacks in America—what they have done and what has been done to them—illuminates the past and informs the present. The father of black historiography, Carter G. Woodson (1875-1950), and his associates and successors have told us much about the constructive role played by blacks in the making of America. But for all his scholarship and perception, Woodson did not fully sense the dimensions of what had been done to blacks. He was, of course, familiar with the well-known U. B. Phillips contention, advanced in 1928, that the central theme in Southern history was that the South was and should remain a white man's country. But Woodson and his black-oriented contemporaries could hardly have been fully aware of the extent of racism in America, a topic which has only recently been given the type of probing scrutiny found, for example, in Winthrop D. Jordan,[1] who feels that, without the blacks, the early whites would have experienced an identity crisis. As Joanna E. Schneider and Robert L. Zangrando have pointed out, one of the ways in which the American past must be reappraised is in terms of the interactions of the dominant whites with red, black and yellow peoples. "Unless we fully comprehend the role of racism in this society, we can never truly know America," they observe, adding that black history "offers us an indispensable opportunity" to do so.[2]

If coming to grips with this component of our national experience confronts us with some of our more sober realities, ironies, and paradoxes, it will also revitalize inquiry. Any loss of innocence should be more than balanced by the virtues of a viewpoint more broadly humanistic in its outreach. Black literature, for example, may offer new insights into classic American literature. William W. Nichols has compared Frederick Douglass' statements in *My Bondage and My Freedom*, written in 1855, with Thoreau's in *Walden*,[3] viewing both as seekers after freedom. Similarly, Leonard J. Deutsch, in an article entitled, "Ralph Waldo Ellison and Ralph Waldo Emerson: A Shared Moral Vision,"[4] sees points of correspondence between the two men of letters despite differences in their exteriors, not to mention in their times and manners. New awareness of the interactions of whites and blacks is making it necessary for many branches of learning to redefine themselves.

Black studies, however, are more than a prelude to cross-cultural understanding; they celebrate ethnic pluralism as a fact in our national life. More and more we are beginning to see America as a multiculture. This heightened ethnic consciousness is not confined to color alone, but embraces non-Anglo-Saxon whites as well. To these people not of the "old stock," the idea of cultural assimilation has lost much of its appeal. In part this has stemmed from a sense of disillusionment. "Are we living the dream our grandparents dreamed when on creaking decks they stood silent, afraid, hopeful at the sight of the Statue of Liberty," Michael Novak asked in 1972. "Will we ever find that secret relief, that door, that hidden entrance?"[5] But the essential feeling behind the rise of white ethnic consciousness comes not from a sense of social acceptance withheld, but rather from a realization that assimilation means "Anglo-assimilation," that minority groups wishing to enter the mainstream must first divest themselves of their own values and traditions. Hence, the thrust by blacks has legitimated cultural diversity, and the push for black studies has served as a spur to studies of women, white ethnic groups, and other minorities.[6] White ethnic groups, while still priding themselves on their true-blue Americanism, no longer feel that they must surrender whatever distinctive Old World ties or traits they still retain. The immigrant past is no longer considered "fringe" history.

This polycultural concept of our country and its past, to which black studies have contributed so markedly, holds that America's diversity is one of her richest national endowments. It says unmistakably, if by inference, that the Northern European types were not the only ones who brought gifts to their new land. And, it might be added, this new acceptance of pluralism by no means connotes a rise in racial antagonisms. We are not unmindful of the admonition of William Dean Howells: "Inequality is as dear to the heart of America as liberty," nor do we forget that many Americans, black and white, forge their identity around the concept of color. A genuine ethnic pluralism, however, would tend less to polarize tension among groups than to reaffirm their mutuality.

Views of Black History

Although black Americans are no longer regarded as an out-group with a blank past, the field of black history is attended by ongoing problems—in the attitudes of its chroniclers, the sources available, and the changes in interpretations.

In the last two decades black history has attained a growing acceptance in learned quarters. White historians could hardly escape noting such statements as those of Robert I. Rotberg that "The existence of African history has, in recent years, achieved scholarly recognition," and of C. Vann Woodward that "so far as their culture is concerned, all Americans are part Negro," and as a consequence, "American history, the white man's version, could profit from an infusion of 'soul.'" If white historians still think of themselves as the custodians of the word and the gate-keepers of the citadel, they are no longer so set on viewing the Negro as a stranger, if not a barbarian at the gates. They now deal more circumspectly with blacks, hoping to avoid what logicians call the "fallacy of initial predication."

However, although they may have succeeded in ridding themselves of preconceptions, and opening their minds to reassessing their sources, they are still subject to some nagging doubts. Many historians have a built-in skepticism concerning innovation, particularly when it comes to a new field of inquiry or a new viewpoint about a low-status minority. The instinct for disciplinary tidiness can be especially strong in a field that is preoccupied with the past.

Still gripped by the genteel tradition of the eighteenth and nineteenth centuries, some historians almost unconsciously believe that society was and is characterized by a high culture and a low culture, and the less said about the latter the better. If a lady (Clio) had her dubious off-moments (mayhap an underworld connection or two), the well-bred and well-trained (the Ph.D.'s) hardly care to call attention to them. And for many historians, despite all their avowed devotion to the canons of objectivity, the mystique of kith and kin still remains strong, making it difficult for them to do full justice to those they regard as beyond the pale. Obviously, too, there are honest differences of opinion among historians; an event that one regards as a watershed may be regarded by another as little more than water under the dam.

Despite assurances from recognized fellow practitioners, many white historians also believe that the whole corpus of black studies is more topical than anything else, a congeries of pressure-group accretions with very little content and a primarily political function. These guardians of the portals see black history as the current faddishness in the profession, its chief result for the discipline a decline in the quality of documentation. Some historians who acquired their basic knowledge and skills when the material available concerning blacks was indeed limited and distorted, feel that new material about blacks must also lack intellectual objectivity and fail to meet valid academic standards. The culture-bound character of their research tools enveloped them in an atmosphere which was nonblack to the extent that black issues were not discussed, and antiblack to the extent that they were. To white scholars, as to whites in general, black history is painful since it forces them to shed the notion that American society is open and fluid, a land where everyone has an equal chance for place and power. As a group, furthermore, blacks have been have-nots and, as Jesse Lemisch points out, "The history of the powerless, the inarticulate, the poor, has not yet begun to be written because they have been treated no more fairly by historians than they have been treated by their contemporaries."

Black chroniclers are not color blind, but they too have their blind spots. The blacks who write history are, in the main, in search of truth, the great canon of the discipline, its very elusiveness making it all the more of a challenge. The search for truth has an intrinsic value, liberating the mind and the spirit. But like many whites in the field, many black historians have "a magnet in their mind," to use Herbert Butterfield's perceptive phrase. There is no magic in skin color, and black historians too sometimes engage in adversary proceedings, with racial vindication the paramount consideration.

Black writers of history for the masses often reflect "the great man" theory of history, presenting a gallery of heroic men and women pushing on to victory against great odds. The black bibliographer, A. A. Schomburg, characterized these glorifiers as "glibly trying to prove that half of the world's geniuses have been Negroes and to trace the pedigree of nineteenth century Americans from the Queen of Sheba." Most writers in this school of "Claim-the-World Negro History" were not as able as J. A. Rogers, the black biographer who died in 1966. That Rogers was an indefatigable researcher on an intercontinental scale is attested to by his wide-ranging, *World's Great Men of Color*.[7] Operating from the premise that "the story of contacts of whites and blacks is usually told from the white angle,"

Rogers designed his capsule biographies as a source of inspiration to the young, particularly to those who were black. But in his desire to project a heroic black image, he was sometimes carried away and his sketches of historical figures are shot through with hyperbole and panegyric.

Another group who view the past from a special angle are the revolutionary black nationalists. They do not feel that history should be hero worship. "Black history does not seek to highlight the outstanding contributions of special black people to the life and times of America," writes Vincent Harding, the eloquent Director of the Institute of the Black World in Atlanta. "Rather our emphasis is on exposure, disclosure, or reinterpretation of the entire American past. We want to know America at its depths, now that invitations to its life are besieging us." The revolutionary black nationalists are exponents of functional research, issue laden and action oriented. Not addressing themselves to pure, theoretical, knowledge-for-its-own-sake investigation, they do not propose to scale the mountain simply because it is there. They hold that black studies, including history, should be a catalyst for the new day a-coming. To Nathan Hare, editor of *The Black Scholar,* "a black studies program which is not revolutionary and nationalist is, accordingly, quite profoundly irrelevant." Scorning objectivity as a species of ivory-towerism, the revolutionary nationalists hold that ideology and intellectualism are not incompatible, and that a person who has leaned too long in one direction may, for a time, have to lean in the other if he is to achieve balance.

Essentially these nationalist intellectuals share many of the beliefs of the sociologist-psychiatrist, Frantz Fanon of Martinique, who held that "African-Negro" culture would develop not around songs, poems, and folklore, but around the struggles of the people. "White America," he said, was "an organized imperialist force holding black people in colonial bondage." The black revolutionaries address themselves to the task of decolonizing America, including her history. Fanon also held that for "the wretched of the earth" the way out was physical confrontation. He thus gave to violence an aura of romance, suggesting that it had a cleansing, releasing effect. Thus disdaining the doctrine of reconciliation and determined not to forget white America's massive assault upon the humanity of blacks, the revolutionary nationalists consciously choose to imprison themselves in the castle of color. The construct of the White Man dominates their thinking, much as the Devil was once the central figure in some Christian theologies.

Nevertheless, we dismiss the black revolutionary nationalists at our intellectual and social peril. Even though we might not share their fondness for rhetorical flourishes and threatening hyperbole, their demand for heretical history must be carefully weighed, especially as they bring to their reflections a tunnel vision so often characteristic of the powerless people whose cause they proclaim. "Let us not decide to imitate Europe," urged Fanon. "Let us try to create the whole man, whom Europe has been incapable of bringing to triumphant birth." The revolutionary black nationalist interpretation of the black experience is somewhat new in American thought, although the nationalist point of view is not.[8]

The Problem of Materials

An old and recurring phenomenon in black history writing is the paucity of sources, the lack of hard data. Many questions must remain unanswered because there are no sources from which to formulate a trustworthy response. Negro sources are not easy to come by; documents, more often than not, are not readily accessible. The formal record is often thin, for most blacks were not articulate in a literary sense. John Chavis, Director of Behavioral Science Research at Tuskegee Institute's Carver Research Foundation, has posed the problem of the investigator: "Where are the diaries, the family Bibles, the correspondence in fancy script tied in bundles? These are not, in most instances, part of the Negro past. Where are the silver services, the porringers, the samplers, the furniture dark and glossy, the oil portraits of awesome ancestors?" Even when Negro memorabilia do exist, they are often hidden away in a basement or an attic, prey to fire or other loss. Such privately held material is invariably unprocessed. All too often even in major research libraries, particularly those of state and local historical societies, Negro-related holdings have never been catalogued.

Fortunately, the available sources are now being more widely publicized than ever before, and depositories are calling attention to their black-oriented materials, including early black newspapers and magazines on microfilm. *The Quarterly Journal of the Library of Congress*, for example, has devoted a special issue to its African materials.[9] In the extent of its black documents, the Library of Congress is rivaled by a sister federal agency, the National Archives. In June, 1973, more than 150 scholars and interested parties attended a two-day "National Archives Conference on Federal Archives as Sources for Research on Afro-Americans," a meeting which addressed itself to the agency's Negro-related materials (a number of them audiovisuals), including the originals of the well-known Emancipation Proclamation and the Civil War amendments.[10] Historical societies have also begun to furnish guides to their Negro-related holdings.[11] This itself is a hopeful sign inasmuch as research libraries, like museums and art galleries, are selective in their acquisitions; they do not buy or accept and certainly do not publicize anything they feel will have too low a yield in public or professional interest and prestige.

During the past decade black source materials have profited from an infusion of oral history, created by interviewing selected persons of note and tape-recording and transcribing their remarks. What is, in essence, a memory bank of formal oral history was inaugurated a quarter of a century ago at Columbia University by Allan Nevins. In the first two decades of Columbia's Oral History Collection, of 200 interviewees only three were black—W. E. B. DuBois, journalist George S. Schuyler, and Roy Wilkins. In orders received for micro-published copies of the memoirs, however, the top best seller as of April 1973 was that of W. E. B. DuBois, and the third-ranking best seller was that of Roy Wilkins.

In recent years other oral history collections have sought Negro-related materials.[12] The largest collection which concentrates on blacks is the Civil Rights Documentation Project at Howard University, dealing with black protest expression since 1954.[13] Currently it includes 703 tape-recorded interviews, 60 conference tapes and 800 transcripts. In Alabama, seven predominantly black colleges have launched a Statewide Oral History Project "to document the personal experiences of black Alabamians in their attempts to cope with racial prejudice and in their struggle to achieve racial equality."[14]

The mounting number of black research materials has led black librarians to seek ways to work cooperatively in providing reliable information on Afro-

American bibliography. With an initial grant in June, 1971, from the U.S. Office of Education, the North Carolina Central University School of Library Science began a project to identify and coordinate all African-American materials in six southeastern states. A year earlier, a group of librarians and scholars, meeting in Philadelphia, formed the Association of African-American Bibliography, one of whose announced aims was the establishment of "a Black Union Catalog on a regional and national basis."

By far the most urgent need in black history (and in black studies in general) is for just such a massive, comprehensive bibliography of black source materials, modeled along the lines of the National Union Catalog, compiled by the Library of Congress. Such a compilation might take a dual form, providing a catalogue of printed works and another of manuscripts. It would serve many interests. Although scholars would be the immediate beneficiaries, the academic community in general would profit. People in public life and in the media would benefit from the availability of a trustworthy guide to materials on black citizens and black-white relationships. Such a tool would also lead reformist groups to the data they need.

Although publicizing the existing data would be a major step forward in black historiography, it should be accompanied by a re-examination of what is considered historical evidence, and an inclination to ask new questions of the data. In fields other than the natural sciences, basic theoretical frameworks have not been staked out, and in an evolving field like black history the play of flexibility and innovation has a special place. With no vested interest in one type of documentation, the researcher in black history can be eclectic in his selection of ways and means. In order to ferret out the true dimensions of the black past he may have to run some methodological risks. Certainly, this is not the place for watertight compartmentalization. Those who work in black studies must be prepared to "stay loose," opening their minds to new approaches while subjecting the familiar ones to constant scrutiny.

Traditional source materials on blacks are in particularly short supply for the periods preceding the Civil War. The African background of the New World blacks is, for example, very difficult to document, and illustrates the need for less traditional methodological approaches. The belief that black Africa had no history has a two-fold origin. With the coming of the European powers, Africa passed into a stage of colonialism. African history was not taught; indeed, the rulers assumed that no such history existed, it being one of their cardinal premises that the history of their subjects dated from their own arrival. Once determined to exploit Africa's human resources, Europeans, as men of conscience and religion, had to convince themselves of the innate inferiority of the natives. Furthermore, written records about West Africa prior to the coming of the Europeans are limited, and thus historical reconstruction is difficult and requires a number of technical skills. Hence, even a historian like Arnold Toynbee was led to believe that the black race was the only one that had made no creative contribution to any of the world's civilizations. Toynbee was careful to disavow the factor of race and color in accounting for the existence of advanced civilizations, but he did tend to make the error common to historians—that of overvaluing peoples for whom written records are abundant and underrating those for whom written records are relatively scarce. In contrast, however, L. S. B. Leakey has pointed out that "men of science today are, with few exceptions, satisfied that Africa was the birthplace of man himself, and that for many hundreds of centuries thereafter Africa was in the forefront of all world progress."[15] As could be expected, the late Dr. Leakey was a social anthropologist.

"The most spectacular feature of the new post-war boom in African history," writes Philip D. Curtin, "has been the development of new techniques for investigation, and the application of older techniques to the African past." In a perceptive booklet,[16] Curtin describes some of the fields which are throwing light on early Africa, including archeology, botanical evidence, linguistic studies, and the oral tradition. The oral tradition is particularly important because most precolonial African civilizations were "oral civilizations" documentable in no other way.[17]

Although the main emphasis in American history writing has traditionally been political and intellectual, areas in which the disadvantaged and anonymous masses did not have much direct impact, other facets of history, whose influence is now growing, take much greater notice of minorities. Social history, for example, views society as a whole, taking into account ordinary people and their patterns of living, and giving attention also to the phenomena of social protest.[18]

The urbanization of black Americans in the twentieth century has had a profound effect not only on blacks themselves but also on America's cities and on the country more generally. A number of excellent books have been written on the daily experiences of ordinary people in American cities.[19] David M. Katzman has illustrated the use of the concept of caste in black urban history.[20] The National Urban League, an agency that has been on the cutting edge of the unprecedented cityward migration in the twentieth century, has been described and assessed by Guichard Parris and Lester Brooks[21] in a book which deals with other major black institutions as well, including the church and the press. Black businesses, small and short-lived as a rule, have not attracted many researchers, but the distinct possibilities in black entrepreneurial history become clearly evident in a meticulous and interpretive study of the North Carolina Mutual Life by Walter Weare.[22] Urban-based reform movements likewise constitute a fruitful line of investigation. August Meier and Elliott Rudwick, one trained in history and the other in sociology, have written a model study of CORE which suggests the desirability of collaborative efforts in black history.[23] The broadening of the kinds of evidence now considered historical is also indicated by new quarterlies like *Ethnohistory*, with its emphasis on general culture, and the *Journal of Interdisciplinary History*, whose avowed purpose, as set forth in its first issue in the autumn of 1970, is to "stimulate historians to examine their own subjects in a new light, whether they be derived from psychology, physics, or paleontology."

Psychohistory, a field of particular importance for minorities, is attracting new attention. This relatively unknown field includes group psychopathology, which touches on the fantasy life and self-image of minorities and on the positive aspects of their differences. It encompasses the best-selling work, *Black Rage,* in which psychiatrists Charles Grier and Price M. Cobbs describe the impact of prejudice on Negro personality patterns. The newest historical periodical is *History of Childhood Quarterly: The Journal of Psychohistory,* which first appeared in the summer of 1973. Earle E. Thorpe, himself black like Grier and Cobbs, holds that "black history always has been cut more from the psychohistory mold than has been the case with modern white Occidental history." In two case studies of Southern life, he challenges the "hate-and-conflict" image of black-white relationships in the antebellum South, holding instead that interracial responses and attitudes were characterized in part by intimacy and affection.[24] Slave-born John Roy Lynch, Congressman from Mississippi during Reconstruction, concurred in this viewpoint, taking note of "the bond of sympathy between the masses of the two races in the South." Thorpe's viewpoints and procedures are stimulating and suggestive. Nevertheless, it is historical revisionism of no mean proportions to view racial relationships below the Potomac as a web of mutuality.

In the less traditional branches of history, particularly those concerned with social behavior and action, investigators of the black experience are turning for information to lesser-mined ores, including church and police records, census publications, city directories, housing and unemployment files, local tax lists, popular culture materials (such as black discography), and legal documents. Court records form the base of historian Letitia Woods Brown's study, *Free Negroes in the District of Columbia, 1790-1846*.[25] Black history stands to gain as more scholars receive training in demographic and family history and in the use of quantitative techniques, including computerized data processing.

New Emphases in Black History

The increasing receptivity to new types of source material for black history has brought about new analyses of familiar topics, such as slavery, and the concept of black uniformity. If, as Staughton Lynd asserts, slavery is "a key to the meaning of our national experience," then we should have as balanced a portrayal of it as possible. Until recently, however, the standard view of slavery tended to reflect the attitudes of the master class. As Henry Steele Commager has pointed out: "The slave-owner was literate and articulate, the Negro slave was illiterate and inarticulate; it was, until recently, the slave-owner's version of slavery which came down to us and which was widely accepted as history." The portrait of slavery that came down from the past was fashioned in the big house and not in slave row. Thus a historian like U. B. Phillips, using sources that represented the views of the masters, tended to depict the slave as contented and his surroundings as pleasant. According to Phillips, plantation life was punctuated by such congenial pastimes as "the dance in the sugarhouse, the bonfire in the quarters with contests in clog dances and cakewalks, the baptizing in the creek with demonstrations from the sisters as they came dripping out, the rabbit hunt, the log-rolling, the house-raising, the husking bee, the quilting party, and the crap game."[26]

Today scholars interested in slavery give more prominence to the slave himself and take little stock in the theory of his total powerlessness. "Any history of slavery must be written in large part from the standpoint of the slave," wrote Richard Hofstadter in 1944. Hitherto consigned to a position as a pawn, the slave is now regarded as a role player, and we are having second thoughts about the allegation that his nature and mentality were servile. We now realize that everybody on the plantation made history, the slave as well as the master.

Something of the slave's experiential world and internal life may be gathered from an examination of his literature—his songs and narratives about bondage and freedom, written or oral. Mark Miles Fisher has opened our eyes to the subtle "this-worldly" character of the ostensibly "other-worldly" religious songs heard along slave row.[27] Sterling Stuckey uses folk songs and folk tales to document his assertion that slaves were able to fashion a life style and set of values of their own.[28] In efforts to reconstruct the slave's world, contemporary slave literature was, of course, a valuable historical source.[29] In addition, the early decades of the twentieth century witnessed a number of efforts to interview ex-slaves and record their impressions. The most comprehensive was conducted by the Federal Writers' Project of the Works Project Administration during the years 1936 to 1938, and resulted in 2,300 recorded interviews, over two-thirds with people over eighty years old.[30]

Used with proper professional safeguards, such nontraditional sources, helped by a fresh glance at the more conventional sources, tell us that slaves found many outlets for their creative energies and social instincts, outlets often hidden from, or un-noted by, their masters. We are now finding that a slave often took as his models of behavior and authority not his master alone, as Stanley Elkins has suggested, but blacks like himself—the sage, the preacher, the bold and defiant, the trickster slave so beloved in black folklore who was adept at "puttin' on ole massa," and even the driver who enforced the dictates of the white overseer. The range of options open to slaves was wider than we had believed, and we are now learning of the myriad ways in which they maintained considerable group solidarity despite the formidable odds against it.

A second example of the many changes in black history is the increased emphasis on the concept that the black is not monolithic, a concept amply illustrated in the rich field of biography and autobiography. In the eyes of others, black Americans often take on a massively uniform quality; if they are not viewed as looking alike, they are thought of as at least thinking and acting alike. This misleading impression stems in part from a tendency to lump all blacks together—to typecast them—and in part from their understandably united and standard response to color discrimination. Blacks, for example, often vote as a bloc against a prejudiced or racially obtuse politician.

Aside from their common cause against an adversary and a shared sense of having been wronged, however, American blacks have been marked historically by diversity. Within themselves, they fall into a congeries of groups reflective of a typically American individualism. They have always had their own class lines. In ante-bellum America, the free black thought of himself as inhabiting a niche considerably above that of the slave. And within the free black group there were further distinctions, including those based on skin color, occupation, schooling, and free ancestry. Slave society also had gradations. House servants had the most prestige; below them came the skilled laborers; and bringing up the rear were the field hands. In the quarter century following the Civil War, skin color (light or dark) loomed even larger as a status determinant; since 1900, however, in line with the national pattern, money has been the most important determinant of rank in the black American's unofficial who's who.

With regard to religious affiliations and political party ties, as in other areas, blacks have had varied preferences. Since they have had no universally held dogmas, they have never had an official spokesman; even Booker T. Washington, although he exercised great influence among prominent whites, could never speak for more than a fraction of his fellow blacks. The Communists made a strong bid for colored membership in the thirties, but found that they could make little headway against the black American's dislike for regimentation and for thinking in lockstep. Indeed, even in fighting discrimination, blacks have never agreed upon one approach or strategy, but have made proposals ranging from going back to Africa to setting aside a portion of the United States for black occupation. Blacks are persons as well as types. There is no such thing as a universally held black ideology or point of view. In America, land of individualism, there is no end to the number of ways of being black.

The field of life-writing bears this out, revealing a multiplicity of disparate personalities. Slave narratives aside, black biography received its first great thrust with the publication, in 1887, of *Men of Mark: Eminent, Progressive and Rising*, by William J. Simmons. A former slave who had become a clergyman and educator, Simmons consistently sounded an inspirational, eulogistic note in the 178 sketches he assembled.[31] Simmons included no women in the hope, which proved vain, that he would be able to publish a companion volume devoted to them. From 1912 to 1952, sketches of black notables were carried in the *Negro Yearbook and Annual Encyclopedia of the Negro*.[32] In more recent years a number of professionally trained historians have published black collective biographies.[33] There are also a number of black biography series in the field, most notably those of the University of Chicago[34] and the Oxford University Press.[35] In addition three of the most prominent of all American blacks, Frederick Douglass, W. E. B. DuBois and Booker T. Washington, are now coming under fuller study and investigation as efforts proceed to publish their papers.[36]

The Periodical Literature

Afro-American History: A Bibliography, edited by Dwight L. Smith,[37] is a compendium of 2,900 abstracts on the black experience, compiled by combing the periodical literature from 1954 to 1971, a period in which awareness of the presence of blacks reached new heights, spurring a vast outpouring of articles. Better than any other single work, *Afro-American History* helps illuminate the new kinds of concerns that have become paramount; it tells much about the kinds of materials that are being used, the questions that are being raised, and the interpretations that are becoming common.

The focus of the bibliography is the United States, but other countries are not ignored and many of the articles come from foreign language periodicals. One abstract gives a sketch of American blacks in Czarist Russia, including the famed Shakespearean actor, Ira Aldridge; another suggests that in Italy the stage version of *Uncle Tom's Cabin* has always been a great favorite, particularly in times of political crisis.

Many of the abstracts carry a concluding sentence on the source materials used; one has only to take a random sample of these to sense their richness. Even when conventional sources, such as diaries and letters, are used, it is edifying to learn, for example, that George A. Matson, who operated as a barber, schoolmaster and clergyman in Lincoln, Nebraska, kept a diary from 1901 to 1903; or that the former slave, Taylor Thistle, while studying theology in Nashville, sent seven letters to his benefactors. Photographs, electoral maps, church and regimental records—conventional though they be—have importance, particularly when they shed light on Negro experience. The family Bible, with its record of births, marriages, and deaths, has its uses, particularly where, as in the case of blacks, other records of vital statistics are in short supply. Nonliterary sources appear infrequently, although some of the authors urge others to make use of them. Certain of the articles are highly personal, essentially exercises in self-discovery.

As David B. Davis makes clear elsewhere in this issue, slavery remains a prime subject of study, and recent literature suggests that the Reconstruction period also retains its fascination. If, on the one hand, we are reminded anew that there was no such thing as black rule and that many carpetbaggers were men of probity, we are also reminded increasingly of the political mind of the Negro, and of men like Richard Allen and Matt Gaines in the Texas legislature, who promoted state and regional measures beneficial to all. We learn of black-on-black political intimidation, with black Republicans using strong-arm tactics on black Democrats. The historiography of the period is still the "dark and bloody ground" that Bernard Weisberger found it fifteen years ago.

Afro-American History includes a number of articles on the age-old question as to whether the mean differences in intelligence scores between white and black children stem from environmental or genetic factors, and, although proponents of the latter have grown more defensive in recent years, they have not left the field.

Contemporary periodical literature indicates an increase in studies comparing blacks with other groups. One author, comparing the Negro with the immigrant, concludes that the factor of race was crucial; the immigrant faced the problem of assimilation, to be sure, but he did not face the insurmountable wall of caste. Tackling the question of why Japanese-Americans have fared better than black Americans, one observer points to the former's smaller numbers and higher educational level. Another writer sees parallels in the relationships between Jews and peasants in prewar Eastern Europe and between Jews and Negroes in modern America; in each instance, he points out, the Jews regarded the other group as violence prone and lacking in culture.

White-black violence is the topic of a great number of articles. Urban racial unrest, including its precipitants and underlying causes, receives its full share of attention. Blacks viewed these disturbances as protests against racial discrimination, whereas whites saw them as conspiracies master-minded by Communists and outside Negroes. A race riot, even when viewed in retrospect, is a sobering experience. Yet, seen in a broader context, it is consistent not only with the nation's history in race relations but with the fact that Americans are a violence-prone people even where the factor of race is not present.[38]

Among the topics which received little scholarly attention is the role of black women. Historically, women were hardly in the public eye; an article on the early history of Negro women in journalism, for example, yielded few names until the appearance of the militant Ida Wells Barnett of Memphis and Chicago at the turn of the twentieth century. As for the women's liberation movement of our own day, this is hardly a matter that attracts blacks or their chroniclers. To black men and women, the battle of the sexes seems almost a diversion in light of the whole range of problems they have in common because of their color.

On the other hand, recent black-oriented periodical literature has devoted considerable attention to the discipline of black studies, a constellation of fields in college curriculum offerings in which history is the largest single component. Supplementing his use of this voluminous literature with visits to more than a hundred colleges, Nick Aaron Ford published *Black Studies: Threat or Challenge,* in 1973.[39] Professor Ford holds that while badly conceived black studies programs pose a threat to effective education, well-conceived programs "are a threat to false and distorted scholarship." Black studies generally are a challenge, calling upon "the national educational establishment" to re-examine "moribund concepts and outmoded methods."

Mirroring the new awareness of Negro history, the literature has put historians themselves under scrutiny, noting their changing images of blacks. There are scores of articles on the treatment of blacks by historians. Some are broadly based; others deal with a particular historian, period, or event. Some indicate topics and themes that are deserving of further research.

In American historiography blacks have sometimes been victimized more by being ignored than by overt prejudice; omission can of course be construed as a form of prejudice. This, however, is no longer a major problem. Although it may be premature to proclaim the full arrival of blacks in American history, they are at least now listed in the cast of characters; if their roles are still too often indeterminate, at least their names are now likely to be spelled correctly.

In fine, this is a day of unusual ferment in black history—in its substantative outreach and in its documentation. In their quest for a usable past, blacks have done two things. They have helped reshape our assessment of "what has actually happened," spurring the use of long-muted evidence. And they have helped alert us to the possibilities of alternate methodologies within the discipline itself. The concept of history "from the bottom up," now so prevalent, is certainly not new, but a good portion of its present sweep and momentum unquestionably stems from the marked upturn of interest by scholars and laymen in the historic role played by Americans from Africa.

In his thoughtful and imaginative book, *The Future as History,* Robert L. Heilbroner bids us not despair as we face the years that seem to loom so ominously before us, but instead to take heart, drawing upon a sense of historical identity and awareness. History does indeed remain the great synthesizing discipline, and Heilbroner is most persuasive in elucidating the grand dynamic of its forces. We must, however, proceed with due caution. A valid projection of the future as history, for all its importance, requires a fresh look at the past as history. "No fact has ever been wholly ascertained, but a fact may be progressively ascertained," observes R. G. Collingwood; "as the labour of historians goes forward, they come to more and more facts, and to reject with greater and greater confidence a number of mistaken accounts of them."[40]

REFERENCES

1. Winthrop D. Jordan, *White Over Black: American Attitudes Toward the Negro, 1550-1812* (Chapel Hill, N.C.: University of North Carolina Press, 1968).

2. Joanna E. Schneider and Robert L. Zangrando, "Black History in the College Curriculum," *The Rocky Mountain Social Science Journal*, 6 (October 1969), pp. 134-142.

3. William M. Nichols, "Individualism and Autobiographical Art: Frederick Douglass and Henry Thoreau," *College Language Association Journal*, 16 (December 1972), pp. 145-158.

4. Leonard J. Deutsch, "Ralph Waldo Ellison and Ralph Waldo Emerson: A Shared Moral Vision," *College Language Association Journal*, 16 (December 1972), pp. 159-178.

5. Michael Novak, *The Rise of the Unmeltable Ethnics: Politics and Culture in the Seventies* (New York: Macmillan, 1972).

6. In higher education in the academic year 1973-1974 an estimated 2,000 courses designed to expand the study and understanding of women were offered in America, a many-fold increase from the "handful" of such courses in the late 1960's. Cheryl M. Fields, "Women's Studies Gain; 2,000 Courses Offered this Year," *The Chronicle of Higher Education*, 8 (December 17, 1973), p. 6. It may be noted that in 1972, Sarah Lawrence College began a master's degree in women's history (if this is not a contradiction in terms).

7. J. A. Rogers, *World's Great Men of Color*, 2 vol., ed. John Hendrick Clarke (New York: Macmillan, 1972).

8. See, for example, the 24-page "Introduction" to Sterling Stuckey, ed., *The Ideological Origins of Black Nationalism* (Boston: Beacon Press, 1972).

9. *The Quarterly Journal of the Library of Congress*, 27 (July 1970). See also John McDonough, "Manuscript Sources for the Study of Negro Life and History," *The Quarterly Journal of the Library of Congress*, 26 (July 1969), pp. 126-148, a description of the library's extensive holdings on black Americans.

10. A quarter of a century earlier, in 1947, the Committee on Negro Studies of the American Council of Learned Societies published its path-breaking and still available "Guide to the Documents in the National Archives: For Negro Studies" (Washington, D.C.: American Council of Learned Societies).

11. For a joint catalogue of the black historical materials—manuscripts, pamphlets and books—in the Library Company of Philadelphia and the adjacent Historical Society of Pennsylvania, see Edward Wolf, ed., *Negro History, 1553-1973* (Philadelphia: Library Company of Philadelphia). For a list of the black history collections in the Maryland Historical Society, see Nancy G. Boles (curator of manuscripts), "Notes on Maryland Historical Society Manuscript Collections: Black History Collections," *Maryland Historical Magazine*, 106:66 (Spring 1971), pp. 72-78; for useful hints on the search for black genealogy, see Mary K. Meyer's, "Genealogical Notes," pp. 79-81, in the same issue. See also John Slonaker, *The United States Army and the Negro* (Carlisle Barracks, Pa.: U.S. Army Military History Research Collection, 1971), 97 pages; Joyce B. Schneider, *Selected List of Periodicals Relating to Negroes, with Holdings in the Libraries of Yale University* (New Haven: Yale University Library, 1970), 26 pages; Earle H. West, *A Bibliography of Doctoral Research on the Negro, 1933-1966* (New York: Xerox Company, 1969). The most comprehensive early-twentieth-century bibliography is Monroe N. Work, *Bibliography of the Negro in Africa and America* (New York: H. W. Wilson Company, 1928). For the fifties and sixties the most serviceable of the various annual compilations is the one published by G. K. Hall, Boston, successively titled, *Index to Selected Negro Periodicals, Index to Selected Periodicals*, and *Index to Periodical Articles By and About Negroes*. For excellent recent bibliographies see James M. McPherson et al., *Blacks in America: Bibliographical Essays* (Garden City, New York: Doubleday, 1971); Louis Harlan, *The Negro in American History* (Washington: American Historical Association, 1965); Elizabeth W. Miller and Mary L. Fisher, *The Negro in America* (Cambridge: Harvard University Press, 1970); Darwin T. Turner, *Afro-American Writers* (New York: Appleton-Century Crofts, 1970); and Dorothy B. Porter, *The Negro in the United States: A Selected Bibliography* (Washington, D.C.: Library of Congress, 1970), a work with a detailed index and 1,781 entries, among them 81 describing other reference sources. Dorothy B. Porter, librarian of the Moorland-Spingarn Collection at Howard University, a treasure house of materials on black Americans, has also edited 72 selections written by early blacks: *Early Negro Writing, 1760-1837* (Boston: Beacon Press, 1971). For a model example of a

bibliographical study which focuses on one state, see *New Jersey and the Negro: A Bibliography, 1715-1966* (Trenton: The New Jersey Library Association, 1967), an excellent work which lists 1,016 entries, divided into 28 headings, and dealing not only with Negro life in New Jersey but also with New Jersey's role in black history plus the racial attitudes of white New Jerseyites. Finally, the black quarterly, *Freedomways,* features annotated bibliographical surveys written by Ernest Kaiser of the staff of the Schomburg Collection in New York.

12. Gary L. Shumway, *Oral History in the United States: A Directory* (New York: The Oral History Association, 1971).

13. Directed from its beginning in 1967 by Vincent J. Browne, this project was sponsored and funded by the Ford Foundation which, in 1973, chose Howard University as the recipient of the collection.

14. The Fisk University Library, in Nashville, has a Black Oral History Program which proposes "to bridge gaps in black history and culture."

15. L. S. B. Leakey, *The Progress and Evolution of Man in Africa* (New York: New York University Press, 1961).

16. Philip D. Curtin, *African History* (New York: Macmillan, 1964).

17. Jan Vansina, "Once Upon a Time: Oral Traditions as History in Africa," *Dædalus* (Spring 1971).

18. Gilberto Freyre, *The Masters and the Slaves: A Study in the Development of Brazilian Civilization* (New York: Knopf, 1946).

19. Gilbert Osofsky, *Harlem: The Making of a Ghetto: New York, 1890-1930* (New York: Harper and Row, 1966); Allen H. Spear, *Black Chicago: The Making of a Negro Ghetto, 1890-1920* (Chicago: University of Chicago Press, 1967); and St. Clair Drake and Horace R. Clayton, *Black Metropolis: A Study of Negro Life in a Northern City* (New York: Harcourt, Brace, 1945).

20. David M. Katzman, *Before the Ghetto: Black Detroit in the Nineteenth Century* (Urbana: University of Illinois Press, 1973).

21. Guichard Parris and Lester Brooks, *Blacks in the City: A History of the National Urban League* (Boston: Little Brown, 1971).

22. Walter Weare, *Black Business in the New South* (Urbana, Ill.: University of Illinois Press, 1973).

23. August Meier and Elliott Rudwick, *CORE: A Study in the Civil Rights Movement, 1942-1968* (New York: Oxford University Press, 1973).

24. Earle E. Thorpe, *Eros and Freedom in Southern Life and Thought* (Durham, N.C.: Seaman Printery, 1967); and *The Old South: A Psychohistory* (Durham, N.C.: Seaman Printery, 1972).

25. Letitia Woods Brown, *Free Negroes in the District of Columbia, 1790-1846* (New York: Oxford University Press, 1972).

26. U. B. Phillips, *Life and Labor in the Old South* (Boston: Little Brown, 1929).

27. Mark Miles Fisher, *Negro Slave Songs in the United States* (Ithaca, N.Y.: Cornell University Press, 1953).

28. Sterling Stuckey, "Through the Prism of Folklore; the Black Ethos in Slavery," *The Massachusetts Review,* 9 (Summer 1968), pp. 417-437.

29. John W. Blassingame, *The Slave Community: Plantation Life in the Ante-Bellum South* (New York: Oxford University Press, 1972). This book includes a "Critical Essay on Sources," which justifies the use of slave literature and comments on some of the major secondary works on slavery.

30. The materials from this federal project, along with two collections assembled by Fisk University and issued in mimeographed form in 1945, were published in nineteen volumes in 1972: George P. Rawick, ed., *The American Slave: A Composite Autobiography* (Westport, Conn.: Greenwood

Publishing Company). See also Norman R. Yetman, *Voices From Slavery* (New York: Holt, Rinehart and Winston, 1970).

31. Although Simmons admitted he was no scholar, *Men of Mark* "is still the basic text in black biography," in the words of Lerone Bennett, Jr. in his foreword to the 1970 edition of the over 800-page volume, published by the Johnson Publishing Company, Chicago.

32. *Negro Yearbook and Annual Encyclopedia of the Negro* (Tuskegee, Ala.: Department of Records and Research, Tuskegee Institute, 1912-1952). This was the brainchild of Monroe N. Work, for thirty years director of the department of records and research at Tuskegee Institute.

33. For a panorama of black notables from Crispus Attucks to Ralph Bunche, etched against a backdrop of three time spans, see Richard Bardolph, *The Negro Vanguard* (New York: Rhinehart, 1959). See also Edgar A. Toppin, *A Biographical History of Blacks in America Since 1528* (New York: David McKay, 1971), half of which is devoted to vignettes of 145 black achievers. Wilhemina S. Robinson, in *Historical Negro Biographies* (New York: Publishers Company, Inc., 1967), includes blacks from Africa and the other Americas. Projected for publication in 1974 is a *Dictionary of American Negro Biography*, ed. Rayford W. Logan and Michael R. Winston.

34. Edited by John Hope Franklin, this series includes biographies of such varying contemporaries as the journalist T. Thomas Fortune (by Emma Lou Thornbrough) and painter Henry Ossawa Tanner (by Marcia M. Matthews).

35. This series, edited by Hollis R. Lynch, is devoted to "distinguished Black Americans and Black Africans." In the first of its published studies Okon E. Uya portrayed the career of Robert Smalls, Civil War hero and Congressman from South Carolina; a more recent study by Carol V. R. George focused on the influence of Richard Allen, the slave-born pioneer black bishop.

36. Yale University has projected a Frederick Douglass Papers Project, under the editorship of John W. Blassingame. The W. E. B. DuBois papers, recently acquired by the University of Massachusetts, are being edited by DuBois' literary executor, Herbert Aptheker. The Washington Papers, like the others, a multivolumed undertaking, are being edited by Louis R. Harlan of the University of Maryland.

37. Dwight L. Smith, ed., *Afro-American History: A Bibliography* (Santa Barbara, Calif.: American Bibliographical Center, 1974).

38. Those proposing to scrutinize the anatomy of black-white outbreaks might gain insight and perspective by first noting the volume by Hugh Davis Graham and Ted Robert Furr, *Violence in America: Historical and Comparative Perspectives—A Staff Report to the National Commission on the Causes and Prevention of Violence* (Washington, D.C.: U.S. Government Printing Office, 1969).

39. Nick Aaron Ford, *Black Studies: Threat or Challenge?* (Port Washington, N.Y.: Kennicat Press, 1973).

40. Robert L. Heilbroner, *The Future as History* (New York: Harper and Brothers, 1959); R. G. Collingwood, *Essays in the Philosophy of History*, William Debbins, ed. (Austin: University of Texas Press, 1965).

THOMAS SOWELL

The Plight of Black Students in the United States

IN THE UNITED STATES black education at the college level expanded rapidly in the 1960's. In 1960, there were 200,000 black students attending college; by 1970 that number had more than doubled.[1] More importantly, the social composition and institutional destinations of these students changed drastically as well. Many predominantly white colleges and universities began seeking not only black students, but lower-class black students.[2] Whereas, until the 1960's, the majority of black students went to the predominantly Negro colleges and universities, an increasing majority now went to white institutions of higher learning.[3] Several factors in this situation led to severe problems.

The leading colleges and universities have been under special pressure to increase their minority enrollment, both because of their general visibility and because of a need to maintain their educational "leadership." Government funds and foundation grants to support special programs for black students were chaneled disproportionately into these leading institutions, just as they are for other purposes. At the same time, the academic preparation of most black students was wholly inadequate to meet the usual standards of these schools. The average College Board scores of black students were often well below the median scores at the high quality schools they attended. In short, a demand was created for black students at precisely those institutions least fitted to the student's educational preparation. Moreover, the incomes of many of the students dictated that they go where large scholarship funds were available. Therefore, many black students moved into education institutions at the top in terms of research prestige, social class and academic prerequisites, whether or not these were the schools best equipped to teach them.

When black students who would normally qualify for a state college are drained away by Ivy League colleges and universities, then state colleges have little choice but to recruit black students who would normally qualify for still lower level institutions—and so the process continues down the line. The net result is that, in a country with 3,000 widely differing colleges and universities capable of accommodating every conceivable level of educational preparation and intellectual development, there is a widespread problem of "underprepared" black students at many institutional levels, even though black students' capabilities span the whole range by any standard used. The problem is not one of absolute ability level, but rather of widespread mismatching of individuals with institutions. The problem is seldom seen for what it is, for it has *not* been approached in terms of the optimum distribution of black students in the light of their preparation and interests, but

179

rather in terms of how Harvard, Berkeley, or Antioch can do its part, maintain its leadership, or fill its quota. The schools which have most rapidly increased their enrollments of black students are those where the great majority of white American students could not qualify. However, since such schools typically do not admit underqualified white students, they have no "white problem" corresponding to the problem posed for them by underqualified black students. This problem must also be seen in perspective: the College Board scores and other academic indicators for black students in prestige colleges and universities are typically *above the national average* for white Americans. Special tutoring, reduced course loads, and other special accommodations and expedients for minority students are necessitated by programs geared to a student body which is not only above the national average but in the top *1 or 2 percent* of all American students. The problem created by black students who do not meet the usual institutional standards may be grim or even desperate for both the students and the institution. Yet it does not arise because students are incapable of absorbing a college education. They may be incapable of absorbing an M.I.T. education, but so is virtually everyone else.

The literature on black college students centers almost exclusively on what the white prestige institution ought to do. This is true whether the individual writing is black or white, whether he "militantly" favors or "traditionally" opposes such things as black studies and special admissions standards. Among black academicians, minority programs like black studies, and other special modifications of academic standards and practices are demanded by so-called "militants" and bitterly opposed by so-called "moderates"; both groups, however, argue in terms of what the given white prestige institution should do to accommodate an increase in black enrollments. This perspective is as plain in moderates like Martin Kilson and Kenneth Clark as it is in militants like Allen Ballard.[4] They share the unspoken assumption of white academicians that students get a better education at a "better" institution. It is, however, well worth considering in what ways prestige institutions are "better."

Prestige universities achieve their standing almost exclusively through the quality of their research output. This has been decried in some quarters and denied in others, but the plain fact is that the ranking of leading departments in any academic discipline closely follows their ranking on quality and quantity of research output.[5] However valuable this special function may be for society in general, there is nothing about outstanding research performance which equips either the institution or the individual faculty member for teaching undergraduates in general, much less those with special educational and psychological needs. Indeed, many of the leading scholars who create a university's prestige have little or nothing to do with undergraduates. Even prestige colleges which emphasize their teaching role are geared to students with test scores in the top 1 to 5 percent. This is true not only of such well-known colleges as Amherst, Swarthmore, and Vassar, but also of lesser-known quality institutions like Davidson, Wells, and Hamilton.

Much of the current literature attempts to convince prestige institutions that they should adapt to serve students who do not meet their highly specialized academic requirements—students, in other words, more like those served by the vast majority of American colleges and universities. The possibility of distributing black students in institutions whose normal standards they already meet has been almost totally ignored. Worse, many institutions have set up special programs specifically and explicitly to do the *opposite* of this, to accommodate black students who do *not* meet the normal standards of the respective institutions. Under such programs financial aid is not available to black students who meet the normal standards of these institutions, even when such students are very much in need of financial aid. Policies of this sort are followed not only in programs established by individual institutions, but also in nationwide programs under both private and government auspices. The best-known program for placing and financing black students in law schools places an upper limit on the test scores students can achieve and still be eligible,[6] a limit well below the average test score in the law schools where they are placed. Many government scholarships for minority undergraduates require academically substandard performances as well as lower socio-economic status. In some cases, such policies are explicitly defined legally; in others they simply exist in practice. Whatever the rationale for them in terms of retrospective justice, what they reward is a low performance level, whether or not a student is capable of more. Black high school students themselves have said that they refuse to perform at their best for fear of reducing their chances of getting the financial aid they need to go to college.[7] Although a number of critics have declared it "bizarre" to deny financial aid to academically qualified black students while favoring weaker ones,[8] their view does not necessarily prevail among academic administrators.

There is some evidence that able black students are often missed by the recruiting and admissions procedures of the leading colleges and universities, or else deliberately passed over. A more grave possibility, however, is that blacks at all levels of ability are systematically mismatched upward, so that good students go where outstanding students should be going and outstanding students go where only a handful of peak performers can survive. The net effect of this "pervasive shifting effect"[9] is to place students where they do not learn as much as they would in schools geared to students of their own educational preparation.[10]

Much of what has happened to black American college students at white institutions was foreshadowed in the earlier experience of African students in white institutions, not only in the United States and other Western countries, but also in the Soviet Union and the Eastern bloc of nations. In the case of visiting African students in the early 1960's, as in the case of American Negroes in the late 1960's, the primary emphasis was on getting their physical presence on campus in significant numbers. This was accomplished not only by special recruiting efforts but by special financial aid policies and special academic standards, including, in some cases, a virtual absence of standards.[11] The results were also very similar to what has emerged with black American students. Both black and white students bitterly resented these arrangements, and the resentment was directed at each other as well as at the administrations responsible for them. An observer of the pattern among African students in the early 1960's commented: "Many African students are uneasily aware that they are kept men. Often they take refuge from this reality in defiantly revolutionary verbiage."[12]

It was observed that African students who studied in the United States tended to become anti-American, while those who studied in the Soviet Union tended to become anti-Soviet. A similar anger at their apparent benefactors became com-

monplace among American Negro students in the late 1960's. The African
students' experiences differed, however, from those of black American students in
several important respects. The Africans had neither sufficient numbers or sufficient
cultural homogeneity or ideological unity to mount sustained campaigns against
college administrators, and therefore produced far fewer dramatic episodes such as
mass demonstrations or disruptions. Also, African students were not granted con-
cessions like special black studies departments.

It is against this background that the literature has discussed such issues as
"open admissions," black studies, and faculty quotas. Several arguments have
emerged for preferential admissions standards for black students. One is simply
that "the number of Blacks qualified for admission to white colleges under
traditional criteria is small" so that admitting "large numbers" of Negro students is
synonymous with "a lowering of entrance requirements."[13] Here the focus is im-
plicitly the institution and its guilt, atonement, or responsibility. Much rarer in the
literature is the position that high costs are incurred "whenever a student is admitted to a school whose normal standards he does not meet, even though he does
meet the normal standards of other schools."[14] Here there is recognition that black
students, with all their educational handicaps, are not underqualified in an absolute
sense, but only relative to the standards of particular institutions. The costs incurred include not only those of remedial programs and special courses, but also
"the intense anxiety and threat to the student's self-esteem." Some indication of
this psychic cost is the high *voluntary* drop-out rate among black students admitted
under programs which do not allow them to be flunked out for some specified
number of years. Personal accounts by students and observations by teachers reinforce the picture of black students under great pressure in unfamiliar settings.[15] A
leading proponent and architect of "open admissions" policies at the City College
of New York boasts of the fact that 30 to 35 percent of the students admitted under
those policies graduate[16]—in other words, the drop out rate is "only" 65 to 70 percent. The national drop-out rate in the United States is about 50 percent but this
includes students with financial problems (unlike the open admissions students
whose expenses are taken care of), students with attractive alternatives, and students
who can return later at their parents' expense. Moreover, the white dropout is not
laboring under the stereotype of mental incompetence which crushingly reinforces
the black's sense of personal failure
One of the most insistent arguments for special admissions criteria for black
students is that the standard mental tests are culturally biased, and thus do not correctly measure a black student's ability and/or predict his college performance.
There is indeed some evidence that tests underestimate the mental ability of lower
income people in general, as well as blacks in particular. Ironically, some of this
evidence is from studies by Arthur R. Jensen, who is better known for his theory of
innate racial differences in mental abilities.[17] However, the question of predicting
college performance is quite different from the question of innate ability or even of
cultural bias. Tests may systematically underestimate a group's natural or potential
intelligence and yet not underestimate their success in college, which requires
many characteristics besides native ability. The predictive validity of a test is an
empirical question, ultimately a matter of statistics rather than philosophy, and a

variety of tests given in a variety of settings indicate that mental tests generally do *not* underestimate the future performance of lower income people, including blacks, and in fact have a slight tendency to predict a better academic performance than that actually achieved.[18] In short, standardized mental tests tend to underestimate ability among blacks but to overestimate performance.

This is not nearly as paradoxical as it may seem. A college education presupposes not only raw intelligence but years of mental habits which cannot be rapidly synthesized in remedial programs. The lack of a given reading speed or mathematical facility may endanger a person's academic survival in a particular institution. And, if blacks are maldistributed, they may run into trouble in most of the institutions they attend. Another factor in the difficulties encountered by disadvantaged students is that the college itself is often as subject to cultural bias as the admissions tests. To some extent this may be a simple social class bias in life styles which creates needless disorientation among students from different social or racial backgrounds. However, insofar as the intellectual process has inherent requirements, there may be little that can be done in the short run to improve the disadvantaged student's chances of academic success at a particular institution, even if he has the same innate potential as everyone else and if all class bias is removed from the collegiate social scene.

It is misleading to depict opposing views on the admission of black students to college as due solely to different assumptions or theories which logically lead to different conclusions. In fact, many of the arguments are opaque moral imperatives: help should go to those who "really" need it; it is not the black student's "fault" that he does not meet academic standards; compensation is due for past injustices, and so on. Such arguments can be met only by shifting the whole basis of the discussion: efficiency requires that help go to those who can best use it, not those who most need it; admission is not a morally based individual benefit but a socially based investment decision; compensation to individual A for what we've done to individual B is not a compensation, and may not even prove to be a benefit. These answers do not meet the original arguments on their own ground, but claim instead that different grounds are preferable.

In one way or another the question of academic standards is central to both proponents and opponents of special treatment for black students. The extent to which black students actually receive special treatment at white colleges and universities is, however, a matter of heated controversy. Clearly "remedial" or "compensatory" courses and reduced course loads are special treatment, but straightforward and above board. Controversy centers around allegations that there are double standards in grading, credits given for courses with little content and no real demands, "incomplete" grades awarded for failing work, and failing drop-outs disguised as temporary withdrawals.[19]

No one has stepped forth to defend such practices, but many argue that reports concerning them are exaggerated,[20] and some argue that black students need courses which cover, at a slower pace, the same material as regular courses at the same college.[21] Why black students should be channeled to fast-paced colleges to get slower-paced courses is a question that does not arise within a framework designed to produce a given demographic profile by institution. As for the prevalence of dishonest and clandestine double standards, its nature is such that it can only be estimated impressionistically. My interviews with academics from coast to coast convince me that double standards are a fact of life on virtually every campus, but not necessarily in a majority of courses. This situation may in fact present the maximum academic danger to the black student: enough double standards courses to give him a false sense of security and enough rigid standards courses to produce academic disasters.

Black academics tend to be especially severe in their criticisms of double standards for black students. The "benevolent paternalism" and "seemingly sympathetic" double standards of white faculty members, they say, tend to "generate feelings of inferiority in the students' hearts and minds in a way unlikely ever to be undone."[22] For some black students it promotes a "hustler mentality."[23] At the same time "it robs those black students who have done well from receiving real credit and the boost in confidence that their accomplishments merit."[24] Often this boost in confidence is very much needed as well as merited. The "lack of feedback," which double-standard grading implies, denies black students clear signals as to their progress and prospects,[25]—signals they need in order to plan their lives rationally, both in college and after graduation.

Not all critics speak in terms of the harm double standards do to black students. Some argue from the more general perspective that "discrimination in favor of X is automatic discrimination against Y."[26] Moreover, in terms of the general racial atmosphere of the country in future years, it is argued that academic mismatching of black and white students in the same institution promotes a white sense of superiority and a black sense of inferiority and thus tends to "perpetuate the very ideas and prejudices it is designed to combat."[27] Finally, it is argued that academically outclassed students will turn to nonacademic means to "achieve recognition and self-expression,"[28] participating not only in "aggressive behavior" but also in attempts to change academic standards and practices in ways detrimental to education in general.[29]

Among the defenses or exculpations of double standards is the argument that various nonblack student subgroups have long concentrated on easy courses or easy graders—varsity athletes and fraternity members being prominent examples. There are problems with this approach, however. First, the least reputable of white academic practices is held up as a norm for blacks. Second, the whole purpose of athletes and fraternity members in attempting to reduce their academic responsibilities is to free their time for essentially nonintellectual purposes. And why should this be the goal of blacks trying to emerge from poverty?

Special recruitment of black faculty and the existence of faculty quotas, whatever they may be called, invoke many of the same arguments as those over special (lower) admissions standards for black students, and a number of others as well. Sometimes the existing black students on campus are cited as a major reason for seeking black faculty; it is argued that they can "relate" better to black faculty members because they tend to be either more sympathetic to the students' problems or more willing and able to impose tough standards, or both. A further argument is often made that a racially integrated faculty is beneficial to *white* students. By seeing Negroes in high status intellectual roles, white students will supposedly carry forth into the world an image of blacks different from the degrading stereotypes of the past, and therefore set the stage for better racial attitudes and actions in the future. Finally, there is the moral argument that black faculty quotas compensate for past unjust discrimination in hiring and, by making blacks part of "the system," provide some built-in protection against future discrimination.

The argument that black faculty "relate" better to black students is not one readily testable by scientific methods. It is clear, impressionistically, that in some cases this is true, but a generalization of this sort requires either much more empirical evidence or much more logical analysis than a general consonance with currently popular racial beliefs. And it is not clear what the intellectual content or consequences of "relating" may be, where it does in fact occur. Some black faculty brought in under lower academic standards have been described as "better examples of continuing disadvantage than of its diminution."[30] The point here is not to claim that this is *typical* of black faculty members, but to suggest the possibility that, although "disadvantaged" faculty members may indeed more readily establish rapport with disadvantaged students, there is not necessarily any intellectual benefit. It would be very useful to determine empirically whether black faculty members with high intellectual credentials (however measured) have more black students in their classes than they would by random chance. My impression is that they do not. However, the important thing is to find out, and it may be significant that no real effort has been made to check this key assumption of those who seek black faculty quotas.

The effect on the racial attitudes of white students, and through them of society as a whole, also turns crucially on the quality of the black faculty hired to fill the quotas. Proponents of quotas (including "targets," "goals," and "preferences") typically state that "of course" they want the black faculty members to be of as high a quality as white faculty members—but this crucial point cannot be "of-coursed" aside. If blacks performing capably in high-status, high-visibility roles can have a positive effect on future racial attitudes, then blacks giving substandard performances in such roles can have a negative effect, one, indeed, which builds on, and may appear to confirm, a whole history of racist beliefs. At almost any institution, of course, there will be black individuals of both kinds, just as there are white individuals of both kinds. The question is, what is the general impression likely to be created by faculty hired to fill quotas?

The past is a great unchangeable fact. That past, for black America, has included very few persons trained o be academic scholars. Moreover, many years of academic education are required for anyone, regardless of race, to qualify, even minimally, as a faculty member, much less as a mature scholar. In short, there are relatively few black scholars in existence, and the number cannot be greatly increased in the immediate future. And it is in this context that faculty quotas must be considered. Any "goal," "target," or "affirmative action" designed to make the percentage of blacks on faculties approximate that in the general population can only mean reducing quality standards. Disputes over reducing the quality of faculty members tend to center on its effect in reducing educational standards, an effect which is minimized by the tendency of good students to avoid or be steered around incompetent faculty members. Not so easily minimized is the effect of substandard faculty members on the racial attitudes of both black and white students.

With faculty quotas as with student quotas, the most prestigious institutions have the greatest incentives to maximize body count. In the case of faculty hiring, they respond not only to the public relations need to maintain visible institutional leadership, but also to the legal need to meet "affirmative action" goals as a precondition for receiving the federal money which is indispensable for maintaining their standing in research competition.

Much has been made of the fact that the government's "affirmative action" programs do not specify exact numbers to be hired from a given race. The government requires each college and university to submit some quota scheme if it wants federal money but allows it to work out its own numbers and mechanics subject to federal approval. All numerical targets, however, need not be rigidly met. This allows the government to use financial pressure to force a certain kind of action, while retaining the option, should it become politically necessary, of repudiating the particular way the action is carried out. In particular, the government can deny that it required lower standards or any form of racial favoritism. It merely created a situation in which certain numerical results would insure the continued flow of government money, while others would threaten that flow and/or subject academic administrations to continuing demands on their time and resources to meet sweeping and repeated investigations. In short, the government has imposed race and sex quotas without accepting responsibility for them, while, in fact, carefully preserving its "deniability."

The importance of federal money for research activity obviously varies according to the importance of research activity in a given institution's scheme of things. This is obviously greatest at the prestige universities receiving the most federal support. Again, as in the case of black students, a great demand for black faculty is created at the top, and the same shifting effect on quality is at work. Faculty members, like students, are neither high nor low quality absolutely, but only relative to the particular institutions in which they operate. A faculty member who would be a respected scholar at a state college may be a second-class academic citizen at a prestige university. In terms of the supposed benefits of quota hiring, a black faculty member who could contribute toward racial respect at a good college, may reinforce racism at a top research institution.

Although in some fields the salaries of black professors are marginally higher than those of their white counterparts,[31] a fact which reflects the demand for additional "affirmative action" professors, there is little evidence that significantly more black faculty members have actually been hired since "affirmative action" policies emerged. Past discrimination in the white academic world is readily documented,[32] but the era chosen for comparison is crucial. *Immediately* before affirmative action, there was little evidence that blacks of a given level of academic preparation and performance averaged less than their white counterparts; a study in 1969 found that less than 10 percent of the black academicians at white universities believed that they had encountered employment discrimination.[33]

Moreover, some of the gains under affirmative action quotas are illusory. The actual hiring of minority faculty members (or women) is only one way of coping with "affirmative action" quotas; another is to generate recruiting activity and practices designed to show "good faith" *attempts* to comply. From the point of view of the black faculty member, this means that the number of *apparent* job opportunities is inflated beyond what is really available to him. Institutions seek to increase their black body counts not only in hiring, but also at the stages of sending recruiting letters or conducting interviews, whether or not they have any intention of proceeding beyond these preliminary stages.

The logic of quotas often extends beyond the hiring process. Faculty committees may also reflect the pervasive desire for minority representation. But to say that blacks must be "represented" in some fixed proportion, where this proportion is greater than the proportion of black faculty members, is to say that black faculty members must serve on more committees than white faculty members. To the individual black faculty member, this is hardly a benefit, and the more interested he is in the intellectual purposes which his position involves, the more of an imposition it is.

To the extent that "black" becomes synonymous with "substandard," the ability of the best black scholars to influence either black or white students is reduced. Indeed, substandard black faculty members have every incentive to undermine competent black faculty members. It is not at all uncommon for officials of black studies departments to acquire a voice or even a veto in the selection of black faculty members in other departments, and to use it against "conventional"—competent—black academics.[34] It could hardly be otherwise, given the threat that able black scholars represent to the less scholarly black academic's personal standing, value orientation, and influence with black students—factors on which his job may depend.

Black Institutions

Most of today's predominantly black American colleges and universities began with predominantly or exclusively white faculties, administrators, and trustees. They were, in short, white-run institutions for black students. The evolution of black colleges and universities can hardly be understood without taking this fact into account. From the earliest times, this raised questions over which was more important, academic quality or black representation in positions of authority and prestige. There were literally only a handful of college-trained Negroes in the United States when most of the Negro colleges were founded after the Civil War, so white domination was inevitable at the outset. As time went on, a small but growing number of blacks began to acquire some higher education, even if it did not fully match that of the whites in the black colleges. By the 1880's, the question of black representation had become a live issue. A black leader declared in 1885 that the "intellects of our young people are being educated at the expense of their manhood," because in their classrooms "they see only white professors."[35] Other blacks—notably the parents of black students—insisted that quality education for black students took precedence over black representation among the faculty or administrators. "We should not allow a mistaken race pride to cause us to impose upon [the students] inferior teachers,"[36] they argued, and their view prevailed—for a time.

The issue did not die, but, despite the sporadic outbursts of rhetoric about black representation,[37] high performance whites or whites with good public relations remained secure in their jobs. Even in the absence of any explicit or dramatic change in policy, however, increasing numbers of educated blacks led to increasing numbers of black scholars and administrators in the Negro colleges and universities. By the time of World War I about half the faculty and administrators of the Negro colleges and universities were black.[38] The post-war "new Negro" and "black renaissance" era of the 1920's had an academic counterpart in a renewed and more insistent demand for black control of black academic institutions. An accelerated substitution of blacks for whites put these institutions firmly in black control by the end of the decade. Contemporary black observers chronicled a decline in academic standards in the wake of this rapid change. The celebrated Negro intellectual and Dean of Howard University, Kelly Miller, described it as "a misfortune barely short of a calamity," and E. Franklin Frazier also depicted it as a setback for black education.[39]

The effects of this sudden change in academic personnel were not limited to the immediate period in which it occurred. Black faculty members and administrators had few alternative occupations open. This meant that black administrators clung tenaciously to their jobs and black faculty dared not oppose them or seem in any way to threaten them. Black administrators not only remained in office for extremely long periods of time but exercised extreme power during their tenure. Academic freedom was one casualty of this situation. The tyranny at black colleges has been bitterly portrayed by black scholars and intellectuals, ranging from W. E. B. DuBois' essays[40] and E. Franklin Frazier's sociological studies[41] to Ralph Ellison's fictional classic, *The Invisible Man*.[42] Phrases such as "authoritarian," "autocratic," "paternalistic," and "domineering" abound in the literature.[43]

Another casualty was academic quality. It was not merely that initially there were not enough good black scholars to replace the departing whites, but also that the first generation of substandard scholars largely determined the atmosphere in which subsequent generations of black scholars would function or fail to function. The young E. Franklin Frazier was admonished for being too bookish at Tuskegee Institute. W. E. B. Dubois encountered hostility on more than one black campus. A list of Negro scholars alienated from the successive administrations at Howard University over the years would read like a Who's Who of black academic scholarship. While the intellectual achievements of these scholars could not be completely stifled, their voice in university affairs was minimized, and the shaping of institutions was largely in the hands of more tractable, but less able men.

The administrators' need for men who would not "rock the boat" was particularly acute in view of the fact that the black administration was typically responsible to white trustees, white foundations, and/or white state legislatures. Since most Negro colleges and universities are located in the South, administrators had to suppress ideas and movements which were unacceptable to Southern white concepts about race relations or the intellectual capacity of the Negro. In short, the black administrators were virtual dictators over black faculty and students, and at the same time fearful clients of white power figures. More importantly, each generation of black administrators chose a succeeding generation after its own image, thereby driving the more intellectual and independent elements to the periphery of institutional affairs, or beyond. Thus the choice of black representation over academic quality had lasting negative consequences, even after large numbers of qualified black scholars and administrators had emerged.

The classic controversy in the black colleges was that between the conservative, vocationally oriented training program advocated by Booker T. Washington and the liberal education with clear overtones of restructured race relations advocated by W. E. B. DuBois. Neither the rhetorical differences nor the personal bitterness between these two men, however, should obscure the large overlap in their respective educational philosophies. Washington repeatedly recognized the need for higher intellectual work[44] and DuBois argued for vocational competence and work discipline.[45] Although their conflict arose partly from a difference in emphasis and partly from a difference in their choice of roles, it was, to a very large extent, a personality clash, exacerbated by the sociopolitical tendencies of the time. Booker T. Washington was accepted by white Americans as *the* spokesmen for black Americans and in that role he was consulted and often held veto power on the advancement of other blacks in important positions in a variety of fields.[46] W. E. B. DuBois had a much smaller base of support, among blacks or whites, and aroused much more resentment and opposition among whites in positions of power.

It should be noted that, during the period of the Washington-DuBois controversies in the early years·of the twentieth century, DuBois was a liberal—a moderate by present day standards—not yet the Marxist he was to become in his later years. One indication of DuBois' moderation during this period is that he was among those who congratulated Booker T. Washington on his famous Atlanta Exposition speech.[47] It was only after Washington's rise to power in the wake of that speech that DuBois turned against him. Even then, DuBois' opposition was directed against particular points on which he thought Washington was mistaken, and against the whites who gave Washington a power which DuBois considered dangerous for anyone.[48] DuBois did not question Washington's desire to promote the advancement of black people; he did not accuse him of a "sell-out," although he did assert that his methods were counterproductive. Washington, as a man with a dominant power position to defend, was much more actively engaged in trying to undercut DuBois' smaller but growing influence.[49] Recent scholarship, however, has brought out Washington's extensive clandestine efforts in behalf of civil rights and political awareness for blacks,[50] so his real differences with DuBois were even less substantial than they might appear from contemporary writings and were, in considerable part, differences in tactics rather than in principle. Perhaps more basically, there were personal power differences and social differences. Washington was "up from slavery" while DuBois was descended from Negroes who had been free for generations—an important distinction in their time.

Both vocational and liberal arts education continued at black institutions, but with a historical trend toward the latter, except insofar as teacher education can be classified as vocational. To that extent, history has followed DuBois rather than Washington. However, the social and political conservatism and accommodation to white Southern racial "realities" which Washington espoused and practiced remained the hallmark of black college administrators for many decades. The fact that many of the leading academics were far more liberal or militant than their college administrators created another source of friction.

Even the best black colleges and universities do not approach the standards of quality of respectable national institutions. Although some black schools are often praised for high quality, hard data provide no support whatever for claims of quality by any Negro college or university. None has a department ranking among the leading graduate departments in any of the twenty-nine fields surveyed by the American Council of Education.[51] None ranks among the "selective" institutions with regard to student admissions.[52] None has a student body whose College Board scores are within 100 points of any school in the Ivy League. None has a library with even one-third as many volumes as the library of the University of Texas, much less the much larger libraries at such schools as Harvard, Yale, or Princeton. Many black schools are so small that a number of predominantly white institutions graduate more black students annually than they do. A study by two white scholars has found black colleges and universities as deficient in spirit as they are in academic matters, and while cries of "racism" have been raised against these men, they have said nothing which was not said earlier and more bitterly by black intellectuals.

Within the past decade, black colleges and universities have been losing their best-qualified faculty and their best potential students to white institutions. The period of integrationist philosophies raised questions as to whether or why they should continue in existence. The more recent period of black awareness has reduced this sort of pressure but led to more scathing indictments of their policies. Black colleges have been defended on the grounds that (1) they were the only institutions realistically available to the majority of black students,[53] during most of the history of black Americans, (2) the social need for black institutions for students who could not feel sufficiently at home in white institutions to realize their intellectual potential,[54] (3) black awareness, pride, and/or ideology can flourish in an all-black setting,[55] and (4) many black students are unable to meet the standards of white institutions.[56] The tone of both defenders and critics has been acerbic to the point of bitterness.

None of these arguments, however, is as strong as it once was. The historical argument for black colleges loses its relevance as the proportion of blacks who attend other institutions rises from a majority to an overwhelming majority. Similarly, the argument concerning the social needs of black students for the companionship and support of other black students is less compelling now that there are large numbers of black students on predominantly white campuses. Wayne State University, for example, graduates more black students than Fisk University.[57] Likewise, the need for black awareness, pride, and/or ideology, however defined or justified, does not logically entail the continuance of all existing black institutions. Finally, the inability of black students to meet white standards is exaggerated by the tendency of circumstances to concentrate black students in institutions where the majority of white students could not meet the standards either. None of this is an argument for the continuation of the deliberate policy of racial integration, which was once central to black organizations. Continued existence of all-black institutions is less urgent than its defenders imply. There is no a priori reason why they must be either deliberately destroyed or sustained at all costs.

In a sense, black studies have existed for generations. Booker T. Washington urged that such black leaders as Frederick Douglass[58] be studied and revered, and later wrote a two-volume history of the American Negro.[59] W. E. B. Dubois wrote the landmark study of *The Philadelphia Negro* in 1899, and followed it with a long series of monographs on various aspects of black American life, as well as more personal sketches and essays. In the 1920's, Carter G. Woodson pioneered scholarly black history and, in the 1930's, Sterling Brown studied and expounded black literature and music. E. Franklin Frazier became the foremost scholar on the sociology of black Americans, with works ranging from narrowly focused academic studies of black residents and family patterns to a wide-ranging critique of the black middle class. White scholars, notably Gunnar Myrdal, have also contributed to the study of black Americans.

Much of the white scholarship on black Americans, however, has been permeated by presuppositions of black inferiority, as are, for example, the historical writings of U. B. Phillips,[60] the sociological writings of Edward B. Reuter on mulatto superiority among Negroes,[61] and innumerable psychological works attempting to prove the intellectual and/or emotional inferiority of blacks. Such writings were particularly dominant during the period of Social Darwinism in American social thought and coincided with an outpouring of scholarship designed to show the inferiority of southern European and Jewish immigrant groups. In sheer volume of material, the writings attempting to prove the inferiority of European immigrant groups may have considerably exceeded that on blacks, if only because of the long controversy preceding the exclusionary immigration laws of the 1920's which are applied to Europeans but not to Negroes, and because the presumption among whites of black inferiority required less "scientific" support.

Black scholars struggled against the myths and misconceptions about American Negroes and, aided by such studies as Myrdal's classic, *An American Dilemma*, slowly changed the interpretation of Negro life reflected in textbooks and popular literature. The civil rights movements of the 1960's created still more interest in the "hidden" history of black involvement in, and contributions to, many aspects of American life. In one sense, the demand for black studies in the university was the culmination of this long trend.

However, the *sudden* and *simultaneous* demands all across the country in the late 1960's cannot be explained in this way. The kinds of black studies demanded reflected far more immediate circumstances—notably the desperate academic condition of black students at many white colleges and universities. It is significant that demands for black studies were most insistent at white institutions, particularly at the most academically demanding ones. The demands for black studies differed from demands for other forms of new academic studies in that they (1) had a strong racial exclusionary tendency with regard to students and/or faculty; (2) restricted the philosophical and political positions acceptable, even from black scholars in such programs; (3) demanded larger areas of autonomy than other academic departments or programs; and (4) sought a voice or veto on the admissions of black students and the hiring of black faculty in the institution as a whole. In short, black studies advocates sought a withdrawal of blacks from academic competition with whites and rejected traditional academic standards, whether exemplified by white or black scholars.

In their justification for the particular constellation of features they demand, black studies advocates shift at crucial points in their arguments from logical or empirical development to assertions as to the perceptions of black students. For example, the "exploitative aspects of graduate school" are asserted to be different "in kind, not only in degree" for the black student, but when it comes to specifics it is stated:

While the objective situation might be the same for both, the subjective state is actually quite different for Black and white students.[62]

Questions of academic qualifications are dismissed rather than discussed. Quality is equated with "white-like"[63]—ignoring the possibility that many whites would not be qualified by the same standards. Such arguments are typically long on colorful characterizations—"academic colonizers," "institutional racism," "house niggers"—and short on specific systematic empirical tests of specific hypotheses. Indeed these very processes of hypotheses-testing are rejected. These rejections are often characterized as "methodological" differences, when in fact they are differences in social-political preconceptions. The very tools of intellectual inquiry are declared to be "conservative tools" and the black intellectual is said to have to add "something extra."[64] But what this something might be is left undefined: "Writing at the beginning of the development of Black Social Science, one can say only what it might become."[65] The black scholar must use "his sense of Black consciousness as the cutting edge to redefine reality"[66] and the black community must "intervene" to prevent any research on blacks that it does not like.[67] The basis for these decisions is left unspecified, and the basis for conclusions already reached is also dealt with summarily: that "racism in America is endemic to capitalism" was "settled long ago" by a writer who listed racism as one of the features of capitalism.[68] That the mass media oppresses blacks is "starkly evident."[69]

Such black studies advocates assume the bad faith of all—black or white—who have a different argument and the only question they give serious attention and space is how to characterize or explain this dishonorable behavior. Essentially, whites are dismissed as racists and blacks are dismissed either as dupes or opportunists "who pant after professional elevation."[70] This literature leaves no place for honest disagreements based on personal differences in the weighing of complex information or different estimates of uncertain future prospects, much less for different interpretations of the elaborate mosaic of the past.

Critics of black studies programs have argued (1) the educational disadvantages of black isolation, (2) the self-defeating nature of the lower standards of these courses, (3) the self-delusions involved in the content of such programs and in their related political activities, and (4) the need for alternative courses as a means of acquiring the skills necessary to better the students' own condition and that of black people in general. The classic criticism of black studies programs, by a distinguished black scholar, asserts that "the way to the top" is through other channels. This needlessly ties the criticisms of black studies to a philosophy of integration and personal advancement, both of which are suspect in the eyes of many black students. In fact, the hard skills needed for personal advancement in a racially integrated setting are even more urgently needed for "nation building" on a separatist model. Any form of black self-sufficiency would require blacks to gain proficiency in a much wider range of scientific and technical skills than they need in a society where they can readily purchase the fruits of such skills from members of other racial groups.

Conclusion

The economic and social progress of black peoples has proceeded in spite of a failure to solve all these problems or even to resolve all differences within the black community. The prospects of a definitive solution to the problems of black education are as remote today as ever, but the continued progress of black peoples seems solidly based in spite of this. Much of the bitterness among black intellectuals, academic and nonacademic, reflects the special problems of a particular set of black people with a peculiar personal and social history. They are, in many cases, products of the cultural and/or physical assimilation process which is now held to be generally shameful and which, in particular aspects, has been and still is indisputably shameful. Their need for expiation or atonement is not conceptually identical with the black population's needs, and in practice the symbolic purifying acts of the intellectuals, including students, may be counterproductive in terms of the economic or other advancement of the black population as a whole. For example, the fields in which black students and faculty members specialize (sociology, political science, etc.) are not the same as the areas in which the black population has expressed its priorities—for medicine, business, and other technical skills.

Despite bitter antagonism among various schools of black intellectuals, there are important areas of agreement. All agree that black faculty and students feel enormous pressures at white institutions—pressures to perform by traditional academic standards and at the same time to be "relevant" to the problems of black people. The pressures to meet standards can only be exacerbated by continuance or acceleration of policies which lead to a systematic mismatching of students and faculty with their respective institutions. The pressures on students could be eased, however, by assigning financial aid to the selected students, and allowing each one to use the aid at whatever institution he chose. This would lead to a distribution of black students in accordance with their own assessments of their preparation and interests, not in accordance with any institution's need for a given demographic profile. For black faculty members, better matching of institutions and individuals could be achieved by a vigorous enforcement of nondiscriminatory hiring policies. This would force institutions to justify their decisions by professional criteria rather than racial percentages. Over a period of time this could lead to a distribution of black scholars to institutions where they could command the most respect rather than a distribution reflecting the institutional needs of white colleges and universities to safeguard their federal money.

Another point on which black intellectuals of widely differing views agree is that education is highly respected in the black community. Historically, education has been the main escape route for those black Americans who have advanced socially and economically. Many understand this who understand neither the educational superstructure nor intellectual prerequisites or traditions. The repudiation of educational and/or intellectual standards by some black intellectuals is more in keeping with the attitudes of some middle-class whites than with the views of the black population in whose name this repudiation is often made. The naive hopes produced among black Americans, as among Americans generally, will undoubtedly be modified by experience to something more realistic, but the central role of education seems more likely to be strengthened than weakened in the long run.

REFERENCES

1. Allen B. Ballard, *The Education of Black Folk* (New York: Harper & Row, 1973), p. 65.

2. Thomas Sowell, *Black Education: Myths and Tragedies* (New York: David McKay Co., 1972), Ch. 6.

3. Ballard, *op. cit.*

4. Martin Kilson, "The Black Experience at Harvard," *New York Times Magazine*, September 2, 1973, p. 37; Ballard, *op. cit., passim.*

5. Kenneth D. Roose and Charles J. Andersen, *A Rating of Graduate Programs* (Washington: American Council on Education, 1970), *passim.*

6. Nancy Fulop, "The 1969 CLEO Summer Institute Reports: A Summary," *University of Toledo Law Review* (Spring-Summer 1970), p. 648.

7. Solveig Eggerz, "Accentuate the Negative," *Call: The Newspaper of Capitol Hill*, July 26, 1973; Sowell, *op. cit.*, p. 136.

8. Fulop, *op. cit.*, p. 649.

9. Clyde W. Summers, "Preferential Admissions: An Unreal Solution to a Real Problem," *University of Toledo Law Review* (Spring-Summer 1970), p. 384.

10. *Ibid.*, pp. 392-393.

11. David Hapgood, "The Competition for Africa's Students," *The Reporter*, September 12, 1963, p. 42.

12. *Ibid.*

13. Ballard, *op. cit.*, p. 83.

14. Summers, *op. cit.*, p. 385.

15. James Alan McPherson, "The Black Law Student," *Atlantic* (April 1970), p. 99.

16. Ballard, *op. cit.*, p. 96.

17. Arthur R. Jensen, "How Much Can We Boost IQ and Scholastic Achievement?" *Harvard Educational Review* (Winter 1969), p. 100.

18. Arthur R. Jensen, "Selection of Minority Students in Higher Education," *The University of Toledo Law Review* (Spring-Summer 1970), pp. 440, 443; Donald A. Rock, "Motivation, Moderators, and Test Bias," *Ibid.*, pp. 536, 537; "Studies of superior Negro high school and college students seem to indicate that they differ somewhat from white students insofar as their achievement is not as high as that of white groups of comparable abilities," E. G. Rodgers, *op. cit.*, p. 22; Ronald L. Flaugher, *Testing Practices, Minority Groups and Higher Education: A Review and Discussion of the Research* (Princeton: Educational Testing Service, 1970), p. 11.

19. Sowell, *op. cit.*, pp. 131-132, 210-213.

20. Ballard, *op. cit.*, pp. 84-90.

21. *Ibid.*, p. 97.

22. Derrick A. Bell, "Black Students in White Law Schools: The Ordeal and the Opportunity," *University of Toledo Law Review* (Spring-Summer 1970), p. 552.

23. *Ibid.*, p. 553.

24. *Ibid.*, p. 552.

25. *Ibid.*, p. 551.

26. Macklin Fleming, "The Black Quota at Yale Law School," *The Public Interest* (Spring 1970), p. 47.

27. *Ibid.*

28. *Ibid.*, p. 46.

29. *Ibid.*

30. Gordon D. Morgan, *The Ghetto College Student* (Iowa City: The American College Testing Program), p. 29n.

31. Unpublished Ph.D. thesis by Kent Mommsen.

32. Michael R. Winston, "Through the Back Door: Academic Ransom and the Negro Scholar in Historical Perspective," *Daedalus* (Summer 1971), p. 695; James Allen Moss, "Negro Teachers in Predominantly White Colleges," *Journal of Negro Education* (Fall 1958), pp. 451-462.

33. "Of 554 black faculty members, eight percent stated that difficulty in finding their present job was caused by discrimination," David M. Rafky, "The Black Academic on the Marketplace," *Change* (October 1971), p. 65.

34. Sowell, *op. cit.*, pp. 214-215.

35. James M. McPherson, "White Liberals and Black Power in Negro Education, 1865-1915," *American Historical Review* (June 1970), p. 1362.

36. *Ibid.*

37. *Ibid.*, pp. 1364-1366.

38. *Ibid.*, p. 1370.

39. *Ibid.*, p. 1378.

40. W. E. B. DuBois, *The Education of Black People*, ed. Herbert Aptheker (Amherst: University of Massachusetts Press, 1973), pp. 46-48, 52-56.

41. E. Franklin Frazier, *Black Bourgeoisie* (New York: Collier Books, 1962), p. 71.

42. Ralph Ellison, *The Invisible Man* (New York: Signet Books, 1952), Ch. 2-6.

43. Tobe Johnson, "The Black College as a System," *Daedalus* (Summer 1971), pp. 801, 804. See also St. Clair Drake, "The Black University in the American Social Order," *Ibid.*, p. 845; Winston, *op. cit.*, pp. 702, 707.

44. ". . . some have gotten the idea that industrial development was opposed to the Negro's higher mental development. . . . I would say to the black boy what I would say to the white boy, Get all the mental development that your time and pocket-book will allow of,—the more, the better. . . ." Booker T. Washington, *The Future of the American Negro* (New York: The New American Library, Inc., 1969), pp. 79-80; ". . . no one understanding the real needs of the race would advocate that industrial education should be given to every Negro to the exclusion of the professions and other branches of learning. . . . There is, then, a place and an increasing need for the Negro college as well as the industrial institute. . . ." Booker T. Washington, "Educational Philosophy," *Great Lives Observed: Booker T. Washington*, ed. E. L. Thornbrough (Englewood Cliffs: Prentice-Hall, 1969), p. 41.

45. DuBois, *op. cit.*, pp. 68-69. See also Myrdal, *op. cit.*, p. 889n.

46. Louis R. Harlan, *Booker T. Washington: The Making of a Black Leader, 1856-1910* (New York: Oxford University Press, 1972), pp. 258-259, 320; Gilbert Osofsky, *Harlem: The Making of a Ghetto* (New York: Harper & Row, 1968), pp. 164-165; Louis R. Harlan, "Booker T. Washington in Biographical Perspective," *American Historical Review* (October 1970), pp. 1584-1585.

47. Harlan, *Booker T. Washington*, p. 225. See also *Ibid.*, p. 265.

48. W. E. DuBois, "The Souls of Black Folk," *Three Negro Classics* (New York: Avon Books, 1965), p. 243.

49. Harlan, *Booker T. Washington*, p. 303; Harlan, "Booker T. Washington in Biographical Perspective," *op. cit.*, p. 1586; Louis R. Harlan, "The Secret Life of Booker T. Washington," *Journal of Southern History* (August 1971), pp. 407-409.

50. August Meier, "Toward a Reinterpretation of Booker T. Washington," *The Making of Black America*, ed. August Meier and Elliott Rudwick (New York: Atheneum, 1969), Vol. II, pp. 126-127, 130; Harlan, "The Secret Life of Booker T. Washington," *op. cit.*, 396-398, 399, 400, 401, 402.

51. Kenneth D. Roose and Charles J. Andersen, *A Rating of Graduate Programs* (Washington, D.C.: American Council on Education, 1970), *passim*.

52. James Cass and Max Birnbaum, *Comparative Guide to American Colleges*, 5th ed. (Harper & Row, 1972), pp. 761-766.

53. C. Eric Lincoln, "The Negro Colleges and Cultural Change," *Daedalus* (Summer 1971), p. 624; Ballard, *op. cit.*, p. 24; Orde Coombs, "Barber-Scotia College," *Change* (May 1973), p. 43.

54. Ballard, *op. cit.*, p. 151; Coombs, *op. cit.*, p. 41.

55. St. Clair Drake, *op. cit.*, p. 877; Henry Allen Bullock, "The Black College and the New Black Awareness," *Daedalus* (Summer 1971), pp. 594-595.

56. Christopher Jencks and David Riesman, "The American Negro College," *Harvard Educational Review* (Winter 1967), p. 42.

57. *Ibid.*, p. 31.

58. "I think we should be ashamed of the coloured man or woman who would not venerate the name of Frederick Douglass," Booker T. Washington, *The Future of the American Negro*, p. 180.

59. Booker T. Washington, *The Story of the Negro* (New York: Negro Universities Press, 1969 [originally published by Doubleday, Page & Co., 1909]).

60. Ulrich Bonnell Phillips, *American Negro Slavery* (Baton Rouge: Louisiana State University Press, 1969 [originally published by Appleton-Century-Crofts, Inc., 1918]); *Life and Labor in the Old South* (Boston: Little Brown, 1929).

61. Edward Byron Reuter, *The Mulatto in the United States* (Boston: Richard G. Badger, 1918).

62. Nathan Hare, "The Challenge of a Black Scholar," *The Death of White Sociology*, ed. Joyce A. Ladner (New York: Vintage Books, 1973), p. 74.

63. Douglas Davidson, "The Furious Passage of the Black Graduate Student," Ladner, ed., *op. cit.*, p. 30.

64. Ronald W. Walters, "*Toward a Definition of Black Social Science*," Ladner, ed., *op. cit.*, p. 212.

65. Walters, *op. cit.*, pp. 192-193.

66. *Ibid.*, p. 199.

67. *Ibid.*, p. 207.

68. *Ibid.*, p. 196.

69. *Ibid.*, p. 200.

70. Hare, *op. cit.*, p. 70.

Notes on Contributors

J. F. ADE. AJAYI, born in 1929 in Ikole-Ekiti, Nigeria, is Vice-Chancellor of the University of Lagos. He is the author of *Christian Missions in Nigeria 1841-1891: The Making of a New Elite* (1965), and co-author of *A History of West Africa*, 2 Vols. (1972, 1974), and *Yoruba Warfare in the Nineteenth Century* (1964). He spent 1970-1971 at Stanford University as a Fellow for Advanced Study in the Behavioral Sciences.

E. J. ALAGOA, born in 1933 in Okpoma, Nigeria is a senior research fellow at the University of Lagos. He is the author of *A History of the Niger Delta* (1973)—a historical interpretation of Ijo oral tradition—and *The Small Brave City-State* (1964)—a history of Nembe (Brass) in the Niger Delta—and co-author of *A Chronical of Grand Bonny* (1972). He has served as archivist of the National Archives of Nigeria.

MICHAEL BANTON, born in 1926 in Birmingham, England, is professor of sociology at the University of Bristol, and director of the Social Science Research Council Research Unit on Ethnic Relations. He is the author of *Police-Community Relations* (1973), *Racial Minorities* (1972), *Race Relations* (1967), *Roles* (1965), *The Policeman in His Community* (1964), *White and Coloured* (1959), *West African City* (1957), and *The Coloured Quarter* (1955).

ROGER BASTIDE, born in 1898 in Nîmes, France, is the director of studies at the École Pratique des Hautes Études in Paris. He is the author of *Sociologie et Psychoanalyse* (1973), *Le Prochain et le Lointain* (1970), *Les Ameriques Noires* (1966), and *Religions Africaines au Brésil* (1959). He has done research on race relations in Brazil, on the formation of an African elite in Paris, and on the Yoruba religion in Dahomey and Nigeria.

EDWARD KAMAU BRATHWAITE, born in 1930 in Barbados, is senior lecturer in history at the University of the West Indies at Mona, Jamaica. His publications include *The Arrivants: Trilogy of Long Poems* (1973), *The People Who Came: A Caribbean History* (1972), *The Development of Creole Society in Jamaica* (1971), *The Folk Culture of the Slaves in Jamaica* (1970), *Islands* (1969), *Masks* (1968), *Rights of Passage* (1967), *Odale's Choice: A Play* (1967), and *Four Plays for Primary Schools* (1964).

PHILIP D. CURTIN, born in 1922 in Philadelphia, Pennsylvania, is the Melville J. Herskovits Professor of History at the University of Wisconsin. He is the author of *The Atlantic Slave Trade: A Census* (1969), *The Image of Africa* (1964), and *Two Jamaicas* (1955); co-author of *Africa and Africans;* and editor of *Africa Remembered* (1967), and *Imperialism* (1971).

DAVID BRION DAVIS, born in 1927 in Denver, Colorado, is Farnam Professor of History at Yale University. He is the author of *The Problem of Slavery in the Age of Revolution* (forthcoming in 1974), *The Fear of Conspiracy* (1971), *The Slave Power Conspiracy and the Paranoid Style* (1969), *Homicide in American Fiction* (1957), and *The Problem of Slavery in Western Culture* (1966). In 1967, he received the Pulitzer Prize for nonfiction, the Anisfield-Wolf Award, and the Mass Media Award of the National Conference of Christians and Jews.

SIDNEY W. MINTZ, born in 1922 in New Jersey, is professor of anthropology at Yale University. He has done anthropological fieldwork in Puerto Rico, Jamaica, Haiti, and Iran, and served as president of the American Ethnological Society. He is the author of *Worker in the Cane* (1960) and of numerous articles, and co-author of *The People of Puerto Rico* (1956).

J. H. KWABENA NKETIA, born in 1921 in Mampong Ashanti, Ghana, is director of the Institute of African studies and professor of music at the University of California at Los Angeles. His publications in English include *Folk Songs of Ghana* (1962), *Drumming in Akan Communities of Ghana* (1963), *African Music in Ghana* (1962), and *Funeral Dirges of the Akan People* (1955). He is also the author of fiction, nonfiction, and poetry in Twi.

BENJAMIN QUARLES, born in 1904 in Boston, Massachusetts, is professor of history at Morgan State College. His publications include *Allies for Freedom: Blacks and John Brown* (forthcoming), *The Negro in the Making of America* (1964), *Lincoln and the Negro* (1962), *The Negro in the American Revolution* (1961), *The Negro in the Civil War* (1953), and *Frederick Douglass* (1948). He is co-author of *The Black American: A Documentary* (1970).

THOMAS SOWELL, born in 1930 in Gastonia, North Carolina, is director of the Ethnic Minorities Research Project at the Urban Institute, Washington, D.C. He is the author of *Classical Economics Reconsidered* (1973), *Race and Economics* (1973), *Say's Law: An Historical Analysis* (1972), *Black Education: Myths and Tragedies* (1972), and *Economics: Analysis and Issues* (1971).

PER WÄSTBERG, born in 1933 in Stockholm, Sweden, is a writer, literary critic in *Dagens Nyheter* (the main morning newspaper in Sweden), and commentator on African affairs on Swedish radio. His fiction includes *The Heir* (1958), *Half the Kingdom* (1955), *An Old Shadowplay* (1952), *Boy with Soap-Bubbles* (1949), and most recently a trilogy: *The Water Palace* (1968), *The Air Cage* (1969), and *The Earth Moon* (1972), which won the Swedish bookseller's prize as best book of the year. His nonfiction includes *A Day at the World Fair* (1967), *On Portuguese Africa* (1962), *On the Black List* (1960) about South Africa, and *Forbidden Territory* (1960), a documentary about Rhodesia. He has also edited anthologies of African writers and published books of poems.